STITCHED UP

a story of heart and a life fulfilled

VIC WIGGINS

Published by Wilkinson Publishing Pty Ltd
ACN 006 042 173
PO Box 24135, Melbourne, VIC 3001, Australia.
Ph: +61 3 9654 5446
enquiries@wilkinsonpublishing.com.au
www.wilkinsonpublishing.com.au

WilkinsonPublishing
wilkinsonpublishinghouse

A catalogue record of this book is available from the National Library of Australia.
ISBN: 9781921804144

Design: Michael Bannenberg.
Printed and bound in Australia by Ligare.

For my family.

All my life I have been
working them angels overtime.

Quote from the song
'Working Them Angels' by Rush

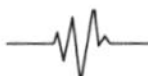

This book is dedicated to the many hundreds of doctors, nurses and all the allied health professionals who have looked after me or been involved with my care for the past half a century and more.
I thank you, sincerely, from the bottom of my new perfect heart that is allowing me to live the life I have always wanted.

MEDICAL TIMELINE

8th October 1970. Birthday.

February 1971. First open heart surgery

January 1984. Corrective open heart surgery.

Dec 2005. First major arrhythmia, NZ.

2011. First pacemaker inserted, NZ.

2016. Cardiac defibrillator inserted instead of pacemaker, Melboune.

2019. Shocked by my ICD defibrillator for the first time.

Mid 2022-mid 2023 .Taken to hospital by ambulance more than 20 times.

Aug 2023. Procedure to ablate my AV Node.

Dec 2023. Procedure to insert CRTD type pacemaker. Saves my life.

Dec 2023. Assessed for Heart Transplant at the Alfred Hospital.

9th Feb 2024. I am placed on the Heart Transplant wait list.

8th Feb 2025. I receive my new heart.

21st Feb 2025. I leave hospital 13 days after receiving my new heart.

31st March 2025. I jog on a treadmill for the first time in decades.

1st April 2025. Fergus and I go on our first bike ride together in years.

CONTENTS

PART THREE

FOREWORD

When Vic asked me to write this foreword, I was both flattered and a bit confused. What had he been up to this time? I mean, writing a book? Wow! But then I thought about it and it made perfect sense as he has quite a story to tell.

My dad, Brian, and Vic's dad, Geoff, had worked together for a number of years. My dad was a lover of motorcycles and I suppose it was inevitable that I would follow in his footsteps. It is all I ever wanted to do.

Vic's dad had been an accomplished cyclist but didn't really know much about motorbikes and in particular trials bike riding. A chance conversation where Geoff had mentioned that he was going to buy Vic a motocross bike had led to Brian suggesting that perhaps trials bike riding would be better suited to Vic, especially with his medical condition.

I was seven and Vic was eight when we first started riding together, our dads giving up their weekends to take us riding. From that day to this we have been friends and while physical distance means we don't see much of each other anymore, we are in regular contact with one another.

For years we battled it out at the top of the schoolboy trials scene both on the mainland of the UK and back on the Isle of Man. And while I beat him most of the time, he made me work for it quite often and was always on my coat-tails.

As we grew older, our mutual love of all things with wheels naturally migrated to cars and I have fond memories of us doing crazy stuff in cars tearing up the roads.

I would be the first to say Vic has always given his all to everything he does. Determined and focused and never one to give up, for years I didn't really realise how serious the heart condition he was born with really was.

He is, without doubt, the craziest person I have ever known on two wheels or four, with skill to match the size of his balls! I have always been amazed by what he has done and continues to try to do even in the face of great challenges.

I am very happy to be writing the foreword to this book. I hope you enjoy it as much as I did as we travel with Vic on his journey with plenty of stories along the way.

Best wishes, Steve Colley.
International trials bike rider, stuntman,
accomplished rally driver and a life-long friend.

INTRODUCTION

In 1971, I was the youngest child in the UK to survive a pioneering 12-hour operation for a rare and complex heart problem. Against all the odds, and despite multiple medical setbacks, I have now reached my fifties – something that few people would have bet on. But my survival has come at a cost, both physically and mentally. This is the story of how I pushed my limits.

I'm standing at the window of our bedroom, looking out across the street. It's a typical Australian suburban area. Most of the houses are single-storey, like ours, but there are a few with two floors. The gardens are, for the most part, well-kept.

There are young families, just starting out on their life journey with their children, then there are the older generation, some have lived in the same house for all their married lives, such as our neighbours across the street.

It's Saturday morning in late November. Summer is just around the corner, and with it, the advent of warmer weather beckons. It's a sunny day with a few clouds in the sky. As I gaze out of the window, I'm not thinking about how great the weekend ahead should be; instead I focus on my heartbeat.

We are taking our son to Bright, about three or four hours

north of Melbourne in the Australian highlands. For the winter months, revellers flock here in their droves most weekends and probably some mid-week travellers too, to hit the ski slopes. For the warmer months of the year, starting mid-spring, the place, like so many other similar destinations around the world, converts itself into a mountain biking Mecca.

Of course we have been before, many times in fact, but that was then. That was before all the recent issues I have been having with my heart.

Things have definitely been getting worse for me health-wise and as the saying goes, if you don't have your health, what do you have? Nothing is the answer and certainly not the way I have been feeling of late.

I'm gazing out of the window with my index and middle fingers of my right hand pressed firmly against the underside of my left wrist, just forward of my watch strap.

I'm taking my pulse again. It's fine. It's regular, beating at around 70 beats per minute. I don't need to count it with the help of a watch or have the aid of a medical device to know; I just know. I'm so attuned to my body that I feel, literally, every skipped beat, every run of irregular heart rhythm.

Even though it's fine, I don't want to go on our trip. I mean, I do want to physically, but I'm fighting the demons in my head that are telling me not to go. For the most part, I am fighting the what-ifs.

What if something happens? The nearest major hospital is hours away by ambulance. I wouldn't make it. What if I don't sleep well? I will be useless the following day.

I'm torn, so torn. I want to go, even though these days I won't be riding much, if at all. I want to be there for our boy, to see him having fun doing the thing he loves to do more than anything else, downhill mountain bike racing. I want us to have a fun weekend as a family. To make some memories together.

But the "what if" feeling that is tormenting me is so loud inside my head, no amount of trying to think rationally, of Susan with her calming logic and reasoning, not just as my wife but as a medical professional herself, none of it helps me to see and understand that I will be fine.

This scenario has become all too familiar for our small family. The overwhelming feeling of trepidation of being in an environment that I feel is unsafe or has the potential to cause me problems if something were to happen is too much to bear.

And it's not just me who is living this, it's Sue and our son Fergus too. I feel terrible that I've let them down, again, but I know I won't relax, I know I won't sleep well there because I'm worried and that in itself perpetuates me feeling even worse than I probably already do.

I'm still taking my pulse. I usually count to five and start again, I don't know why I do that, habit I guess. It is still regular, maybe a little faster than it was, but it's OK right? I feel OK, it must be fine.

This is the dance I do with myself many times each day. It's awful, I hate it and I hate myself for allowing myself to do it. I go and talk to Sue. I've decided I can't go.

It's got to the point that she half expects it and, in fact, has started to make hotel bookings for just her and Fergus, almost sure that if she books for me too then it will be a waste of time and money.

My anxiety has beaten me once more. They will go anyway and have a great time. I miss out and I will miss them.

PART ONE

BIRTHDAY

Winter weather in Britain, as most people know, is inherently poor in the colder months. Luckily for me, October 8, 1970, was by all accounts a decent day. This worked in my favour and was perhaps the first of many good fortunes that came my way in those first few hours of life.

Joyce Wiggins, my mum, was no doubt elated at the arrival of her only son, but also terrified when I was whisked away to be given oxygen along with immediate and essential medical treatment.

I can't imagine the emotions she would have been going through. That she had already been through this twice before, albeit that some 10 years had passed since her last child arrived into the world, she surely would have thought things would be fine.

Get dropped off at the Jane Crookall maternity hospital, say goodbye to my dad while he returned home to hold the fort, looking after my two sisters, as was the custom in those days. She would have her baby, stay a night or two in hospital and take her new bundle of joy home.

I'm not sure I was planned, I've never asked, but given there had been a 10-year gap between this visit to the hospital and the previous time, I'm sure I was a surprise! I would deliver many surprises to them over the next several decades!

Regardless of them being seasoned parents, I never really understood the emotions or stresses that she and my dad would have been going through. Not just in the minutes and hours after my birth, but ongoing.

It wasn't until I became a parent myself that it all kind of clicked and I gained perspective. More on this later!

Her obstetrician that day, Dr Townsend, who delivered me, was an experienced doctor and that was the second stroke of good fortune. He recognised immediately that all was not well and almost 100 per cent accurately, as it turned out later, diagnosed my condition.

When you think about it, that is an incredible feat, as I was born on a small island in the middle of the Irish Sea, a place better known for motorbike racing and cats without tails, rather than its medical prowess.

In fact, it's probably fair to say that if you were going to pick a place to be born with a serious, life-threatening medical condition, the Isle of Man would not be it!

Added to that, the condition I had been afflicted with was rare. So rare, in fact, that I was probably the only person on the island (population 70,000 then) to have it. So, it's not the kind of thing a doctor would see and treat regularly, quite the opposite.

But thankfully, Dr Townsend (whose son I would end up going to school with years later) was on top of his game and made the call that I needed to be transferred to the nearest major hospital. That needed a plane ride!

It's a shame that I never really asked my mum about the finer details of how that day unfolded.

Sadly, my mum is no longer with us and my dad wouldn't know anyway (no offence, Dad!) But what I am going to write is my summary of events.

A plane was organised and, within hours of being born, I was safely delivered to the Royal Liverpool Children's Hospital, at Myrtle Street. This was the nearest major children's hospital to home for us. Of course, there may well be better-known ones, such as Great Ormond Street in London or Addenbrooks in Cambridge, but these were much further away and time was of the essence.

We would have departed the Isle of Man at Ronaldsway Airport, the only civil aviation airport on the island, although there is an old airfield, two actually, which served as air bases during World War 2.

I don't know what type of plane it was but typical transport in the 1970s would have been perhaps a Dakota or a Viscount. Either way the flight would have been around 30-40 minutes. Upon landing, an ambulance would have met the plane and taken me swiftly into the centre of Liverpool, where my home for the next nine months awaited.

The hospital isn't there now – having moved to Alder Hey, another well- known children's hospital – and while I haven't been there for many years, I could describe it in detail. Also, I could drive you there without directions or a map.

That place is in my DNA. I loved that building, I still do. Not so much for its aesthetic qualities; in fact, it was quite scary looking really, but for what it meant to me. It was typically Victorian. Opened in the 1850s, it was foreboding. In common with many other institutional buildings of that era, it could just have easily been the façade of a prison, or a museum, or even a boarding school (in some ways, it was the latter!)

The hospital was on a corner of a busy road and in later years, when I was there for another operation, I remember looking out of the window by my bed and watching the cars, buses and taxis go by in winter. I yearned to be outdoors, too.

Liverpool has always been my second home.

I identify with it; I love the humour of the locals and their unmistakable Scouse accents.

Of course, the city itself has seen a huge transformation over the past two or three decades. From being a very blue-collar centre with shipbuilding and heavy industry being at its forefront, to having to adapt to the changing times, by way of reclaiming old warehouses on the docks and turning them into shops, bars, restaurants and so on.

But without doubt my favourite landmark in the city used to be the Tower Restaurant. It was perched high above the cityscape and best of all used to turn around so that you get 360-degree views of the city while munching down lunch! My mum used to take me there as a treat during the years that I had to go back to the hospital for checks and procedures. In fact, when the check-ups were carried out back home on the island, I was a little disappointed. Firstly, I didn't get to go to the Tower Restaurant as much, but also, I didn't get long off school!

DIAGNOSIS

When I was older and able to understand more about my condition, people used to say all the time, "Oh, you probably have a hole in the heart. I had one of those." Or they would know someone who had one.

But a hole in the heart is common and here is why (bear in mind I am not a physician) .... When a baby is in the womb it is 100 per cent reliant on its mother for food and oxygen, so the mother's blood is the source of survival via the placenta and umbilical cord. However, when the baby is born, its circulatory system must turn on.

To do this, some amazing things occur. Of course, the umbilical cord is clamped, cutting off the lifeline that it had relied on for the past nine months. The baby's lungs inflate and, crucially, the part of the heart that had allowed blood to flow from the placenta is closed off.

Sometimes though, the hole doesn't close fully or at all and this is a hole in the heart. Usually, it's no big deal and the hole will sometimes close on its own in time, or the child needs a surgical procedure to fix it.

I kind of wish that this was all that had been wrong with me. Sadly, my condition was much more serious. It's known as TGA-D, or to give its full name, Transposition of the Great Arteries. A bit of a mouthful!

It took me years to really understand and get my head around the complexity of my condition, too. I went from thinking that my heart was back to front, inside out, upside down, on the wrong side and all the above at the same time. Even now, it's quite hard to fully articulate to someone exactly what's going on, but here's my very rudimentary human biology lesson.

In a normal heart, the flow of blood goes like this (we will begin our journey with the de-oxygenated blood): as it returns from providing nutrients, minerals, oxygen and other life-needing components, the blood enters the right atrium from the main veins and is pushed through a valve into the right ventricle.

It's easy to remember the atriums and ventricles as being the receiver and sender, in that order. From the right ventricle, blood is sent a short distance via the pulmonary vein to the lungs, where an exchange of gases occurs, carbon dioxide being swapped out for oxygen.

I like the analogy of a pit stop in Formula 1. Old tyres off and new tyres on (and a refuel, too, of course!). Then it makes its way back out of the "pit lane" – continuing the motorsport analogies – to the heart, where the left atrium receives the freshly oxygenated blood. The atrium contracts and pushes the blood through a valve into the left ventricle.

This is where the serious stuff happens, and this incredibly powerful chamber contracts and sends the goods out for another lap of the body, via the aorta, and on to the many arteries and capillaries that make up our amazing bodies.

All of this happens in about 45 seconds. So, if you could put a marker somewhere in the blood and watch it go round, you would need less than a minute from pressing start and stop on your stopwatch!

For me, things were (and are) different. When I arrived in the world, a genetic mutation had caused my heart essentially to have two separate circulatory systems, which crucially didn't talk to one another.

So, the system of pumping blood to my lungs was fine, except that at no time did it cross over with the circulatory system that pumps the blood around the body.

The result of this was that there was no "clean" or oxygenated blood getting to my organs, tissues, brain, etc. Think of two trains heading in the same direction on two different lines, except that at some stage they need to swap lines. There is no intersecting point, no junction where the controller can pull the lever from his little box. So, the result is that those two trains never interact. I was what is called a blue baby, the colour of my skin because of a severe lack of oxygen.

If you have ever had an accident or a medical procedure, you may be familiar with a little clamp-like device that medical staff pop on your finger.

It's called an oximeter and it measures, via a light source that shines through the finger, the amount of oxygen in your blood. A normal reading is anything above 95 per cent. Anything below 90 per cent and doctors and nurses start asking questions and running around being very busy.

When I arrived at the hospital a few hours old, my oxygen level was 67 per cent. This meant, as a result of being very cyanotic, that I was critically ill and needed immediate intervention to survive. Luckily, I had been taken to one of the best heart centres for children in the UK. I was in good hands.

I say I was in good hands and obviously I was. I am still here, after all. But the good hands that I was in were all very inexperienced at looking after babies with this condition.

Without getting too gloomy or morose about it, until the early 1960s the chances of survival from being born with TGA were virtually nil.

The reason being, back then, there was no procedure in place to help save these lives. It's a little confronting at times to know that, in fact, I am one of few people in the world (relative to population) who have survived this long. It's also an amazing gift and one I literally cherish each day. I know my luck will run out one day and I will talk about that later.

These days, a very different operation is used to save children born with TGA and is regularly carried out on babies that are just hours old.

Back in 1970 when it was my turn, I was considered very young to have an operation at five months old. So, between birth and operation day, there needed to be a mechanism to keep me alive. That came by way of a balloon via a catheter from my groin into my heart and a hole was created by inflating the balloon once inside the heart. This allowed the "dirty" and "clean" blood to greet each other for the first time.

But this was only going to sustain me for so long and the conversation that no parent would want to hear was had.

I am guessing it would have been along the lines of: there are no options, it's do, or quite literally, die. I am sure the phraseology would have been more tender, but succinct, nevertheless.

From the notes I have read from those days, it seems that I had a cardiac arrest caused by a cyanotic attack in early February 1971, while still in hospital. I wasn't going to go home anytime soon. I had never been home, where even was home?

In the early 1960s, a clever chap named Dr William Mustard devised an operation to correct this condition. Of course, it can never be fully corrected, but the hope was that an operation could give kids like me a chance at life.

Dr Mustard (not to be mistaken for the Cluedo character) was a Canadian surgeon who pioneered two operations during his career. The first was to help children afflicted with polio. The other was the procedure I needed to have.

Known as the Mustard procedure, it is a complex operation that, in my case, lasted 12 or more hours. Some perspective is needed here. A newborn baby's heart is about the size of a large walnut. Within that area, you have four chambers to navigate and work through.

The degree of accuracy, patience and care that needs to be executed, to me, is staggering while operating on such a tiny organ. So small is the subject that the surgeons wear the same type of glasses that a jeweller would use.

Dr Mustard must have been so nervous, yet excited at the same time at the prospect of being able to allow these tiny infants the opportunity to have a life, however short those lives might be.

Can you imagine the burden he must have placed on himself to succeed, knowing, probably, that he might not and even if the operation itself was a success, how long would these kids survive? I can't possibly fathom that level of responsibility.

On February 5, 1971, at five months old, it was my day. My day to do what I needed to do. To behave myself, to be a fighter, to not cause problems; in short, to survive.

Most of these major procedures start early in the morning. I would have been the only person on the list that day; there wouldn't have been time for anyone else. The previous week, a young girl with the same heart condition as mine had been operated on, she was a little older than me, apparently. The night before my operation, sadly she passed away.

My mum told me that it was one of the hardest things she has ever had to do, sending me for surgery, not knowing whether she would ever see me alive again. Then to hear the news of this other little girl magnified that hesitancy, that guilt, that indecision.

Ultimately, as she knew and as she told me, there was only one decision and that decision had been made.

I am very lucky that many years later I was allowed access to most of my medical notes, so I can recount with certain accuracy how the operation unfolded.

By all accounts, the procedure itself was fairly unremarkable as far as the medical side of things was concerned; however, I dare say that it would have been the longest 12 hours of my parents' lives. I imagine they paced the corridors, maybe went for a walk outside, perhaps they had something to eat.

I'm not sure of any of this, but what I am sure of is that whatever it was they did and however they passed the time, their minds would not have been on any of those activities, they would have been fairly and squarely worrying about their son.

Of course they would have also been missing their two elder daughters. My sisters had remained on the Isle of Man, attending school and being cared for by close family friends. I was talking about this with my sister recently and she told me that they would call the hospital at the same time every evening to get a progress report, she even recited the phone number as if she had just dialled it. Amazing!

By all accounts, at that time I was the youngest child to have survived the operation in the UK. I am quite sure it wasn't a title that I held for long; indubitably, the medical advancements were coming along in leaps and bounds and with them the chances of survival.

Basically, the surgeons to whom I owe my life replumbed my heart as follows:

In a normal heart the left ventricle pumps blood around the body. It's built and designed to do that. But for me, the physical outcome of the operation meant my right ventricle was adopted as the main pump and the left ventricle was only being asked to pump blood to the lungs.

The condition's name gives the clue as to the plumbing. In essence, the two main arteries that flow out of the chambers are transposed.

The simplest analogy I can give is that the hot water hose is on the cold tap and vice versa. The long-term issue and ongoing concern with this is that the right ventricle, unlike its opposite number, is not designed to pump blood under heavy load. The left ventricle has thicker walls and much more muscle to get the job done.

Over time, as we will explore later, the right ventricle becomes tired and the tissue becomes hard, less pliable and unable to pump the blood in an efficient manner.

To get the blood to mix, a tunnel called a baffle is cut into the heart to join the right side of the heart to the left. This allows the dirty and clean blood to be combined. This is the crux of the operation. Without the baffle, there is no chance of long-term survival. The baffle is made from artificial material.

There was a Gore-Tex one, which the replaced the original, having been crafted from my own tissue.

My body would never look the same again, five months old and 50 inches of silk suture woven into my chest and abdomen.

I was placed in the ICU and everyone crossed their fingers.

It was a bumpy ride at times, infections, thrush and some other complications, but on April 2, 1971, I was allowed to be taken home, back to the Isle of Man, to begin a life there with my adoring family.

I was seven months old. I had spent 75 per cent of my first year on the planet in a hospital, but I had been fixed and now it was playtime. I had some catching up to do!

FAMILY

Geoff and Joyce Wiggins (née Anderson) met at University, but not in the traditional sense! They had both been invited, separately, to an afternoon tea on the grounds of the University. Apparently, it was a lovely summer's day, unusual for Scotland at any time of the year!

My father had come by his invitation by way of a couple of friends who had recently completed their National Service. My Mother, on the other hand, had been evacuated during the war to Dumfries just south of her hometown, Glasgow, and very close to Lockerbie, which would of course become very well known in years to come, for all the wrong reasons. She had attended an all-girls school and was the Dux Literarum while there.

My mum was a very intelligent lady, an academic at heart!

Woe betide if you beat her at Scrabble, she wasn't keen on that at all! Scrabble was a family staple growing up, mostly contested on a Sunday evening after one of my mum's delicious roasts. Often, the Collins English Dictionary had to be called upon to adjudicate on various words.

Mum had yearned to go to university; she really wanted to further her education, but when she was old enough to go it was the late 1940s and mostly women didn't go to university then. My understanding is that her father prevented her from going, which is very sad, but not uncommon for the era.

However, her two friends did go to university and had invited my mum along to the afternoon tea party on the grounds of the campus. It was there, where fortuitously my future parents ended up sitting next to each other and the beginnings of a long, happy life together began.

One of my favourite movies is *Sliding Doors*. I am a hopeless romantic, but I have always believed in the power of chance or fate, of being in the right (or wrong) place at any given time. How they both came to be invited to the tea party that day, was it fate? I like to think so!

Mum was the daughter of a merchant seaman who saw active service and was torpedoed not once, not twice, but three times, in the Atlantic. The ships he served on were deployed to be the vital supply lines between the US and Britain.

Her mum, my grandma, was a stay-at-home mother who was raising four children. My mum was the second eldest and she had two brothers and a sister. I can briefly remember my grandma and while there is a picture somewhere of my grandad holding me, I was very young and have no recollection of him. I don't remember my uncles either, but I do know and remember my mum's sister, my aunt Olive.

While my mum's family may not have been as cohesive and as loving as I experienced, she did at least have a family. My dad, on the other hand, had none.

Geoffrey Wiggins wasn't born with that name; he was given it later. I don't know his original given name. I once found some paperwork as I was "exploring", as most kids do, when I came across an old identity card with the name E. Wiggins on it. Maybe it was Edward, maybe it was Euan, maybe it was something else, or quite possibly it wasn't his at all.

My dad's story has always been shrouded in mystery. Even now the details are still somewhat sketchy, but a few years back, while on a flight with him from Melbourne to Auckland, he opened up.

It was one of the most emotional moments we have ever had

together, and there have been many!

I was gobsmacked by his story. His mum basically disowned him at a very early age. For a time, he lived with his grandparents whom he loved and who loved him in return. But then, aged nine, he found himself, along with so many other young children, evacuated from his home in London, not knowing where he might be going, but ending up in Cumbria, in the north of England – near Scotland!

My father was taken under the wing of a man to whom he would refer on the rare occasions he would offer some insight into his past, as Uncle. It turned out Uncle was a character in his own right. This was wartime, my dad was a young man trying to find his way in life, hard enough to do with the support of loving parents, but he had none.

Uncle and others like him had recruited and vouched for young men, plucked from the numerous orphanages, which, as a further result of the war, were filling up very rapidly. He would then educate them in terms of being a young gentleman, how to act, how to dine correctly and of course how to engage with others. It was akin to finishing school, I suppose.

Instead of being cast off at the age of 18 or so into the big wide world, my father was helped into a career by Uncle.

My father and I had an extremely close relationship when I was growing up, he literally was my hero. I know this is probably common for lots of young boys and their dads, but the devotion, the love and the time he gave me was incredible. When I became a father myself, I hoped that I would be half as good a dad as he was. Maybe it was the lack of family he had personally that drove him to want to have a cohesive one himself. I think everyone would understand that.

And so, the courtship began and in 1955 my parents married.

They tied the knot in Coventry in the Midlands of England, near Birmingham. Coventry itself had been battered during the war and my dad was working for an industrial paint company, having tried his hand at being a car salesman – he was shown the door after crashing a customer's car on their test track!

As it turned out, Uncle was the owner of a paint company, with its head office on the Isle of Man, and my parents were given the chance to move there soon after they were married.

Dad was a keen cyclist and had been to the island several times riding his bike and loved the place, so it was an easy decision when the offer came.

My father's love of cycling had come to him by accident, I suppose. As a young boy he had suffered terribly with asthma.

He has told me how he can remember standing in his cot, so very young, hands gripping the sides and fighting for air. Years later, while still afflicted with this frightening condition, he went to a doctor whose prescription was to buy himself a bicycle and get pedaling out in the fresh air. This did two things. It gave him a huge geographical knowledge of the British Isles taking in just about every square mile of the land, but it also cured his asthma. The doctor was right.

A couple of years later, having settled into married life on the island, my eldest sister, Jacqueline, came along. She was known to us as Jacqui or more commonly by her family pet name, Ninee. She is 13 years older than me and has always been my other mum in many ways.

I remember vividly when she was in London at university, her coming home to surprise her six-year-old baby brother for my birthday party, or the time that I spent a week with her in London, her taking me to Trafalgar Square and HMS *Belfast*.

I stayed at her student house with her uni friends; it was such a great week. Ninee became a teacher; after she graduated from university she returned to the Isle of Man and began working at a local primary school. But her real passion was, and always has been, the performing arts.

She absolutely loved speech and drama, and it was through her when I was a little older, say 10 or so, that she got me involved. I enjoyed doing some plays, I took part in some school productions and was in a couple of stage shows at the local theatre too, but I never had the passion for it that she did and still does to this day.

She left teaching some years later and set up her own stage school, which has grown and thrived into a very reputable business. She and her staff put on lots of shows and help lots of kids find their confidence, their voice and even their careers! I am extremely proud of her and her achievements, but undoubtedly her greatest ones have been her children. All four have turned into amazing people with flourishing careers and families now, too.

Three years later my other sister arrived. September 1960 saw Vivienne, Viv to us, or more commonly called Gump as her family pet name. Gump actually came from the fact that Jacqui's eldest child, born in 1982, couldn't say Dumpty, which had been the pet name my parents gave her. The story goes that she kept falling off things, rather like Humpty Dumpty. So Gump arrived and it's probably fair to say that my parents' lives got a whole lot busier.

If Ninee was quiet, well-behaved and compliant, Gump was the opposite, mischievous, loud, headstrong and intelligent beyond her years. She managed to excel at everything she did, be it at school, university, in business, or in her various passions such as show jumping, carriage driving and dog breeding. She was just a natural winner.

I say "was" because tragedy struck our family in 2000 when, around the time of her 40th birthday, Gump was diagnosed with breast cancer. The next few years were a roller coaster ride for her and us all. From a double mastectomy and reconstruction surgery to the joy of remission, to the absolute heartache of accepting that one day she would lose this battle and with it we would lose an incredible human being.

While Ninee and I had a great relationship, the fact that she was 13 years older meant she was in a very different phase of her life from where I was.

Although Gump was 10 years older than me, we got to spend lots of time together. I was her little sidekick, she took me everywhere, well, almost everywhere! There are some places an 18-year-old girl doesn't want to take her baby brother. Understandably, she wouldn't want me cramping her style.

Viv met a boy and love bloomed. He was a car mechanic, or at least training to be one. My parents didn't approve but we knew my sister was headstrong and was pursuing this relationship. Naturally, I had no idea of their displeasure and, to be honest, I approved greatly! His name was Adrian and he was a rally driver. Not only that, he took me out in his rally cars and if my love of cars, motorbikes and anything with wheels wasn't already deeply seated, at eight years old, this guy was like a superhero to me.

Some of my very fondest memories of spending time with Viv were sitting on the sides of hedges watching Adrian come past in his Mini rally car. In later years, I got to live with them both in London and it was magical. Silverstone, Brands Hatch and all manner of other exciting places were on the regular visit schedule to watch all manner and forms of motorsport.

When I was old enough to drive, she and I used to race everywhere. God could she drive. I don't think I ever beat her, but I think she had a faster car to be fair!

As you can imagine, all throughout my single-digit years, into my teenage ones and to this day, I have been monitored closely by cardiologists specially trained in congenital heart disease.

Initially, these visits meant a plane ride to Liverpool, but around the time I was 15 the doctors started coming to the Isle of Man as there were more "customers" for them to see. It was on one of these visits in 1996 that I called Viv up after the appointment in tears.

Until that point, I had not had to take any ongoing medication; my heart had been working really well, allowing me to take part and compete in my love of motorcycling, the sport I chose and the sport that chose me. But that day things changed.

On reflection, they didn't change too much, but at the time I honestly thought it was the beginning of the end. The docs wanted me to take a small tablet each day to help relieve pressure on the heart. The medication is more commonly used to control high blood pressure (hypertension) but for me they were using it for another purpose.

My sister was amazing as she always was, reassuring me that I wasn't going to die anytime soon and that taking a small tablet each day was no big deal really and she was right, it wasn't.

These days, I still take that same drug each day. The dose has never changed in over 20 years, except now there are a few more to go with it!

Viv was often right about things. She taught me so much. From helping me to understand algebra, to taking me under her wing when I was 18 and out into the big wide world on my own in one of the biggest and busiest cities in the world.

But it all ended, for us all.

DARK DAYS

The first time I encountered death was at the age of six. It was the school summer holidays, if memory serves me right it was August.

A beautiful summer's day had seen me and some other friends, including one of my best friends, Sam, taken to the swimming pool at the school I would be attending in a few years' time. During the school holidays, the school allowed families of pupils attending the school (or its sister school, where I spent the first number of years of my educational journey) to purchase a season pass. I am sure it was 10 pounds for the whole summer, which seems very cheap now, but in reality in 1976 was still a decent amount of money, I suppose.

My friends and I played our games, our favourite being walk the plank, which saw one person standing at the end of the diving board having to battle another person and whoever fell in first won. If you didn't fall in, it was winner stays on!

Sam had a younger sister named Anna who was in my year at school. While in the pool, she blurted out to me that Michael had died, just almost dropping it into conversation, perhaps as you would at that age. I wasn't sure what to think. Was she joking? It was certainly a strange thing to say. I'm not sure I believed her, but there again, why would she lie about something like that?

We all got out of the pool, and I think Sam and Anna's mum gave me a lift home. In the car, Anna's mum was visibly upset and indeed confirmed the awful news that Michael had died while out riding his bike with his dad. That is all that was said.

The next part I remember vividly as if it were yesterday. Arriving home, my mum was standing at the kitchen sink with her head scarf on and a light blouse with slacks. Clearly, she had taken the opportunity to catch up on a few chores on Saturday morning while her son was out at the pool with friends.

I tapped her back and as she turned I said, "Mummy, Michael has died." She looked at me as if I had just sworn using the worst language possible. She couldn't believe the words that had come from my mouth and immediately told me off for telling such terrible and horrible lies. She sat me down and explained that to say such awful things about someone, let alone one of my best friends, was despicable behaviour.

She asked me how and why I had come to tell this atrocious prevarication. "Anna told me" I said, and just as I had said it, the phone rang. Mum answered, her gaze still reflecting her sentiment towards me at that moment; she wasn't done with me yet, I feared. But her usual healthy glow quickly changed as blood drained from her face. One of our other family friends had been put in charge of ringing around the close-knit group of mums and dads to deliver the shocking, yet no longer a tale, news.

She apologised to me immediately for not believing me, taking me in her arms and squeezing me tight. Tears were streaming down her face and I looked on quizzically. Michael had indeed died while out riding his bike with his dad on that sunny summer's day. I wish he had come swimming instead.

Of course, at age six, I don't think dying and death are understood; I know they weren't by me. "But will he be OK Mummy?" I asked. Thinking that, OK, he's had an accident, he is asleep at the hospital, but he will wake up and we will be able to play again soon, when he is better.

It must have been heart-wrenching for her to have to try and explain that death doesn't work that way. Michael would never wake up again and I would never see him again. She was right on both counts. He had been eight years old when he was taken from us.

Not only was his death the first death I had been close to, certainly the first I remember, so too was his funeral. A week or so later, as the dawn of realisation arose that I would never see him again, it was his funeral.

During those years and indeed for most of my early childhood, we lived in a small, quaint village called Ballasalla, the Gaelic translation being "place of the willow trees." Ballasalla had been built up around Rushen Abbey, an ancient monastery, which had been founded in the early 12th Century. It had one church, which came many centuries after the Abbey, dedicated in the late 19th Century.

Again, I unfortunately remember the day of his funeral quite vividly. The church was packed. He was a popular boy from a popular, well-known family. I solemnly recall the remaining members of the family, Michael's parents and his younger brother David, with whom I would attend "big school" a couple of years later.

What I recall mostly though, is the grey skin on the faces of Michael's parents. His dad had his arm wrapped around his wife, who was barely making it down the aisle to take her seat in the front row of the pews. I remember the many flowers atop his coffin, but most of all, I remember being sad.

For years later (and I do mean years – well into my twenties), I would have a recurring dream about Michael's death. I didn't dream of his crash; I dreamed about the funeral car crashing into a set of railings on the roundabout in our village. The car had several coffins in it, on trays, rather like a tool box that folds out. Michael was in one of them, but the car had crashed on the way to the church. On one of the occasions, I had the dream, the following day I rode past the railings at the roundabout on my bike, only to discover the railings had been bent, a car had crashed into them during the night. This in itself scared me.

Of course, Michael's death had a profound effect on me; how could it not have? I used to visit his grave regularly and whenever I am back on the island I make a point of going. Such a tragic end to what I am sure would have been a very well lived life.

The next death to have a profound effect on me was that of my sister, Viv, AKA Gump. Of course, this was many years after saying goodbye to Michael and this time I knew exactly what death meant, it's finality. As mentioned earlier, Viv had been diagnosed with cancer around her 40th birthday in 2000.

We were all relieved and at the same time hopeful that the post-operative remission that had been declared would remain in play. It didn't. It was 2am in New Zealand, November 2, 2003. I knew, we all knew, she was ill. The cancer had returned; it was taking over her body, rapidly. It was in her bones, in her brain and was trying to extinguish her, rather like a boxer that keeps hitting their opponent even when they are clearly defenceless and unable to come back. It was pummelling her from inside out.

Donna, my previous wife, and I had not long been in New Zealand. We had decided to move there for lots of different reasons, but it had been a hard decision.

While, understandably, my parents did not want to accept or even contemplate her fate Viv and I had talked a number of times about the fact that one day this vile disease would take her.

Perhaps it was because I had been born with a serious medical condition that I understood you don't want people to keep saying you will be fine, almost as lip service, if you are unwell and there are facts to be discussed or contemplated.

Don't skirt around those facts, however hard it may be. I don't say this being critical, or cold of others who don't want to hear or accept bad news, I completely get it and understand. Surely things don't get much rock bottom in life than losing a young child.

I recall some funny moments with her in the latter months of her life. By this time, she was in and out of hospice regularly. She was willing herself to get better and remain positive but at the same time being realistic.

Her evening penchant was a gin and tonic, and why not? While the staff at the hospice encouraged the patients in their care to enjoy whatever time they had left with as much fulfilment and quality as possible, I suppose there were still boundaries and guidelines.

Of course, Viv, just like she had all of her life, decided her own rules, marched to her own drum and certainly wasn't going to be constrained by some "silly" rules.

So, her regular instruction to me was to buy her some of those ready-made G&Ts and sneak them in. We discovered the easiest way to do this was to pass them through one of the sash windows of the imposing Victorian building, as conveniently all of the patients' rooms in this delightful looking building were on the ground floor. Problem solved! There was the day that she asked Donna and me to pick her up from the hospice and take her for lunch. We were always more than happy to do so, as by now we had decided, though torn, on moving to New Zealand for a year. There were a number of reasons why we had decided to make the move. On reflection, some of them positive and some of them negative.

So we collected her from hospice and made our way to a dine-in fish and chip shop, a kind of upmarket one if there is such a thing! Over lunch, she tackled us both and was very blunt with her instructions to us. "You must go to NZ", she said. "I don't want you both hanging around here waiting for me to die."

I cried almost immediately. I suppose, a bit like Michael all those years earlier, it became abundantly clear that there would come a time in the not-too-distant future that her life would end. Amazingly she was at peace with it. Braver than anyone I have met before or since. Her stoicism was incredible. How could anyone facing their end be so accepting of their fate? I knew I wouldn't be. What I did say to her was that she had bloody better stay alive long enough for us to get home and say our goodbyes.

Little did I know that September 3rd, 2003 would be the last time I saw her alive. It was her birthday and we all headed out to celebrate at our local restaurant. That night we had a picture taken together, Viv, my mum, my other sister, her husband Tony, Donna and me. My dad must have taken it. It would be the last picture of us altogether. I treasure it to this day.

Viv's face and body ballooned from the high doses of steroids being pumped into her to help her pain and to make life just a little more comfortable as she endured yet more chemotherapy. She looked nothing like my sister really, no hair, a body and face that was, for all intents and purposes, unrecognisable to us, but I didn't care. I just wanted her to live.

When the bad news came, we were at a nightclub to celebrate my getting a job. Just as we went to sleep, the phone rang; it was my other sister on the end of the line. Viv had gone. Every ounce of my being broke. I just couldn't believe it. I knew it would happen, but I had promised her, promised myself, promised my parents that we would be back before the end. I had failed to deliver on that promise and to this day I hate myself for it. I should have been there, I wasn't and now I would never get to talk to her, to hug her, to share time with her ever again.

It really, really hurt. Time makes things easier but 20 years and there isn't a day, in fact, there are multiple times per day that she is in my thoughts. While I am not religious, I know she is with me; I feel it. I feel her presence regularly.

GROWING UP

To be honest, by and large I had what I would deem to be a normal childhood in the sense that I wasn't really restricted in what I did.

My parents were amazing in how they balanced the protection they very clearly wanted to give me, with the freedom to live. They didn't wrap me up in cotton wool at all.

In fact, I am sure there would have been a few raised eyebrows from other parents in later years once I started riding motorbikes competitively. My parents' philosophy was for me to be careful but to have fun. Not to overdo it, but not to hold back either. I cannot recall a time when either one of them said no to me if I wanted to try something and I have the utmost respect and love for them because of that.

I had been at school since I was four years old, and at nine I went to an amazing school, a private school on the island called King William's College (KWC).

My first day there in September 1980 was so scary! I had gone from a small prep school where I knew everyone and was one of the oldest kids, to this enormous school that was centuries old – think Hogwarts! Both my sisters had gone to KWC's partner school, which acted as the prep school for boys, but the girls stayed all the way through to their senior years.

Before being accepted into KWC, it was a requirement that an entrance exam be taken. I can recall being shown around the area of the school where we were fortunate enough to go and we would spend most time in. There was one area called The Octagon. It was a sort of central hub of, funnily enough, eight converging points. It seemed such a large area and had a mosaic tile inlay on the floor, the red tiles with various other coloured tiles making up the pattern. The best thing about it though, was it was slippery so you could run and do skids across it!

Dressed in my shorts, blazer and cap, off I went for my first day at 'big school'. I just couldn't believe that we had to change classrooms for each different lesson. Then there was lunch. Each day, before we ate, grace was read in Latin from the balcony above the dining hall. Every morning except Wednesdays, we had chapel.

The teachers (we called them masters) were dressed in their robes. There were much older boys, some of whom were prefects, who bossed us junior kids around no end. So, it was all very formal really, and while I have never been the most studious or academic of people, the school gave me an excellent grounding for life.

But school life wasn't without its challenges; boys will be boys, after all. Mostly, I could take part in the extra-curricular activities, such as cricket, swimming and so on.

During one of my check-ups, I asked my doctor if I could play rugby. I told my mum I wanted to play because I liked it, which was in part the case, but the main reason was that I was getting what these days would be called bullied by others for not playing. The doc wasn't keen; he was more concerned about me being hit in the chest very hard than the actual physicality of it, but I persisted anyway.

I wasn't going to be called names and thought of as a weakling by anyone. However, cross country was another story. I have never been a runner, even when I was young, I just didn't have the stamina to sustain running for more than a minute at a time before I needed a rest! I didn't mind and I was happy not to participate.

I enjoyed some other aspects of school. I became involved with speech and drama, as I mentioned earlier, and I also enjoyed being involved with the Duke of Edinburgh's Award Scheme.

A legacy of the war years saw many private schools have a cadet scheme for the army, navy and air force. We had to choose one, so I chose the army. I enjoyed the formality of it; the discipline of polishing rifles and boots, and ironing shirts with a razor-sharp crease for inspection every Tuesday afternoon. It was fun; we got to go on overnight exercises, ride in a helicopter from time to time, and generally pretend to shoot one another. What could be better?

School was tough though. It was hard, it was competitive and there were some very bright and talented kids there, some of whom I am still friends with today.

Around 1983 when I was 12, my mum had started to notice that I was much more tired than I had usually been. My schoolwork wasn't so good (not that it had been fantastic to begin with) and I was just struggling much more. I had virtually stopped growing too.

Interestingly, many years later I attended a lecture while living in Auckland about the lesser-known effects of congenital heart disease. One of the topics of discussion was the impact that an impaired circulatory system had on the long-term development and, thus, the cognitive ability of a person. It was certainly a light-bulb moment for me (no pun intended!). Was this the reason I had struggled at school, particularly with my ability to concentrate over long periods of time. My mind would wander off the task very easily. In all honesty, it's the same these days.

I have to take regular breaks from activities like reading a book, doing an Excel worksheet for work, or even writing a book! OK, so maybe it was/is just my personality, but I am quite sure that the initial starvation of oxygen has had its implications.

At one of the regular check-ups, my mum mentioned all this to the doctor, and he thought it might be a good idea to investigate. So, in July that year, I was flown over to Liverpool once again to have a heart study done. This was by way of a catheter placed into my veins via my groin, just like the life- saving procedure I had had 12 years earlier. The tests were all about measuring the various pressures in the heart, as the doctors believed that the baffle was not working as well as it should have been.

When someone grows up with a chronic condition that needs ongoing care and follow-up, no matter what it is, the person becomes used to being poked, prodded, examined, talked about and tests being carried out. It's just part of the gig.

To many people this may sound awful (and to many people it probably would be), but I didn't really mind. It meant time off school (never a bad thing), having a ride on a plane (always a good thing) and staying in a hotel with my mum for a couple of nights (also fun). We would usually stay at the Atlantic Towers hotel, certainly my favourite place in Liverpool. The hotel was located near where the Isle of Man ferries to-ing and fro-ing would tie up. It also had a great view of one of the most well-recognised landmarks in the UK, the Royal Liver Building at Pier Head.

Mum was fantastic at offsetting any worry or anxiety I may have had about any of the procedures or tests I would be having, enveloping me in her love and reassuring me all the time, even though I am sure her own anxiety about her son's uncertain future must have been a heavy burden.

The letter written after the tests was candid. I suppose there is no use in beating around the bush, is there? The sentence that discusses the quality of my life being likely to be "significantly reduced if the present situation remains unchanged" is the focal point for me.

By then in 1983, the Mustard procedure had been carried

out many, many times across the world. The operation was sound, it worked, but as I would find out much later in life, many of the kids needed a follow-up operation, as was now being recommended for me.

So, my parents had another critical decision to make. Should they put me through another gruelling 12-hour operation, with no guarantee of an improved outcome? Albeit the doctors were confident that they could fix me up once more and give me back better exercise tolerance and general wellbeing. The end of the letter referred to a planned operation for the end of the British summer in 1984.

I am not sure why, but fortuitously, this date was brought forward to January 1984. As it turned out, it's a good job it did.

REDO

Christmas of 1983 I can remember well. I can't remember many around that time of my life, but this one is crystal clear.

It didn't register with me then, but now I know exactly what was going on. Just before Christmas, my mum took me to have some portrait studio pictures done. I was wearing a red shirt and a god-awful V-necked tank top jumper! My hair had been brushed to look like a choir boy. Angelic I was not! This was clearly my parents' opportunity to get some last pictures of their only son, if things did not go as planned.

It's heavy stuff really, but I absolutely understand why they did it. They may only have memories of me to reflect on in a few weeks' time. How awful for them. Again, their emotions must have been all over the place. But they didn't show it, at least not to me. They exuded strength, positivity, support and love.

While I didn't appreciate it at the time, I know now that I was stressed, I was scared. I was 13 and old enough to know how things could go. That said, the thing I was looking forward to the most was time off school! The thing I was looking forward to the least was being off my motorbikes for a while, although not as long as some had estimated!

People have, through the years, when they have heard about my story and others like me, said we are brave. I don't think so. I am not being gallant or modest when I say this. Bravery doesn't come into it. It's a mindset of choice.

You want to live, or you don't. The brave people are the doctors and nurses who give their all to help make that happen. Brave is running into a building that's on fire when others are running the opposite way, or going into battle when most of us wouldn't, or putting themselves before others in order to help augment a better outcome than would otherwise occur.

If I must put a word about how a patient accepts their plight and faces what is sometimes overbearing adversity, then I think it's courage. Courage to face what is before you head on. To withstand fear or a difficult situation. I am not brave, but I will say that I, and others like me in this position, have shown courage.

Christmas was lovely, it always was in our house. I suppose we were a traditional family in the sense of following a fairly well-accepted plan of the day. If I had been a good boy, Santa would have left some presents for me at the bottom of the bed, which was very exciting.

Before Santa came, one of our traditions was for Mum and Dad to take me out to dinner, generally at a lovely restaurant in our village, La Rosette. The food was sumptuous and it was good practice for what was typically to follow the next day, more food!

My parents were married on Christmas Eve, so it was also nice for them to go out and celebrate their anniversary. I suppose they would rather have done so without me, but as both my sisters had well and truly left home by then, they probably had no choice but to take me with them!

After dinner we headed to the local church, the same church that Michael's funeral had been in almost eight years earlier. While none of my family are religious, there is something very magical about going to midnight Mass, even though we usually went to the earlier service, as a midnight start is a bit late for a 13-year-old!

With church done, it would be home and to bed, not forgetting to leave whisky and a couple of mince pies for Santa first though. (You are welcome, Dad!)

So Christmas Day was always busy. I would accompany my parents to a couple of drinks parties in the morning, while my sister Viv would be left in charge of cooking the lunch. This arrangement had come to pass after one year when my mum may have had one too many gin and tonics in the morning and almost tried to kill us all with a very undercooked turkey!

One of the more interesting aspects of our Christmas was that my dad insisted that the family presents, i.e. the presents we had bought one another, couldn't be opened until after lunch had finished, which given our "lunch" usually only started around 3pm and was always a long affair, meant that presents didn't get unwrapped until around 7pm!

This was purgatory, but it's a tradition I have now carried on with my own family and again it's the cause of great frustration each year! My parents' reasoning was that if all the presents were given out at the start of the day, then we would be distracted by the new presents and wouldn't want to sit down for lunch!

The Queen's speech was a tradition, probably similar to many British families. The day would be rounded off with either a game of charades, or a James Bond movie, or sometimes both, it really depended on how much wine had been consumed by then!

Although not much was said about my impending operation that Christmas, there was a certain air that this could be the last time we were all together as a family. Me, my mum and dad, my two amazing sisters, Ninee's husband and my nephew, who by then was two years old.

YES, MATRON!

January 5, 1984. Walking across the apron towards the Viscount aircraft operated by Manx Airlines, the National flag carrier of the island, I turned back to see my dad and my two sisters waving.

Fingers crossed, I would be seeing them again in a few days. I was wearing my favourite jacket. Thick and warm, it had been bought for me at Christmas and was just what I needed for this crisp winter's day. I had seen it in the shop several times and had hoped that Santa would get it for me.

As the four Rolls-Royce engines pulled us up off the ground for the short journey to Liverpool, I looked out of the window, wondering if I would see this land I had called home for the past 12 years again. It was a beautiful day for flying but as we made our way across the Irish Sea, I snuggled up to my mum, she smiled, put her arm around me and that sense of safety came over me. I would be OK, of course I would, my mum would make sure of it.

As previously mentioned, I have always considered Liverpool to be my second home.

I can think of no other reason for this than it's the location in which my life was saved, not once, but twice. Unusually perhaps for a Brit, I have never really followed football, or soccer as it's known in Australia. Many of my friends did, and their parents too, but back then if it didn't have wheels or an engine, I wasn't really interested! That being said, if there was to be a team I supported, it was then, as it is now, Liverpool FC.

As a youngster, I had never been to a football match. I had seen it on TV, but coming from the Isle of Man, where we didn't have a team that played in the Premier League, it wasn't that prevalent, at least not for me.

In my late teenage years, one of my friends who had originally come from Manchester, around 30 miles east of Liverpool, took me to a couple of games. He was a huge fan of Manchester United, a proper Red Devils follower.

One match was between Manchester United and Nottingham Forest, and the following day we went to watch Liverpool playing Everton at Anfield, the home of Liverpool FC. To that point in my life I had never seen such a large crowd. The noise, the emotion, and even though it was winter, the heat was incredible. The thing I remember most was when there was a goal or even an exciting part of the game, such as a free kick, the surge of the crowd was ridiculous. You couldn't fight it, there was no point. Your feet were just lifted from the ground as the energy from thousands of revellers enveloped your own personal space. You literally were along for the ride.

But of course, it's much more than just the soccer team that draws me to Liverpool whenever I'm there, though sadly, it's been far too long. It's also more than the hospital I was being looked after in, more than the skills of the highly trained medical professionals that saved my life, quite literally. It's also more than the cheeky Scouse sense of humour and accent. It's all of these things and more. It's a place that seems to exude love. Love for all, no matter your background or circumstance, the people are super friendly and my memory of them is that they would give you the shirts off their backs (so long as you gave them a tenner – just kidding!).

I feel it would be impossible not to be drawn to a place that has so much meaning to your life, and for me, that place is Liverpool.

Sister Wynn had been a junior nurse back in 1970 and 1971 when I was operated on for the first time. Now, as the nurse in charge of the ward – the matron as they were called in those days – she was somebody who made sure things happened. A no-nonsense, forthright, but kind-beyond-words lady, her demeanour was reassuring to me but I am sure it could be frightening to junior doctors and nurses if they got on her wrong side.

Known to me as Aunty, she was there at the entrance to the Royal Liverpool Children's Hospital, waiting as our taxi pulled up. She embraced my mum, then me.

In 1970 and 1971, while I was in hospital, my mum spent most weeks to-ing and fro-ing between the Isle of Man and Liverpool, balancing the attention she wanted to give me with the attention that my two sisters, aged 13 and 10, also needed and yearned for.

My dad, too, had pretty much been a solo parent for the first six months of my life. My mum told me about some of the ferry trips she had been on during those winter months after my birth; they sounded awful. I remember her telling me about one journey where, after four hours of sailing, the ship hadn't reached the end of the River Mersey to enter the Irish Sea. In normal conditions, a sailing would take four hours from Liverpool to the Isle of Man. Twelve or 13 hours later the ship arrived in Douglas, the capital of the island. I am sure there would have been some green faces disembarking that day! The Irish Sea can be a torturous place. These days when the waves are that size, the ships don't sail.

During the weeks that she was by my side, my mum became friendly with many of the nurses. In fact, she slept in the nurses' home most of the time. This was before the days of family accommodation and support. It was a time when the hospital looked after patients, but parents and family had to make their own arrangements.

So, my mum and Sister Wynn became good friends and with that she had a bit of a soft spot for me.

We went into the hospital and up to ward five, which was on the second floor. The smell of disinfectant, that unmistakable hospital odour of the time, met my nose almost immediately. I think it was then that it dawned upon me that this was more than just one of my regular checkups, this was the real deal and there was no backing out now.

I'm quite sure I held on to my mum's hand that bit tighter in that moment, looking for the "you will be OK" squeeze back from her, which I inevitably received.

Sister Wynn showed me to my bed. It was the first cubicle on the left after the big double doors that separated the ward from the rest of the hospital. I thought it unusual that my bed didn't face the middle of the corridor, as was usually the case. Instead, it was parallel to the corridor.

What this allowed, though, was for me to see out of the large window. This was my link to the outside world for the following two weeks.

The hospital was on the corner of Myrtle Street, a bustling road with a steady procession of buses, taxis and pedestrians going about their daily lives. As I leaned against the ward's old-fashioned radiator – you know the ones, cast iron with huge grills and painted institutional white – with my head against the glass, I remembered wondering if I would get out of here alive?

Maybe it was then that I had my first realisation in life that, ultimately, we all just exist, have our own paths and our own stories, mine was no more important or less so than anyone else's. The person crossing the street a couple of storeys down had no clue, no interest and no need to concern themselves with my plight, in the same way that I didn't theirs. Even though at the time you think, what can be more precarious than me awaiting open heart surgery for the second time in my 13 years.

"Victor," Sister Wynn snapped me out of my trance. I turned to see her. "Come on, I have something to show you," she said. I followed her into the kids' play area at the end of the ward. The room was on the right, just past the doctors' offices where they wrote their notes and consulted the patients and their parents, as had happened to us a few months earlier.

The playroom, as could be imagined, was painted in kiddy colours, bright and vibrant with pictures of monkeys, the alphabet and so on stencilled on the walls. I am too old for this room, was my initial thought. However, Sister Wynn said: "Look what I have for you!" It was a ride-on toy, but not just any ride-on toy, this was the milk float! This was my milk float, I owned it. I mean I didn't, but I did at the same time!

The milk float was my favourite toy growing up, from as early as I can remember (maybe aged three or so). When we used to go back to the hospital for regular check-ups, usually every six months, I would whizz up and down the ward on this machine. Trust me when I say it was the fastest milk float in all of Liverpool. I could truly make that thing zoom, sliding around corners scaring the bejesus out of the medical staff and other parents and generally causing havoc! No one would get a look in for a turn while I was in town. No sir, she was all mine!

I smiled at Sister Wynn and said it was time for someone else to take over the milk float, complete with plastic bottles that looked more like Skittles and certainly reacted like them once I was behind the wheel. After all, I was now 13. Aside from even being able to fit on the thing, it wasn't good for my street cred – Adrian Mole would agree!

I had arrived at the hospital four days before my operation so that a whole barrage of tests could be carried out. Everything from X-rays, to having blood taken to cross match for the operation, to ultrasounds and pees and poos were tested. The doctors had to make sure I was as fit and as well as I could be to give me the best chance of survival. Those tests started right after the playroom visit with a decent-sized needle about to be sunk into one of the veins in my arm.

I know some people are really scared of needles; I am happy to say I am not one of them. I mean, I don't relish them, who would? but I have always understood that they come with the gig of having a heart condition.

I have never kept count, but gosh, I would love to know how many I have had over the years – literally thousands. Not always to take blood, of course. There are lots of different reasons I have found myself with a tourniquet and a needle shoved into my vein, or artery.

It's most definitely a skill that, unfortunately, not all medical practitioners seem to have! Over the years I have seen the full range, from incredibly skilled phlebotomists to others who just seem to shove it in and hope for the best.

It was one of the latter I would encounter many years later while living in Auckland, New Zealand. I was having a procedure and needed a cannula put in my arm. I will confess I am not the easiest of specimens to get a needle into. It's a good job I have never had a penchant for illicit drugs of any variety, otherwise I would have been devoid of getting my high on a regular basis!

Unfortunately for the nurse that day, my veins were shy, not cooperating. I think the rules must vary from jurisdiction to jurisdiction, but at this hospital, she was allowed three goes at getting the needle in my arm. We were up to the last attempt. She decided that there was a nice popping vein on the inside edge of my left wrist, just by my watch strap. She was wrong. In she went and pop ... she had literally hit a nerve. Holy shit!! My god, the pain was unreal! I immediately went clammy and tried my best not to swear at her or out loud.

In fairness, she was very apologetic and suggested that the consultant could throw the line in when I was in theatre. Good plan, I winced! Still to this day, my wrist is tender from that.

Sister Wynn did all my pre-op procedures on the ward. Anything she could do, such as taking bloods, she did.

When not being poked or prodded or wheeled around the hospital to various departments like X-ray, I could do what I wanted, although I was under house arrest of course! So, I listened to music. I had been given a tape player, which had headphones, for Christmas, so I had "borrowed" some of Viv's tapes to play. Viv had bought me my first-ever vinyl LP a couple of years earlier. It was Status Quo's *Rocking All Over The World*. I didn't particularly like them as a band, but I did like the fact that their drummer, John Coghlan, lived in the same village as us back on the Isle of Man. That fact alone was enough to listen to their music! Tapes were the order of the day though. I had brought plenty with me, some having been recorded off a vinyl record, as was common back then, mostly on a Sunday night listening to the Top 40. Tape recording was an art. I wasn't necessarily very accomplished at the art of not missing the number one song for that week!

My two sisters were always trying to educate me in various ways. Viv would help me with maths and science subjects as she was amazing at them herself. She would also "educate" me with music. It was with her I went to see my first ever big music concert in 1989 at Wembley – Phil Collins *No Jacket Required* tour. Just like at the football match I couldn't believe the size of the crowd. It was incredible. It was quite overwhelming when she told me that there were more people inside that arena than lived on the Isle of Man! I couldn't believe it.

She and I went to see lots of bands together while I lived in London with her. Aside from Phil Collins, Black and Steve Winwood were my favourites.

She also introduced me to Guinness! One night we headed off to meet some of her friends, she was around 30, me 10 years younger. "I got you a pint of this," she said. I knew what Guinness looked like, and the fact that it came in a glass with Guinness on the side was a bit of a giveaway, but I had never tasted it to that point. Oh no, I thought, this stuff is amazing, I loved it! Several pints later I was having a great time! Less so the next day, however!

My other sister, Jacqui, aka Ninee, was more traditional in her education offering. She wanted me to read, and while I have never been a huge reader, I know that any interest in literature came from her.

At school, I was fairly good at English literature, speech and drama and the classics, I guess you would call them. Around the time of my O-levels, when studying writers such as Chaucer and his *Canterbury Tales*, I couldn't read the prose properly, it just didn't make sense. "Read it with a German accent if you can do one," she said. Huh? I tried it, it made sense! Ninee had bought me a slightly less intense book to take to the hospital, *The Secret Diary of Adrian Mole, Aged 13 and ¾*. I am not sure the medical staff appreciated me laughing out loud from my bed in those few days before my operation, but it was so funny and really helped to take my mind off the upcoming operation.

OPERATION DAY

January 9, 1984. The day had come, the day that would hopefully restore my health, give me more years to live. To finish school, grow into a man, maybe have a family someday and for me, above all, to be able to ride my trials bikes again.

A few years earlier, while on holiday in America, my mum and dad had taken me to all the kid hotspots; Disney World, Cape Canaveral, to name a couple. During the second week of the trip, we had been staying in Sarasota when my parents decided they needed a more low-key day. We ended up on one of those Mississippi river boats, the well-known ones, huge paddle steamers that back in the day would have ferried passengers and goods up and down the river. The one we embarked that day was purely a tourist attraction and had a restaurant, allowing passengers to dine while taking in the delights of the Gulf of Mexico.

As we were dining, a family near us overheard us talking and were taken with our British accents, mine in particular I believe! Of course, this was at a time in the late 1970s when it was still not that common for people to travel long distances, and I guess it was a bit unusual to have a family from the other side of the world dining alongside you. Either that, or they were just very outgoing, which, as we found out, they were!

I have never been shy and so when I was beckoned to join them, I did. The same fascination was at play for me. Wow, I thought, I am making friends with American people, this is amazing!

These guys hailed from far north America, somewhere near the border of Canada. Half of their year was in temperatures that, even today, I find hard to appreciate, and the other half was baking hot.

During the conversation they asked me what type of motorbike I had. Not if I had one – that was assumed. No they just wanted to know what type. I think their assumption was reinforced by learning that we hailed from the Isle of Man. Why wouldn't I have a motorbike?

Upon learning that, in fact, I didn't have a motorbike of any type, they immediately whistled my dad over and told him that the first thing he needed to do upon returning home was to get this young boy a motorbike. A boy cannot be a boy without one!

As it happened, I had been asking my dad for a scrambler bike for some time. Fortunately for me, one of my dad's colleagues was really into motorbikes. He had a son a year younger than me who had just got his first trials bike. His son's name was Steve Colley. He would go on to become one of the best trials riders the world had seen. He would also go on to become one of my very best lifelong friends.

So, my dad asked Brian, Steve's dad, for advice about what kind of bike to get me. Not a scrambler bike, Brian advised. Vic won't cope with the physical demands of a scrambler bike, get him into trials-bike riding.

And so, on October 8, 1979, my ninth birthday, I was the happiest kid on the planet when I came home from school and there in the garden with my name on it was a brand-new Yamaha TY80 trials bike. And so began many years of riding, competing and making new friends. Trials riding saved me.

But today, the trials bikes were in our garage at home. This was a different trial. I don't mind telling you, I was scared. I can feel that emotion still today when I think back. I was old enough to know that this was a big gig.

The trolley had come to collect me from the ward to take me

to theatre. I was about to get on it when Sister Wynn came by. "We won't be needing that," she said to the porter. She picked me up off the bed and literally carried me to the operating rooms!

I had said my goodbyes to my mum and dad. I had my favourite teddy. It too had a scar down its chest from when I operated on it some years earlier! I held on to him and Sister Wynn tightly as we made our way to the theatre.

My parents no doubt would have been pacing the hospital corridors just as they had all those years earlier. Waiting for news, good news.

From this point to when I woke up, I have no recollection of the procedure at all. Good job, too! But I do have the operation notes, which go something like this:

The holes they thought had been causing me to lose energy, slow my growth, struggle at school and affect my general development, were much worse than they had seen back in July the previous year. But, as it turned out, these holes had saved my life.

The main issue was that the baffle, or tunnel that was created 13 years earlier (almost to the day!) had narrowed badly. So the blood was backing up, and were it not for the several holes that had allowed the blood to bypass the blockage, my number would have been up.

The rest of the notes are unremarkable, except for the last paragraph, which details the "cardiac takeover." My heart wouldn't restart. Several attempts to restart my heart using electrodes placed around it had failed. This, no doubt, caused a few raised eyebrows. But then my heart decided of its own accord it was time to get going again and fired into life.

My next memory was as I began to come around from the anaesthesia. I remember vividly and dream about this regularly, even today, that one of the medical staff said: "We cannot lose him." These words have stayed with me this whole time. Unfortunately, my heart had started to leak blood from somewhere, so I was taken back to theatre urgently, and repaired.

The team having fixed me up again, the next thing I can recall is opening my eyes to see this bar thing across my field of vision and me going cross-eyed trying to focus on it. It was the ventilator tube. It was breathing for me.

The nurse said to me, relax, let the machine do this for you. No way! I wasn't having that in me any longer than was needed, and I had decided by then that it wasn't needed!

To those who've never experienced a ventilator, which I am guessing would be most of the population, it's the most bizarre sensation. While you want to breathe for yourself, you can't. If you try, you kind of cough and splutter. But breathing for you isn't like holding your breath either, you have to kind of do nothing. Very odd. Of course this can't continue, so as soon as the medical team sees that you want and need to breathe for yourself, the intubation tube has to come out.

"Cough, Victor!" came the instruction, and as I coughed, a tube was pulled from the depths of my chest out through my mouth. Not the most pleasant experience, I will confess! I was free, albeit still hooked up to many machines, drugs and monitors, but I was alive, I was breathing for myself and I had made it.

It had been about 36 hours from going into theatre to being taken off the ventilator. To me, it had seemed like five minutes. I was alive!

RECOVERY

Before the procedure, the physiotherapists had come by to tell me what would be happening post op. There were two distinct things I recall. The first was that they said I would struggle to raise my arms above my head and touch the back of the bed, but not to worry, this was normal and that they would help me get stronger each day. The second was that I would need some help with clearing my chest, which would likely be full of gunk.

The first of these was no issue. Two days after I woke, they came by as promised to see how I was doing. "Fine," I said, "I feel great." "Let's see how far you can put your arms behind your head, Victor," one of them said. I stretched my arms up towards the head of the bed and touched the iron bar behind me with ease. They looked at one another and then said, "OK, Superman, that's impressive!" Yeah, I thought. I have got this.

But before I was allowed to start gloating about my physical abilities, then came part two.

"OK, we are going to help you lay on your side."

They did so. Then they started playing drums on the side of my rib cage, it honestly felt like I was being hit with a hammer! This action started to dislodge phlegm and other disgusting nasties from my chest, lodged there from having been on a ventilator and not moving for a few days.

Next thing, I couldn't breathe. I was so blocked up with this stuff that they had to get the suction machine. Not a pleasant experience! As the tube went into my mouth, I felt a sense of panic, as I can only imagine a similar sensation would be with drowning.

Over the next week, my cry to the medical staff was: "Suck me out! Suck me out!"

Soon though, a routine was established. In the mornings before breakfast, in would come the bloods lady. She would stab me with a needle in my toe. It was not a needle as such, more of a pin that clicked. Placed upon one of my toes, she would then shoot and squeeze whichever toe had been the victim that day so that blood would come out of it.

I believe this was to ensure that my blood counts were fine and that I wasn't getting an infection of any kind. Then, after breakfast, I would go for a walk around the ward. Then a biscuit or something, then the physios would come by and knock seven bells out of me! After lunch, another walk, and then rest for a while. To break up this monotony, an odd trip to X-ray or for an ECG would occur. They were the best because I got to leave for a short time and see life outside ward five!

After I was out of intensive care and back on the ward my sisters could come and see me. They arrived separately; I don't know why, maybe as not to overbear me and wear me out, I am not sure. My recollection is that my oldest sister, Ninee, arrived first and after gentle hugs and so on, she started to read me my Adrian Mole book. Singularly, and without exaggeration, this was the best but also the most painful thing about my stay in hospital.

Open heart surgery obviously involves your chest being cut open with a scalpel, but to get access to the organs below, a special saw is used to cut through the breastbone and create access via large clamps or vices that pull the two sides of the chest part. This is fine really, while asleep. The real struggle comes when upon waking up and start laughing at Adrian Mole (or some other juvenile comedy). The rib cage is wired back together and needs time to heal, just like any other broken bone. Any laughter, cough or sneeze was excruciating! Meanwhile my other sister, Viv, aka Gump, had arrived in all her usual glamorous splendour. Viv had not long finished a course at the Steiner beauty college in London and had set up a small beauty business back home on the island. I am unsure if it ended up not being enough of a challenge for her, or she wanted to have an opportunity to earn more money, but not long afterwards she decided that investment banking was the way to go. Just like anything else she touched or tried, she excelled at that too!

But here she was, she had come to see her little brother and, oh, what was that smell? Her perfume and I took an instant dislike to each other. I don't think she had changed brands and it never used to bother me, but right then, right at that moment I couldn't breathe, it was so bad. The poor thing had to go and wash it off then come back to see me.

The doctors had said that I might stay in hospital anywhere from two to four weeks, depending how things went with the operation and my recovery. I continued to get stronger, to be suctioned out each day, in fact several times per day. I also decided that Twiglets, the crispy stick snacks covered in Marmite, were the best invention man had made so far (apart from motorbikes). And I continued to be tortured with the inevitable laughter that came with being read Adrian Mole.

Just over two weeks after arriving in the hospital, it was time to go home. It had still been school holidays when I had arrived at hospital and that kind of sucked, having to use my holidays to come into hospital, but of course now I would have lots more time off recuperating at home. I was fixed, I was getting stronger each day, and now my focus and attention was getting back to my beloved trials bike riding.

But before I went, there were a few goodbyes and thanks to do.

I saw the two surgeons who had given me a new lease of life. Their names were Mr David Hamilton and Miss McKay, surgeons who had been brave enough to put their skills to the test.

David Hamilton died in 2017 after a remarkable career, saving the lives of many children in all corners of the world. Originally from County Durham, he was the son of one of the main engineers responsible for designing and building the Forth Road Bridge near Edinburgh.

During his tenure as the lead surgeon for cardiothoracic surgery at The Royal Liverpool Children's Hospital, the hospital became well known as one of the best centres for paediatric cardiac care in Europe, if not in the world. I remember Mr Hamilton as a tall, handsome, athletic man. He was kind, but business-like. Like Sister Wynn in many ways. A traditionalist, someone who just got things done and knew his craft inside out (no pun intended!)

It goes without saying that I will be forever indebted to his skills and the skills of his colleagues, all of them. I don't say that lightly either, I really, truly mean it. It actually stirs significant emotion for me. It's one of the reasons why, in my adult years, I have always struggled with two things.

I would be the first to admit that I have no right to struggle, or maybe even think about these things, but I do, I can't help it. I get angry and frustrated.

The first thing is members of the general population who don't take care of themselves. Whether it's drinking too much, smoking, taking illicit drugs or being obese, I look at these people and I just think, wow, what a waste. I would give anything to have a body that functions normally, that works, that is able to train and get fit and be very healthy.

The second thing is those, like me, who have had surgery and then go and do that stuff anyway. I personally think it's just a pure insult to those incredibly talented and dedicated medical staff. I know that my second dislike is a little confrontational and I understand that. Who am I to judge anyway? It's not my life, it's theirs, that should be the end of it. But it's not. In both cases, I feel it's just such a waste.

Back home on the island, I had some catching up to do with schoolwork. In all honesty, I didn't really enjoy school that much. I wanted to ride my motorbikes. While I am grateful for the education I was given – it cost enough, as my parents used to remind me regularly – looking back on it now, I just didn't really fit in. I thought it grossly unfair that some non-curricular sports, such as golf, were encouraged and supported, whereas my chosen sport was frowned upon.

I became fairly good at trials bike riding; I could hold my own. I mean, I was never going to be a world champion or anything even close, but I won a few events along the way, got some sponsorship here and there and managed to get myself to a reasonably decent position domestically and even nationally for a few years.

It was during those few years that my school really took a dislike to my sport. I had to attend school on a Saturday as was the tradition; the morning was taken up with lessons and in the afternoon, until 3pm, there were sports.

But for me, on most weekends there was a boat to catch. My dad would roll up around noon, with our VW camper van all packed up and my motorbike on the back in a special cradle. My school friends would gather round and ask me where I was off to that weekend. Could have been Yorkshire, or the Midlands or maybe Hawkstone Park in Shropshire. Wherever it was we were going, it was a bloody damn sight better than staying at school, that was for sure!

The ship, like the ones my mum spent much of her time on during those first few months of my life, would leave around 2pm each Saturday afternoon.

Sometimes, instead of sailing to Liverpool, we would go to Heysham in Lancashire. It was a bit faster to get there, about three-and-a-half hours. Dad would then drive to where the event was being held and we would set up camp for the weekend.

Invariably, my best mate Steve Colley and his dad would be there too. Generally, but not always, we were the only two schoolboys who rode regularly in the UK at that time.

It would be an early-ish night and then competition the next day. After the event, we would make our way back to Heysham, but sometimes, if we had time, we would head into Morecambe or even Blackpool to go to the fairground rides. Steve and I used to love the huge slide drop in Blackpool. The slide was near vertical at the top and the sensation of falling only to be saved by the curve as you slid down in a hessian bag was fantastic. Such good times.

The tradition was that we would usually get the midnight boat back to the island. They called it a midnight sailing but, in fact, it went around 2am, so we were absolutely exhausted by that time. Once aboard, we would find a bit of floor, and with a pillow and a sleeping bag, bunk down for a few hours' rest.

The ship used to arrive at about 6am. We would head home, Dad would have a wash and a shave, Mum would make him some breakfast, and off he would go to work. I generally pulled the "I am too tired to go to school" card and ended up having the day off. School didn't take kindly to this either.

Eventually my number was up, and my parents got the call from the principal. He politely suggested that if they wanted their son to continue being educated at their school, it would be dependent upon my regular attendance.

At first, I wanted to leave; motorbikes were all I wanted to do with my life. Each day after school, I was straight to the garage, helmet on, riding boots on, and I was practising over the obstacles Dad had built for me. This was my Narnia, my Zen, my happy place. I honestly didn't give two stuffs about anything else, friends, school or pretty much anything else. I was 100 per cent committed to trials bikes and that was that!

However, with a bit of tough love and a few life lessons, my parents convinced me it would be important for me to do well at school, to knuckle down and pass exams so that I had options in the future. I used to exclaim that Steve didn't have to be so diligent and that he could continue his dream of becoming a professional trials bike rider.

While they never said it to me, not once that I can recall anyway, I knew what they were thinking, and they were right. Steve Colley was a cut above when it came to trials bike riding. A natural, a god on a motorcycle, born to ride. I was not at that level, never was, never would be. Sure, I beat him a handful of times when he had a rare off day, but there was a chasm of difference in talent between me and him. I started to understand where my priorities lay, at least a little bit, anyway.

I am guessing about four weeks after the operation it was time to go back to school. I can recall being nervous about it. Even though I had been doing some schoolwork at home, I was worried I would be so far behind that other boys would tease me for being stupid. They didn't necessarily tease me about that, but there was plenty of bullying and teasing to come. Kids can be cruel at times.

I have always been resilient, to a point I really didn't care, at least outwardly, about what people think of me. But inside, probably like most of us, I am sensitive. My upbringing had been that of a stiff-upper-lip and get- on-with-things kind of approach.

I remember sitting at the dinner table when I was about 16 and the subject of stress came up. My mum slapped me down, verbally, not physically, as I discussed that stress was an actual thing. "You have no idea about stress, Victor!" came her retort. Try living through a world war, walking miles to school each day, no matter what the weather, having nothing to eat, no heating. She was right, of course, but it was relative. I wasn't articulate enough to fight from my corner back then and, to be fair, I probably knew better!

I never ever told my parents that kids had been cruel or unkind to me. Academically, I was middle of the road. I was too smart for the kids who really struggled academically, but I wasn't anywhere near the boys who were so smart that most of them would go on to Oxford or Cambridge with unconditional offers; boys who would potentially run for government one day or be high-powered lawyers or doctors. No way I could compete with them. So, I was doomed!

I was in a class for most subjects that saw me trying to keep up with those very gifted kids, and the pace of learning was fast, particularly around the sciences. Ironic then that I ended up working in the chemical industry years later.

The clever kids would take the mickey out of me for not understanding certain aspects of physics or maths.

Then it would be time to go swimming. I had a huge scar down my chest. They all knew why it was there, but of course I was quizzed at each swimming lesson. In the end I started to make up a story. I was in the war, or I was bitten by a shark, something, anything to shut them up.

One day, I was getting changed after sport (it was compulsory to have a shower or a bath), a kid referred to my chest as representing a vagina and then went on to insult my mum about giving birth to such a "freak". I remember the word he used as clear today.

I didn't care about his analogy of female genitalia (I am not sure to this day what book he was studying biology from), but I did care about him insulting my mum. Without a second thought, I hit him, hard. He hit the floor like a ton of the proverbial. He never said a word ever again. I don't condone violence, but I do condone sticking up for yourself.

School was, in some ways, like the movie *A Few Good Men*. There was a code, you never "snitched" or told tales; that would make more trouble for you long term. There was very much an unwritten rule that you sorted out your own battles. I was never the strongest kid or the handiest with my fists, but I held my ground. I also had some really good friends who knew me well and the battles I had been through, and they always stood up for me. I have never forgotten that.

My own son has experienced bullying at school. I had a very off-the-record conversation with him once along the lines that some bullies only respond to physical retaliation and while it should never be your first line of defence, sometimes there is no other option.

But, I said, "Pick your battles. If you aren't sure you can win a fight, don't start one!" Luckily for our son, he was probably the strongest and most definitely the fittest in his class, so with my awesome parenting advice in mind, the next time this kid had a go at him, our boy flattened him.

The difference these days is that there is no code, everything is so by-the-book, so controlled and so politically correct. Personally, I am not sure that is always a good thing, in fact I know it's not.

In many ways, the comments and bullying that occurred were water off a duck's back, then. But now, I know it did affect me and I believe it's why I pushed myself harder than most in my cohort. If my family were ever to read this, it would be the first time hearing me talk about it. I never talked about it, ever. There was a code.

NO COTTON WOOL

Two weeks after going back to school and nine weeks after surgery, I rode in a motorbike competition again. I could not wait.

The event was held at one of my favourite venues, Lower Sulby Farm, land owned by Merv Caley, whose own boys used to ride too, although they were a few years older than me and in a different class.

The joy and excitement that each minute, hour or day on a motorbike brought me is so hard to explain, but it was my sanctuary. I am so grateful to those lovely American people on the riverboat, to my friend Steve Colley's dad, Brian, and of course to my parents, for not only buying me the motorbikes and supporting me but also allowing me to participate in a sport that has inherent dangers.

It's probably fair to say that there would have been a few people along the way who would no doubt have had a dull opinion of a kid with a serious heart condition riding a motorbike. Perhaps the odd subtle - or less subtle - quip was received by my parents from "concerned" bystanders, aka nosy do-gooders!

The fact is that trials bike riding is, without doubt, one of the safer forms of motorsport. It has much lower speeds than, say, scrambling (these days called motocross), and is certainly much less physically demanding.

In trials riding, the idea is that the rider navigates a predetermined, marked-out course across varying terrain, from muddy banks to tree roots, to rivers and rocks. These courses are known as sections of different lengths, from maybe 30 to 100 metres on average. While the rider is in a section, the idea is not to put a foot down to help balance. If a foot is put down, a point is added. We call these dabs. A maximum of five marks, or dabs, can be accumulated during one section. In fact, five would mean that, for whatever reason, the rider hasn't completed the section. They've either stopped, fallen off or maybe gone outside the section borders. So that the rider knows where to go, the course is marked with flags and/or tape. The rider must keep the blue flags to the left and the red flags to the right. Of course, the closer the flags and the harder the terrain, the more difficult the section is.

The winner and the results are decided by the rider who had the least number of marks. If you navigate the section "cleanly", meaning you didn't put your foot down (or any other body part touched the ground, such as an elbow etc.), then no marks were given against you and this was called a "clean". The idea was to get as many cleans as you could.

A typical event might have 10 to 15 sections, with four or five laps of those sections making up the event. It is called a trial.

The great thing for me was that each section might last from perhaps 20 seconds to a minute and while standing on a trials bike, negotiating all manner of terrain was intense, the intensity was in short, sharp bursts.

Unlike motocross, where a rider is racing for periods of about 20 minutes non-stop with extreme physical pressure on the body, trials riders are more like long-distance runners. There are breaks between sections. The pace was much slower, but that's not to discount the physical requirements of the sport. These days, professional trials riders are like any other high-performing athlete, extremely fit, with swimming, gym and mountain-bike riding as common training aids.

My mum, I think it's more than fair to say, was not necessarily eager to see her son, her delicate boy, riding motorbikes of any variety. But, good on her, she let me do it with one condition. Before I got my first motorbike, she made me promise that if ever I got a bike, I would never ever ride a motorbike on the road. A deal I agreed to without hesitation. I mean, I would have agreed to anything quite honestly!

Little did I know when I made that deal that my love for bikes would inevitably lead to other forms of riding. Also, little did I know that once I was 16 and legally allowed to ride on the road, I could compete in events with road sections, meaning I needed to ride from one venue to another as part of an event. So, while I agreed, that was a deal that was never going to stick. I am sorry, Mum!

I mentioned that it wasn't until I became a parent myself that some things became clear, that my empathy and understanding for how my parents must have felt clicked into place.

Any good parents want to protect their child, their pride and joy. It's entirely natural and I always understood that. I have immense gratitude and respect for the way my parents dealt with my condition. I am not sure that if I had been in their shoes, I would have been so easy on the reins. I think I would have kept a much firmer hold on them in terms of allowing me to do things.

Maybe it's because of my dad's upbringing, his own background, that he had a live-and-let-live view. Maybe it was his love of adventure sports, too, that he didn't feel he could or would want to deny me those experiences. Maybe it was my mum being told as a young woman that she couldn't do this or that. Maybe it was because they knew that my world could end at any time, and they wanted me to experience as much as I could. Maybe it was all these things. I am not sure what it was, but I am so glad they didn't wrap me in cotton wool.

My escapades on two wheels took what seemed to me to be a natural progression. Trials riding was always my number-one passion, as far as sport and fun were concerned, but I naturally wanted to try other forms of motorcycle riding.

Monday nights were time for me and my dad. By the time I was 12 or so, both my sisters had long since left home, so it was just Mum, Dad and me. On Mondays, Mum went to yoga with her friends. Afterwards they would settle in for a couple of gin and tonics at a pub in Port Erin, on the island. This allowed for a few hours of dad-and-lad time, and I made it count.

One cold winter's night, when Mum was out, Dad asked what we should do. Until then, Monday evenings had been taken up with playing table tennis in our summer house, which my dad built, or we would race one another at Scalextric. Or, if I had been competing on a Sunday, we would maybe strip the bike down, him teaching me about the importance of not losing the parts and doing things in a methodical manner or using the right tool for the job.

He taught me so much; those hints, tips and tricks never left me. Dad was not a mechanic, not by a long stretch, but he was methodical and able to work stuff out, and if he couldn't, we rang the Colleys!

This night he asked me what I wanted to do, and I said, aged about 12, "Please teach me to drive." I think it was spurred by a trials-riding friend of mine, Jonathan Kelly, who had driven his dad's car down a long track on the way to an event, and while Jon was a year or two older than me, I wanted to do that.

My dad owned a business supplying building materials, located nearby on an industrial estate. Back in 1982 there were not many buildings. In fact, for me and my mates, it was our go-to place to ride our BMX bikes, building jumps and generally having fun. Dad once built us a half-pipe up against a wall for us to ride on; it was so much fun and made me the most popular kid in the village!

So, he said, "You aren't old enough to drive Victor! Plus, where can I teach you? You are not allowed to drive on public roads." But what he hadn't counted on was me remembering that he had once told me that the industrial estate was on private land! I am sure there was a bit of me begging, but eventually he relented and off we went for my first driving lesson.

Propped up with an extra pillow or two, off we went in a Mazda 323, bronze, registration number 101MAN. All our family's cars were 101-something. By the time I had my own car I was given 101VMN, my sister Viv had VMN101. Jacqui had WMN101 and she still does to this day!

With great patience Dad explained what everything did and of course, I knew anyway. I had been changing gears from the passenger seat for ages. I knew the drill. Plus, I was mad about wheels and cars, so why wouldn't I know? Stall! Another stall ... Geez, this is a little trickier than it looks. But soon I had it, and after a few Monday-night lessons, we were zooming around the industrial estate doing 60mph along the bottom road. At the end of that road there was a grassy area. "Teach me how to do a handbrake turn, Dad."

I should explain that my dad, in his own right, could really steer a car. I think it's fair to say – and I am sure he won't mind me doing so – he was a bit of a nutter behind the wheel when he wanted to be. Other than on one occasion, I never ever felt scared. Back then, there were virtually no speed limits on the Isle of Man, so drivers could go as fast as they wanted, and Dad did. I will never forget the first time we went 100mph in a car. It was down a long straight called the Ballamodha, near where we lived. It was a straight for sure, but it was also downhill. We used the road a lot really, as it was the main road to get to where I rode my bikes.

I used to egg him on, and one day in his Capri he hit 100mph. It was absolutely awesome! Ecstatic.

So, I had a great teacher, and our Monday-night lessons became more and more involved. From learning to do proper three-point turns to parallel parking in tight spaces, to emergency stops to handbrake turns, he had me doing it all.

Sometimes in winter when it snowed and the police shut the roads, he would take me up to the hills in the car and there he taught me how to drive in snow and ice. It may sound reckless, it may sound foolhardy of him, but I know that having those skills has saved my life on more than one occasion.

The winter of 1988 was brutal. I was living in London with my sister Viv and her partner (the rally driver) and I was due to drive to Liverpool to get the ferry home to the island. It was the biggest snowstorm the UK had seen for years, with freezing fog and black ice everywhere. The M1 and the M6, the two main motorways to get from London to Liverpool, were both being closed as I was driving up them. There were cars spinning out of control everywhere and accidents all over the place. I was so grateful for all those illegal lessons. They quite literally saved my ass!

But my enthusiasm to get behind the wheel earlier than was legal almost cost me greatly. By the time I was 14, my best friend and I, who had been on a similar trajectory when it came to cars, were regularly flouting the law.

Paul McArd was 10 days older than me. His mum was coming out of the maternity hospital as my mum was going in to have me. Margaret, Paul's mum, was a tiny, beautiful Irish lady, with a temper like you had never seen. She had married Keith, a successful builder and property developer; their family business was now three generations in and well known. In fact, Paul would end up taking over the reins from his dad in the future. They had three kids,

Paul being the youngest. We ended up at the same schools, both interested in motorbikes. Paul rode a bit of motocross on his green Kawasaki KX80 from around the time I started to ride trials bikes. But he had other passions too. He loved the water, having fun and it's reasonable to say he just loved generally having a good time. Growing up we were almost inseparable, especially up to about 15 or 16. Their eldest child was several years older, so by the time Paul was 14, Gary, his older brother, was maybe 18 or 19. Gary had bought a Mini Metro MG to drive and this was then given to Paul as his first car to learn in when he was about 14.

Around this time Paul broke his left leg playing rugby at school and was somewhat incapacitated. Not to be deterred, Paul and I devised a cunning plan which saw him steer the car and use the accelerator and brakes with his good leg, while I used his crutch pressed against the clutch to change gears.

Our audacity continued and we became ever bolder in our escapades. By now, both of us were competent drivers and we could easily hold our own on the roads, the only issue being that we had no licence and no insurance!

We didn't let these seemingly minor details slow us down. Initially, we would go for drives locally, mostly during school holidays and in the dark so as not to be seen. Inevitably, our lust for the thrill became more and more brazen. We decided that a disguise was what we needed, so we dressed up with false moustaches, hats and other absurd costume accessories. This, we thought, would allow us to drive during the day too. What a great plan!

We never actually got caught driving his car; I don't know if blind eyes were turned or if we just got away with it. That was, until one night when my parents went out for dinner at a friend's house. They took the Mazda, leaving my dad's 2.8 litre Granada Ghia in pearl white in the driveway. I was 15. It would be another year before I could legally learn to drive, not actually drive, just get a learner's licence.

But heck, it was Saturday night. I rang Paul's number. "Let's go for a drive, my parents are out. I'll pick you up!"

By now, such was the level of our confidence in driving, I am pretty sure we both felt we were entitled to be on the road, regardless of the lack of credentials. We were just as capable as anyone else, right? Paul lived about six or seven miles from my house, perhaps a little further. By now, I didn't think twice about going out at night for a drive. So, I collected him and off we went. "Where shall we go?" We didn't care, we just wanted to drive and listen to music.

It was decided to venture into Douglas, the island's capital. I was extremely hesitant about venturing that far and into the capital on a Saturday night. On reflection, it was a ridiculous thing to do.

We drove towards the town. It was uneventful. By then we didn't even panic when we saw a police car. This activity had become so second nature that our arrogance was off the charts!

But on this night I did get spooked. I don't know why, but something was telling me that what we were doing wasn't a great idea. We turned the car around. I was driving and we headed back home. The main road between Douglas and the village that I lived in, Ballasalla, was known to us like the back of our hands. Every twist, every turn, every bump or crack in the road, I knew it. I had travelled this road many times, sometimes more than once per day with my parents or my sisters or my friends' parents. It was a thoroughfare.

Nearing Ballasalla there was an infamous corner, called The Blackboards. It had been responsible for multiple car crashes over the years. Approaching it from our village, the driver had to negotiate a 90-degree bend going down a hill. The approach to it was fast and in those days there was no speed limit, so 70, 80 or 90mph was commonplace. But if you were not ready for it, the corner, that spanned a bridge over a railway, could easily catch a driver out and did so with alarming regularity.

It was not unusual to see cars in the field below the bridge or even caught in a tree like a fly in a spider's web. The corner was very different when approached from the other way. Again, it was fast, but the advantage was that it was uphill to help slow the inertia of a vehicle. The apex of the corner was slippery, and the camber dropped away, meaning that the physics of forces on the car made it "go light", so less traction was at the wheels.

My dad's car was rear-wheel drive, as was common back then. I came into the corner on this autumn evening a bit hot. I wanted to get home; I had been spooked, and I just wanted to get Dad's car back home in one piece. Paul could stay the night at our house.

As I rounded the bend, I became a bit eager on the power. Being used to driving the Mazda, which was front-wheel drive and much less powerful than the Granada, I wasn't ready for the back end of the car to step out as it did.

"Fuck! Oh no!" I shouted as the front of the car now aimed towards the oncoming traffic, and I frantically applied the opposite lock in a bid to save us from disaster. There was no skill; it was blind panic. There was no calmness, no precision and no control. This was a journey in which the car was in charge. Paul and I literally were passengers. By now we were on the opposite side of the road and a collision with an oncoming car seemed inevitable.

Somehow, the rear wheels gripped and the car, with its front wheels pointed back to the left-hand side of the road, made its way in that direction, this time heading for a stone wall that was painted and had chevron arrows across it to warn of the severity and direction of the corner.

I steered away from the wall and braked hard. We missed it, God knows how, but all that mattered was that we had. We stopped, and for a moment, I had forgotten that we were on a public road with other road users about to arrive at our location. I looked at Paul, he was as white as a sheet, as was I, no doubt. "Fuck. That was close, mate," he said. Closer than close, I said, as I felt my heart pounding in my chest.

I started the car and we drove, very gingerly, the last couple of miles to the sanctuary of home, very aware that we had averted a disaster.

I can remember three times when my dad totally lost his shit with me. I am sure there were more, but these three really stand out in my memory.

The first was when I broke my foot as I was warming up my trials bike at Tholt-y-Will, a popular trials venue and location of the yearly Schoolboy Manx two-day trial. The combined scores for both days dictated the results. Day one for me was OK, not brilliant, I was in fourth place. Steve was winning, as he usually was, and I had probably made a couple of silly mistakes here and there. Often a few of the good riders from the UK would come over for the event.

It was usual before an event to mess about or warm up, trying different settings such as tyre pressures maybe, or perhaps the suspension had been changed and that needed to be checked. The second day was no different. I hopped on my bike and started to ride, except that I had "forgotten" to put on my riding boots that offered protection. Not only that, but my choice of footwear had been a pair of slippers, not ideal!

I had been going along the bottom of a bank and hadn't seen Steve coming down the bank. He couldn't stop and T-boned me. It wasn't his fault, it was mine and, fortunately, it was me who paid the price. The impact broke my foot, although this wasn't confirmed until later that day at hospital.

That day, my sister Viv had come to watch, and I am so glad she was there. My dad had completely lost his shit with me and, to be honest, I didn't blame him. What I did was so stupid and totally avoidable.

Trials riding back then was a serious business for us. We wanted to do well, we wanted to get decent results, and while I am sure he was concerned about my foot, he wasn't going to let it get in the way of riding!

I was in tears, I was sore, but I was also upset that my dad was upset. I hated him being upset with me. He was my hero, the one person in the world who I wanted to please all the time and right at that moment, it had all turned to lumpy custard. My sister came and gave me a hug and told Dad to leave things to her.

She took me down to the edge of the river and took my slipper and sock off. My foot was already bruised and swollen. "Put it in the water," she said. It was instant relief. With the cold water easing my pain, though just temporarily, she pulled my foot out and quickly dried it. She put on some duct tape, the most common and most useful item in any toolbox, and then pulled my thick riding socks over my foot. Next, she rammed my foot into the boot and then told me off for being an idiot. She told me to go and ride the bike and not put my foot on the ground, as it would hurt. And so, that was my motivation for keeping my feet on the pegs that day.

I came second at the end of the event, behind Steve. Maybe I would have anyway, who knows? One thing was certain, the motivation to keep my foot on the pegs that day was never stronger. I ended up in emergency with an X-ray and a plaster cast for my troubles!

The next time my dad lost it also involved pain. The house we lived in for most of my upbringing was on a quiet estate.

Most of the residents were retired but there were a few families around with kids. One of my school friends, Chris Kelly, lived there too. His family home was 300 metres down the road from ours. Chris had been a gun BMX racer before his family moved him and his brother, Mick, to the island.

Originally from Manchester, his dad had been in the Greater Manchester Police and when Chris and his brother arrived, our school had never seen the likes. Put it this way, you wanted Chris and his brother, but more so Chris, on your side. Their streetwise approach was a revelation to us quiet naive boys who had been raised in an environment that largely shielded us from the real goings-on in the world. So, Chris and I became mates, and he rode a few trials with me too.

One day we were "racing" our bikes from my house to his when I had a huge crash. I tore skin off my face, my arms, my back, in fact just about everywhere. This was long before it was common to wear a helmet on a pedal bike. I had beaten myself up pretty bad, and in my pain I screamed out several expletives.

My dad had been in the garden at the time and heard the commotion. He ran down to where I was lying in the road and made sure I was OK before lambasting me in front of Chris and some other boys about my language.

The third and last time that I can remember was the morning after the near-crash incident.

I was outside riding my motorbike; it was a Sunday morning. Dad asked me straight out: "What did you do last night?"

"Nothing much, Paul got dropped off and came to stay, we watched a movie," I said.

"Really?" came his reply? "Then why would it be that when Mum and I came home from dinner, I felt the car bonnet and it was warm?"

"Erm, I'm not sure, Dad."

"Well, I know," he said. "You were out driving my car."

"No, I wasn't!" I exclaimed, but there was no use denying it any further when he told me what came next.

"You were seen, Victor. You were seen by someone who was on their way to dinner with us. They saw my car and wondered how it could be that I was at dinner with them when they had seen my car driving in the opposite direction."

I had nothing.

He didn't lose his temper, which was almost worse; he was quiet and calm, at least outwardly. He proceeded to tell me that the person who saw me driving knew it was me and, worse yet, was a police officer.

"I am not sure what we should do, Geoff," said my dad's friend. "I am happy to leave it to you but if I see Victor out driving before he is 16 and without supervision, I will have no alternative but to book him."

I think it was more that my dad's integrity had been questioned, too. How could he have allowed or even augmented in any way the ability for me to go joyriding in his car on a Saturday night?

My dad gave me more than a stern lecture on the consequences if something had happened. "Fuck me! Something very nearly did happen," I thought to myself. I metaphorically shit my pants.

I waited another year before I drove on my own again, although those regular Monday night lessons continued because they were on private land.

NEAR MISSES

By the time I was in my early 20s I had been driving, legally, for about five years. I was the youngest person to have passed my driving test on the Isle of Man at that time. I'm not sure if that record still stands.

I turned 16 on October 8, 1986. I passed my driving test first time, on November 24. My parents would lecture me almost daily about the responsibilities of driving a car. "It's a lethal weapon, Victor," my mum would say.

They worried about me, probably not so much about my actual ability to drive but I was extremely impressionable, and I wanted to show off. I was a show-off. I know now why. I was making up for something, I needed to show the world and myself that even though I had this chronic illness that I could, and would, do anything anyone else could do – and not only that, I would do it better.

If it was a jump on my BMX, I would go further and higher than my mates. Or in driving a car I would be faster, be more daring, do more crazy things than the others.

I wasn't like this in trials riding. Maybe because I knew I could be, and was, beaten with regularity by Steve mostly, or because people already knew I was capable, I am not sure, but for some reason I rode my bikes with thought and focus, not for any other reason. My first harsh lesson wasn't a near-miss at all, it was a hit, a direct one.

One of the conditions my parents had for allowing me to drive to school, which I did the day after I passed my test, was that I didn't take anyone in the car with me. As always, I agreed to whatever I was being asked to do.

But perhaps not meaning it, I never had the intention of dishonouring the promise, it just happened.

At this time, we were living on the outskirts of Douglas, having moved there a year before. I ignored my parents' instructions and made a diversion on the way to school, to pick up buddies.

The journey from where I picked them up to school took us along some back roads, narrow roads through countryside and past farms. I had driven these roads several times as a learner, but this could well have been my first time as a driver in my own right. One corner tightened up faster than I was expecting. I panicked and braked so hard that the car began to skid on the wet, muddy roads. Inexperience meant that instead of releasing the brakes and just steering around the corner, which would have been perfectly achievable, I collided with a VW Polo being driven by an elderly man. The impact was so severe that I remember watching in slow-motion as the whole of the front windscreen of my car came out in one piece.

The noise was horrific, the sound of metal crunching metal, glass smashing, the engine revving, the tyres screeching and then, complete silence, nothing.

I undid my seat belt and asked my friends if they were OK. One was, but the guy in the back had broken his wrist. He hadn't been wearing a seatbelt. The impact had thrown him between the front seats and rotated him, leaving his arm behind, which snapped.

I got out of the car. I didn't think the damage would be so bad, but it was horrific. Both cars were mangled. My attention turned to the man in the other car. I walked over to him; he was slumped against the steering wheel and I noticed that while he had been wearing a seatbelt it didn't look like it had done its job too well. He was very pale, and I was starting to panic.

My reaction was to run away, not from the scene completely but far enough away that I didn't have to look at the destruction I had caused. No one else had been responsible, this was all on me and that was too much to bear. I started screaming "No! No! No!" I was also terribly frightened of what may parents would say. This was my mum's car, she loved it. I had killed it.

After a while, the police and an ambulance arrived. There were no mobile phones, of course, so I am not sure how they were alerted. Probably the same way as most incidents were in those days; someone running to a nearby house and asking to use the phone.

The ambulance arrived and attended to the poor man I had hit, and my mate. Later, my dad arrived. I will never forget the look on his face when he saw the mess I had caused; disappointment, sadness, relief that no one was dead, but he wasn't angry. He was calm, he came and gave me a hug and reassured me that it would be OK.

We heard later in the day that the man I had crashed into was OK. He had some injuries but would survive. I cannot even begin to describe the relief I felt hearing that news. I was taken to hospital to be checked over, as was my friend in the front seat.

I still had to face my mum. I was not looking forward to that! In some ways she was like my dad, clearly relieved I was OK and that no one had been seriously hurt, but man-oh-man was she angry. Not then, not later that day, but she was angry for a very long time after. I had disobeyed her, and she wasn't going to let me off the hook that easily. At almost every meal we had together, every time we were in each other's company she reminded me of what I had done and the outcome of it.

From losing her car to my parents being sued by the boy who broke his arm, to the other party claiming on our insurance, to her telling me how stupid I had been and that any shine I had for passing my driving test so quickly was now gone and that I was being looked at as just another young stupid driver. She made me pay, not financially but emotionally. I had let her down, I had let both my parents down and that was terrible to bear. I deserved to be punished, have my wings clipped and repent at leisure.

I recently received a text from Steve Colley; we were catching up and I told him of my intention to write this book. He claimed that I was the wildest person he had known, that he expected me to be dead by 20, not from my heart but from an accident of some kind.

I thought that a bit rich coming from a man who literally has pummelled his body in pursuit of his sport, crashing and smashing his body against rocks and so on; racing his rally car at nutcase speeds and not always keeping the panels on the car as they had been intended!

But then I thought, and realised he was right, I was a bit crazy. While he took risks, they were measured, the risks I took were, on reflection, foolhardy and idiotic. It really is by the grace of God that I made it this far! It was his text message that led to me asking Steve if he would write the foreword to this book.

Moving forwards to when I was about 27, and that promise I had made my dear old mum years earlier – the one about not riding motorbikes on the road – had by now been broken many times over. I hadn't though just gone and bought the fastest machine available, I had, in fairness, built up from a scooter when I was 16 and now car-less after my accident, to a Yamaha TZR125 which was my first proper road bike, to a ZXR400 and eventually to a 1000cc Honda Fireblade which I bought when I was around 31.

I initially had been working for my dad's company, which by now had evolved from just supplying building materials to another business he started, supplying cleaning chemicals for industry.

I met a girl, too. After I returned from Australia in 1991 in time for my 21st birthday, Alison (Ali), and I became closer. A couple of years later we bought a house together in the suburb of Douglas, quite near her parents' house where she had lived all her life. We had a lovely time together, we both had decent jobs, we were young, we had fun and we were trying to make a go of things generally. But I was immature, I wasn't ready emotionally for all the aspects that came with a serious relationship. They say a young man's frontal lobe doesn't fully develop until the mid to late 20s. I don't think mine is fully developed yet!

I wanted to ride bikes in my spare time, and she was supportive of that, but maybe not all the time. I think I was about 25 when we parted ways. Ali moved to London where she met the man of her dreams and had a very beautiful family. I am happy for her; she is a wonderful human being and deserves the best that life can bring. We are still in touch from time to time keeping a caring eye out for one another. The near-miss was hers, not mine.

So, my mid-to-late 20s were about work, work and more work, trying to help build a successful business with a guy my dad had employed to run the chemical business. An ex-policeman from Manchester, Tim Rush was a foreboding character, larger than life in more ways than one. My dad had explained that while he wanted me to benefit from the growth of the business, I was too young and too inexperienced (definitely the latter) to run things. I needed to learn and as my dad would no doubt attest, I needed firm direction and impartiality. I was never going to get that from him.

Tim joined the business and immediately I could see that my play-days were over. If I was going to survive in this business I needed to grow up and grow up fast. I could recount countless great stories and not-so-great ones, but safe to say, the time from my mid-20s to turning 30 were the happiest but hardest of my life.

Tim and I eventually became "joined at the hip." We worked so hard to build the business, employing more and more staff and all the while me being his protégé; learning, understanding how to conduct myself, how to think commercially, what hard work really meant, but also enjoying the trappings that success could bring.

We ate out, we travelled on a whim, I bought toys that I could never have done had I continued along the path I had been on. In business, he taught me almost everything I know today, certainly the foundation of it. He was more than a mentor, he was in many ways my older brother, my second dad, my guardian.

Being a pursuit police driver in days gone by, he taught me how to drive a car very quickly and very safely. But there was one thing he didn't know that I taught him. He had seen the things I could do on a motorbike, and he wanted to try that too. He quickly realised it was harder than it looked but he did end up taking his motorcycle test at the age of 40-odd and together we toured Ireland and Wales, folding in business trips to suppliers with riding some of the best roads the UK had to offer outside the Isle of Man.

In the summer after work, most nights we would either get on his boat and head out for a spin, sometimes venturing to Portpatrick in Scotland for dinner or Strangford Lough in Ireland, then power back again before dark. The boat was a RIB, a rigid inflatable boat, with two monster 250HP motors strapped to the back. Six metres long, the thing could get up and dance, making easy work of the Irish Sea.

If we weren't boating, we would take the bikes out for a lap of the TT (Tourist Trophy) course, the world famous 37.75-mile track that nestles itself in the mid to north of the island. Started in 1907, the TT is the toughest motorcycle road race in the world. These days the top riders lap at more than 135mph average speed and hit top speeds of well over 200mph!

Of course, when the track is not being used for racing, it's a regular road used daily by island residents and businesses. Although now it is much more regulated and restricted than it was (isn't everything?), there are lots of sections of the course which are still free of speed limits.

It was on one of these sections that I had a severe dressing down from Tim one evening. Again, I had been showing-off and pushing myself past my limits. We had finished doing a lap and twilight was fast approaching. "Let's go back over the mountain to Ramsey and do another quick run," I had suggested.

Tim agreed. So, we set off the "wrong way" round, and while I knew the roads well, very well, it wasn't common to ride the course this way. The road ascends towards the mountain section. When going the right way round the rider often gets a feeling of weightlessness as the bike becomes light as it crests the drop. The front wheel comes up and it's fun!

However, going the other way, the step is much more noticeable, especially at speed. I was probably doing 120mph as I hit the step up and the next thing I knew the front wheel was so high in the air I couldn't get it back down. Ordinarily, this wouldn't be a problem, but the road then curves to the left round a corner known as Kate's Cottage. I managed to get my foot on the back brake to help bring the front wheel down, only to be met with a brick wall 50 feet away, which sounds a long way, but at that speed it takes a second, maybe less. I tipped the bike into the corner, praying it would behave.

Alongside the TT track are white lines so the riders can clearly see the edge of the road. I was in between the white line of the left side of the road and the wall. My feet were off the pegs as I scrambled with all I had to keep from hitting the wall, which even at 50mph (probably the speed I was doing by then) would be very nasty.

Somehow, and still to this day I don't know how, I saved it. I pulled up a few hundred metres up the road where it was safe. My heart, just like in the incident in my dad's car, was going at a hell of a rate. I took my helmet off and Tim pulled up behind me. He tore a strip off me, which was fair enough. He never wanted to have to be the one to tell my parents that something awful had happened to me. I got it. I had made a mistake. I was going in too hot, and I knew it had been a very near-miss. He was right. I needed to be more careful. I wasn't a TT racer.

I am happy to say that I have never fallen off a road bike, not once, never even dropped one, but if the encounter that Tim had seen that evening was bad, what was to come was worse and scared me so much that I didn't ride my bike for a while after.

It was a few years later. I had my Honda Fireblade, a very quick bike. It was Cadbury blue, the same colour as a Cadbury's chocolate bar wrapper. The thing was epic, so much power, so light, well balanced. To all intents and purposes, it was a race bike and by far the best bike I owned – and there were a few over the years!

I used to hang out with some of the boys that raced. I didn't race, I was still very much into riding off-road, be it the odd enduro event or riding my beloved trials bikes. But I did love having a "scratch" as we called it on the roads.

In all honesty, now that my frontal lobe is possibly a bit more developed, what we did and the speeds we did it at on open public roads was insane. In a 37.75-mile lap perhaps up to 15 or so miles of that was through unrestricted speed limits, most of that was on what we call the mountain section of the TT course, where we would easily be averaging over 100mph and hitting speeds of 140mph-plus.

The fastest I ever remember going was just over 160mph up a stretch of the course called the Mountain Mile. It wasn't straight but you could see the whole way and you could easily use both sides of the road to get a "racing" line.

One particular evening though, we had just turned right and that meant north at the only traffic lights on the track – a famous corner called Ballacraine. Just up from the corner, maybe 300 metres, the road goes left around a blind corner with high walls and grassy banks on both sides. Nearby is a horse-riding school. The power of these bikes was such that in a very short distance, maybe 300 metres, it was easily possible to be doing towards 100mph.

I was following a guy who I knew, but not well. I saw his bike just sneak out of view as I tipped my bike into the corner. Hitting its apex, there were two horses in the middle of the road. Paul (the guy in front) managed to tip the bike over even more and went inside the horses. The horses moved to the left a touch, but one of them reared and I threw the bike upright, clipping one with my wing mirror. By now, I was on the other side of the road, so grateful that there was nothing coming the other way, otherwise it would have been game over. The main thing about the whole incident was that Paul just kept going.

I couldn't believe it. We had cheated death. The carnage that could have unfolded is hard to comprehend. Like the other incident, I pulled up when I could and took a breath. I got back on my bike after a few minutes and carried on.

By now I was riding on my own and took it nice and steady, catching up with Paul around 10 miles later as he had stopped for a break. "Bit close that one, yessir," he said to me. "Er, yeah," I said. "Thought I was a goner." Although I didn't know him well, Paul sadly died not long after in a motorcycle crash. I heard he had a medical event before crashing, perhaps a heart attack. Sad though it was, I wasn't surprised given his attitude towards danger. I knew I couldn't keep riding like this, that my luck would run out one day.

KINDRED SPIRITS

Growing up in a small community I'd never really met anyone else with a heart condition. I hadn't really met anyone who had even had open heart surgery, except perhaps a couple of family friends who had received a bypass operation, although I can't recall them specifically.

During those crazy days of work, we got word that a new nursing home was to open on the island. Of course, it was incumbent on me to at least try to secure the supply of cleaning and hygiene products to them. Duty called and I picked up the phone to the newcomer. "Oh you need to speak to my daughter, Zandra," came the answer. That's an unusual and nice name I thought to myself ! Zandra and I organised a meeting and a few days later I found myself at her home. In a beautiful location, the home was made of exposed stone. I thought it very grand indeed driving up to the door with the crunch of gravel below my wheels. Sometimes in life when you meet someone, you kind of just know that there is a connection. It's hard to explain it exactly but I'm sure we have all had those times when you're sure that the person you meet will somehow or other be in your life for a long time, be it romantically or platonically, or, as in this case, both. This was one of those days and it soon became clear why.

Her blonde bobbed hair (bobbed was all the go then!) caught my eye immediately. Then she introduced herself. Her accent was one of someone who was well educated and certainly upper middle class. I soon found out why. Her father had been in the Royal Air Force, a Wing Commander! Zandra's mum, Pippa, was a very elegant lady. She had been involved with owning and running nursing homes in the UK and had evidently been very successful at it.

Zandra had followed in her footsteps and trained as a nurse. They had moved to the island not long ago and had decided that the island needed a new, better, standard of care for elderly folk. She was right.

What became clear very quickly was that Zandra's father had passed away at a fairly young age, in his 60s, suffering a massive heart attack. As if this wasn't enough, I soon noticed through her low-cut top that she too had a scar, just like mine! I had to ask if she had a heart condition and she explained that while she wasn't born with it, she had actually had a heart attack while on holiday in Spain when she was 29. At this stage she was in her early 30s, so not long ago!

I was really surprised; to be honest I didn't quite understand how someone so young, who looked very fit and healthy had managed to suffer a heart attack. I know now that she did have some underlying conditions, which coupled with her DNA had led to this most unfortunate event in her life.

The long story short is that over time Zandra and I became romantically involved. We just clicked. Whether that was due to personality, or whether it was due to our determination to live life to the full, or whether it was kindred spirits of sorts, I'm not sure. Perhaps it was all of those things.

I'd found myself recently single and had rented a small house on the outskirts of the main town on the island. We spent many days and nights together, enjoying each other's company, understanding each other's lives perhaps more than someone without a heart condition could do.

I think the hook for her was that she found out I rode bikes and she was an avid motorbike fan, again something I hadn't expected at all from this very well turned out, well spoken and educated young lady. Never judge a book!

In the end the romance finished; she knew that one day I wanted a family and that was something that she wasn't able to give me, but that wasn't before we had lots of fun together. Zandra and I are still friends staying in contact quite regularly via the newfound world of social media!

And of course I won her business, she had no choice in the end!

HOOK, LINE AND SINKER

Donna Picton had been on the Isle of Man for two weeks. She had never been to the island and the likelihood of her and I meeting before was at best unlikely.

I had seen her walking through the nightclub, our regular haunt in those days, called Paramount City at the northern end of the mile-long promenade in Douglas.

Paramount was owned by a friend of mine, his second venture into night-time entertainment, the first having been a huge success and innovative for its time. Paramount City took that success and upped the ante. The first of its kind on the island, Paramount was set across three floors. Each floor had a different genre of music, and the top floor hosted an American-style diner, too. It was epic.

I asked my friend who she was, he didn't know. It was a Friday night, people out letting their hair down after a busy week.

I used to go to nightclubs more often on a Friday, as opposed to Saturday, as on Sundays I often had to compete in a trial.

Honestly, I was mesmerised by her. Her look and style were different to the usual on the island at the time. A low-cut top, skin-tight jeans and a small tattoo of a Chinese symbol just above a pierced belly button. She was fresh, and I needed to say hi! A strong Welsh accent, instantly recognisable, said hi back. She was loud, she was confident and as I looked into those beautiful, big brown eyes and I could tell almost immediately that she was a lot of fun.

Donna Picton, as I later found out, had recently arrived from south Wales, transferred to the island with the high-street bank she worked for as a personal banker, the ones people you can seek advice from for a loan, mortgage or insurance. I had never really met anyone quite like her. Her vibrant personality drew me in, made me want to know more.

The usual exchanges took place: "Can I buy you a drink?" "Would you like to dance?" Her reply to the latter being "I will dance with you but give me your hand first." Unusual, I thought, but there in the darkness of the nightclub, moments into meeting this girl, she read my palm.

As I have said, there is no way we could have met each other earlier; she didn't know me and vice versa. What happened next was just incredible. She told me that I had been sick as a child and that she was very, very sure that it was something to do with my heart. I just looked at her, gobsmacked with my mouth wide open wide. "Erm, how on earth do you know that?" I asked. "I read palms," she said. We spent the rest of the night in the club together and while I tried very hard to get her to come home with me for a nightcap, she was having none of that. "Are you free tomorrow?" she asked. "I am now!" She told me where she was staying, a temporary flat that the bank had found half a mile from where I lived. "7pm. I'll wait outside for you."

The next evening, I was there on the dot at 7pm. We drove west to a fish restaurant in the only official city on the island, the historic port of Peel. It was a wonderful night, I was hooked. She was so different, bohemian, fun, intelligent, an adventure seeker, a huge breath of fresh air.

The days and weeks unfolded and just like in any new romance we tried to spend as much time as we could together.

Donna and I learned about one another and for me it quickly became clear that our backgrounds could not have been more different. I don't say that in any class sense, far from it. I say it because it was a fact, and I knew there would be aspects of my life she would find very different and there were aspects of her life that I had no exposure to and couldn't comprehend.

She was the eldest of four kids, and later five, with her mum remarrying and having a child in a new relationship, and how she ended up being a surrogate mother to her siblings. Also, she had to answer the door to bailiffs who came knocking to recover outstanding debts, because her mum was a gambler and didn't have the money to pay. She got so fed up with this happening, that at 14 she got a job in a newsagency – the money she earned went straight to the bailiffs, not spent on herself. Her father, who had walked out when she, her two brothers and sister were young, headed to the UAE to work as an electrician, ended up dying young, most probably from alcoholism.

All these things made me quickly understand that she had grown up far faster than she should have, that her childhood had been cut short and that if my life had been gilded, hers had been austere.

As I would later discover, Donna had dreamed of becoming a doctor. Her home life prevented this though, as she had to get a job as soon as she could to help her siblings survive.

Understandably, her relationship with her mum was fractured at best. Resenting the fact that she couldn't go to university to chase her dreams, resenting the fact that her mum favoured her brothers, both of whom had spent time inside for various misdemeanours, and knowing that the only way she could remove herself from this environment was to get a job, she joined Barclays Banks, one of Britain's largest high-street banks.

She started on the first rung of the ladder and worked her way up. She was at least now free to support herself, to find a better life and to make her own way. Part of making her own way saw her accepting the transfer to the Isle of Man in the summer of 1996.

I loved my mum, a strong, loving, caring woman who, like

most parents, only wanted what she felt was best for her kids.

My eldest sister had married, at what would these days be considered young. She was 24. She married her childhood sweetheart, they had met at school and stayed together during their respective university days. Their wedding was a traditional affair and my parents, I am sure, were proud and very happy that she was marrying him. He was educated, successful and could provide her with anything she wanted, except for the things she yearned for, none-material things, not to spend on herself – love and attention.

Years later, when things started to fall apart in their relationship, my parents, especially Mum, became upset and maybe even embarrassed at the prospect of her daughter no longer being with a respected businessman but instead with another man who had been a prison guard. Rather than supporting her, my mum made her feelings very clear.

My other sister, Viv, had met a rally driver at a young age. He was entirely unsuitable in the eyes of my mum. Completely from the "wrong side of the tracks," the prospect of her daughter marrying or even just being with this guy was just too much for my mum to deal with.

Then it was my turn. My mum hadn't necessarily thought that Ali had been entirely suitable. She hadn't gone to a private school; like me, her parents, while actually financially sound, weren't my mum's kind, although I am not sure they ever met!

Then Donna came along. Everything that could be wrong with her was wrong in my mum's eyes. She had come from a very different background and was "out there" in terms of her appearance and her personality. She was loud, she could be uncouth and, at times, inappropriate. She was lacking polish.

Both my sisters, though, and in particular Viv, absolutely loved her and said to me that I needed to follow my heart even if following your heart could be painful and cause pain to others, including those close to you.

It wasn't that my mum wouldn't talk to Donna, but she made her feel so uncomfortable, picked on her and tried to show her up, especially at family gatherings.

My mum always believed she was a good judge of character, but her judgment was often based on who the person was in society and how much money they had, rather than who they were as a person. My mum was the matriarch of the family; in most respects she wore the trousers, and my dad would go along with her views and wishes. When out of range of Mum, Dad would be lovely to Donna, and I know he thought well of my sisters' chosen partners. But we all want an easy life. I understand that and while it's not what we should do, we sometimes just go with the flow.

The irony of this little story is this. My eldest sister went on to marry the prison guard, they have had a wonderful life together, they still are having a wonderful life.

The happiness they have brought each other is so lovely to see, and as her brother, all I ever wanted was for her to be happy, and she has been happy for more than 20 years with him.

Furthermore, her husband was far from being bitter towards my parents for how they had initially viewed him. The things that he did for them both, and later for my dad, are extraordinary. From house maintenance to latterly, as my dad has had health problems over the past 12 years or so, he has slept the night with my dad to make sure he is OK, taking him to the bathroom and caring for him. One thing I know 100 per cent is that there is no way that my father would have got that help or care from his first son-in-law.

My parents have been blessed that my sister found a man that could rise above the extreme dislike, the obvious shunning of him, to forgiving them for that behaviour, and moreover for that same man to have given so much to them, an amazing quality. My sister's husband is the salt of the earth. A great example of what a man should be. A further irony is that my other sister's partner, the car mechanic and rally driver, went on to be one of the most successful motor trade dealers in the UK.

In the late 1980s he became a protégé of the VW Audi group, chosen by them because they saw his potential. He was sponsored financially to buy his first dealership, after he decided a mechanic's career was not for him. He went from strength to strength accumulating more dealerships for his network, selling everything from VW-Audi to Porsche and other high-end marques, to these days being the chairman of one of the largest dealer networks in the UK.

Long retired from day-to-day activities, he now enjoys having time to rally his beautiful Mini Coopers and his classic Porsche. Though my sister and him did not stay together, it was a true love story. They remained close right to her death. If only my mum could have seen the potential in him rather than what he was at that time.

Donna and I were growing closer. We bought a house in a village called Ballaugh, famous for its hump-backed bridge on the TT course. By now, I had left my dad's business. He sold it to Tim and I had started my own little company.

I sold chemicals, oils and lubricants, workwear and all sorts of other peripheral items that complemented the range of products. I had a warehouse in the south of the island near where my dad's business had been and where I had learnt to drive!

Donna was now in charge of one of the bank branches in the south of the island, near where I worked. Life was good, we socialised in the local pub, we hung out with our mates touring around each other's houses most weekends for a curry or a BBQ. I was happy, she was happy. It was time to put a ring on this girl's finger.

WILL YOU MARRY ME?

The flight to Mombasa in Kenya was terrible. The plane was filthy, it stunk to high heaven and the toilets were swimming in human waste.

We didn't care, though, we were on our way to the Nyali Beach Hotel to get married and go on safari for our honeymoon. About a year earlier, Donna had agreed to marry me when I popped the question after a boozy lunch with my sister and her husband.

We had retired to Viv's house and put the world to rights, as we often did over several glasses of wine. We were all pissed, it was spur-of-the-moment but though the following day came with a decent hangover, there was no regret. I knew she was the girl for me.

We had set the date for the wedding for May 1999. A few weeks before we were due to marry, Donna had an awful accident on, of all things, a moped!

The damage she did to herself was almost incomprehensible given the relatively low speed that she had been riding. But as she landed, she caught her knee on the side of the pavement and the kneecap got decimated. A month in hospital and many months of rehab saw us having to postpone the trip and the wedding to November of that year.

I must confess that before meeting Donna I hadn't really travelled much. Aside from a gap year-style trip Down Under, which ended in its own disastrous way, and that trip to the USA with my parents, most of my travelling had been to European destinations.

For Donna, someone very unmaterialistic, the "possessions" she wanted were amazing experiences and the memories that came with them. The first holiday we had been on together was to New Zealand, although she went on ahead as I was running my own business then, and getting time off was hard.

She collected me late at night after the plane touched down in Christchurch. I remember thinking how few lights there were, like there was just nothing there. As I would find out later, the flight path across the Tasman Sea takes you over the spine of mountains that runs down the South Island of that wondrous and incredible country. It was no wonder I couldn't see much, there was only a beautiful landscape below and it was dark.

We spent the next two weeks exploring South Island in our Maui motorhome. We decided to head south first, down to historic Dunedin and then fun-drenched Queenstown, then we made our way up the west coast towards Hokitika, still today one of the quaintest places I have ever been. It just filled my heart with happiness that small town. From white water rafting to kayaking on Doubtful Sound, it was breathtaking. We then cut across the island via Arthur's Pass and I remember saying we should come back and tour on a motorbike. But what a holiday, what an experience. We both knew we would be back someday. She had given me the bug and I couldn't wait until we could go on another trip.

My parents had made the journey to Kenya to see us getting married. By now, I guess, my mum "got along" with Donna; she knew I was marrying her and that was that, so maybe better to keep the peace? But even on our wedding night sitting in the beautiful restaurant in the hotel there was an air of disapproval. Nothing was said outright, but sometimes no words are needed to know the lay of the land.

The following day, we left my parents at the hotel and we joined a few other couples on a three-night safari through the Masai Mara National Park, a vast landscape, home to all the "big five".

As we got jolted about in the back of the four-wheel-drive vehicle for the first leg of our trip, most of the conversation was about which animals we most wanted to see.

A few hours later we arrived at our first overnight spot, a remote resort that looked more like an army barracks than a hotel. But once inside, oh my goodness, this was glamping on another level.

Like most people, I had never seen big-game cats in the wild and after dinner that night as the lights went down, a large hunk of meat was skewered onto an enormous hook and dangled in the air. As darkness fell, with one spotlight shining on the area, in came a leopard to devour the meat. She had her fill and so did we.

How amazing was it to see this wild animal feeding in front of our very eyes. The sights got even more spectacular from then on. Water buffalo and hippos were going about their daily routine, but for me the elephants were my favourite of the big five. Their majestic nature and sheer size were incredible. With the safari over it was time to head home.

By now I well and truly had the travel bug, but an event of which the world had never before, either in scale or impact, was about to unfold. For me, it changed quite a few things.

TURBULENCE

For any of us old enough to remember that fateful day, we probably know where we were and what we were doing.

I was sitting in a pub called the Glue Pot, in Castletown, the ancient capital of the island, having lunch with Donna and a friend.

Just like it was in New York, 9/11, it was a sunny day on the Isle of Man. Autumn and spring have always been my favourite seasons, the colours of the trees changing from winter into spring and summer into autumn. The temperatures dropping or increasing, relative to the time of year, the daffodils sprouting, the leaves forming a brown carpet that kids love to kick and play in.

This autumn was no different. The summer had been one of riding bikes and having fun. We had been over to the mainland to watch a concert and to Dublin to watch U2 at Slane Castle.

But all was not well on the home front. Unfortunately, my relationship with my parents had taken a backward step. For just about all of 2000 and into 2001 we hardly talked and didn't see much of each other. It was sparked by my parents' perception that Donna was making me do things and go places that we could not afford financially because I was trying to build a business and that my focus was not where it should have been.

They – in particular, my mum – saw her as a disruption. What my parents didn't know was that during that time Donna had two miscarriages. She had been unwell mentally and the push-pull effect of me trying to appease both parties was beginning to take a strain on us.

I didn't know what to do or how to help Donna with these

emotions. I didn't understand them and for sure I was far too immature to support her.

I'm ashamed to say it now, but at times I thought her threats of suicide were just for show. Was it a ploy to make me side with her more than my parents? Was it just an attention seeking stunt? I just didn't know, and I wasn't equipped to really look at what was going on and be man enough to help her fix it.

I felt like I was trying to please everyone, but in the end it became too much and there was only one answer. We needed some time alone, with no extended family and nothing to influence me one way or the other.

I had never been afraid of flying. I enjoyed it. No, I loved it. I loved the whole experience from wearing some nice clothes and having a glass or two of wine in the departure lounge, to sitting back watching a movie and enjoying the in-flight food. The first trip to NZ a few years earlier had been my first true taste, certainly as an adult, of long-haul flying and all its trimmings.

As we watched the planes plough into the Twin Towers, in utter disbelief at what we were seeing, little did I know what a profound effect it would have on me in terms of flying.

It's fair to say I have always had a type-A personality. As numerous psychologists have told me over the years, it's not ideal with my heart condition. Some lesser-known negative traits of a type-A person would be overthinking, hyper-imaginative, catastrophising.

Of course, with it comes the competitive spirit, needing to win and utter impatience. I can give big fat ticks to these boxes!

In the northern hemisphere winter of 2002 with my business now part of a national supply chain group and a great crew of staff able to take the reins in my absence, Donna and I decided to spend Christmas and New Year back in New Zealand.

It was a tough call, if I am honest. We had been away for the millennium, but this was the first actual Christmas that we would be away from family. I wasn't used to it, and my recollection is that I was also not really looking forward to it. Again, I felt torn. I hated feeling torn; why couldn't things just be easier?

Coupled with this, my sister Viv's cancer had returned. She made it seem OK, she didn't want to make a fuss; that was her all over. But in reality, and on reflection, I hated that I wasn't there for what would turn out to be her last Christmas. Her life had become like the soap opera Coronation Street, too! I say this with an air of comedy, because honestly if you didn't laugh, you'd bloody cry.

To divert for a moment. Winding the clock back a while, Viv had split up with her long-term partner somewhere around 1989-ish. They had lived in London but she had returned to the island and met a very jolly fellow by the name of Frank.

I could just about write a book on Frank alone, but in the name of trying to stay on point, he was one of the most charismatic, outgoing, benevolent, kind-hearted and just bloody-good-fun souls I had ever met.

As I returned from my trip to Australia in 1990, my sister called me and said she had someone she wanted me to meet. I knew immediately it was a bloke. My sister had been hurt in her previous relationship for a whole manner of different reasons which are not relevant or necessary to delve into here, but safe to say I began the relationship between me and Frank with scepticism and some slight aggression! Some near 20 years his junior I made it clear the first time I met him that if he hurt her, I would kill him! The fact that he was bigger and probably stronger than me was immaterial, I would have found a way.

Frank just had an aura around him. He was an accountant, but so far removed from being a stereotypical bean counter that it was hard to reconcile (excuse the pun!) that his day job was looking at numbers and spreadsheets.

It turned out that wasn't really his job at all! He was one of three partners in a firm, his prime role was as the entertainment partner, meaning he did lots of wining and dining clients, telling stories, keeping them entertained.

They were an unlikely couple, but for many years it worked. They built a very successful business together and shared a beautiful home, until one day it didn't, and their relationship ended. By now Frank had become sick too; years of entertaining had caught up with him, I think.

I am sure, we were all sure, that in her final year or two Viv, now single, had become lonely and maybe not as lucid as she once was. She had been as sharp as a tack, with great judgment and now that judgment had diminished significantly.

A "man" came into her life, and we all felt at the time that he was there for one reason and one reason only, to get a quick cash grab. He insisted that was not the case but knowing her worth and what she would leave behind, it seemed quite likely that was his main motivation.

They married, then they weren't! The marriage was annulled. For many different reasons it was an extremely stressful time for everyone.

The 2002-03 trip to NZ was amazing, but right before it – and I mean literally the day before we left – I received word from the organisation that my business was a part of, had been sold to a much larger entity. While you would think this would be a good thing, I knew for my small business and its unique position on the island that, in fact, it could be disastrous.

With this weighing on my mind, I decided to use the time away in NZ to really think about our future and what we wanted to do.

The NZ trip had two parts. A week on the North Island, arriving at Auckland and then making our way down to Wellington. We quickly realised that we had seriously underestimated the time needed to do that given all the fun stuff to do on the way. So, we made a call to end the first part of the trip at Rotorua, the North Island's playground, before continuing to the South Island.

As we were checking in – bearing in mind that this was a little over a year since 9/11 – the man in front said to the check-in clerk: "The bomb is in that one," pointing to a small bag. Well, as you can imagine, the next minute the whole place was essentially locked down. The face of the poor woman who was checking him in, lost all colour. She knew the potential ramifications about the call she was just about to make.

Incredibly, after around 30 minutes of fuss, the man and his luggage were allowed to carry on with their journey, with us, to Christchurch! No way that would happen nowadays, he would have been in the clink faster than you could say "boom!"

The whole way there, I was on edge, just waiting for us all to explode and rain down on earth in a million pieces; it was the first time I was truly terrified of being on a plane. There would be more to come.

At last, we arrived and spent the next two weeks fulfilling our promise to each other to tour this incredible place courtesy of a BMW R1100 motorbike. It was nothing short of an amazing holiday. Donna and I talked a lot about the business, our lives together, the family dynamic, my sister Viv and her illness. Before all of this I had been approached by a customer several times to see if I would ever sell my business. I had always said no. I had now decided to say yes.

PART TWO

GREENER GRASS

My mother told me many times during her life that the grass is not always greener on the other side of the fence.

We all know what this means. Sometimes it's better to appreciate what you have rather than what you believe could be better elsewhere.

But for me, I was feeling at the time that a new start, away from all that had been going on, was what was needed.

I knew Donna was unhappy living on the island in part, it's fair to say, because of how my parents – in particular my mum – had been with her. I found it increasingly difficult to be neutral and try to support her while still seeing my parents, whom I loved so much.

It really boiled down to their belief that Donna was not good enough for me. But she was good enough, she was more than good enough.

I was so hung up on not offending anyone in those days. I really did want happy families. It hurt so much that no matter how much I tried, how much I "promoted" Donna, stuck up for her and tried to make them see that she was a great person, it was to no avail. It was not her fault that she had been born into a life very different to mine. We had very different upbringings, different education and a different standard of living.

In fact, there were so many differences that perhaps it was hard to see why we were suited, but we very much were. I was looking for something different, exciting and adventurous. For someone who had seen a bit of life and who could teach and show me just as much as I could show her.

When I first visited the very green valleys of South Wales, where Donna came from, around three or four months after we had been seeing each other, I was definitely in for a cultural surprise.

As we all mature and find our way and our voice, there is no way on earth that these days, if that situation arose again, would it be a reprise.

I did take inspiration from my sisters, especially Ninee, who in many ways had a huge amount at risk and to potentially lose during her separation and subsequent divorce. Four children, a beautiful house and lifestyle, all nice-to-haves, but worthless if you are not happy, for whatever reason.

She followed her heart; she made a life with her true love, and it was a romance that has survived the test of time. It has all worked out fine. Her children have all done well, her ex-husband has also found love and they are still friends. It has been a great outcome all round.

On reflection, I feel rather than being a new start it was a case of just having to remove myself from the greater situation.

My sister Viv was born on September 3, 1960. September 3, 2003, was the last time I saw her alive. She was sick, puffed up like she had been inflated, a side-effect of the large doses of steroids she was taking to help her body through the bouts of chemo she was having. She looked terrible, nothing like the sister I had known all my life. I really struggled seeing her like that, it just was so unfair.

But that last day we had together was a very special one. Not only was it her birthday, but Donna and I were leaving the following day to start our journey to NZ.

Looking back and perhaps this is blind naivety, I didn't really either understand or accept, or just know, that she was as sick as she was. Had I done, had I known that less than eight weeks later she would be gone, there is no way I would have left her on September 5.

We all have regrets in life. I don't believe people when they say they have none. I just can't accept people's lives are that perfect. Certainly, leaving Viv has been the biggest regret of my life, so far. There have been others, but God, what I would do to roll back time to have had another eight weeks with her. I hope she knows that.

Sadly, that evening came to an end, and as we had done for the past six months, Donna and I took Viv back to her home. We had moved in with her earlier in the year after we had decided to give living in NZ a go. It worked out for us all really; my sister needed help on her 10-acre property, looking after her dogs and numerous other animals ranging from donkeys to chickens and just about everything in between.

We, on the other hand, had rented our home out for a year, but the tenants had wanted to move in almost immediately. So, with many of our possessions in storage and some at my sister's place we became housemates.

By now, she was single again, having managed to break off the whirlwind romance, which had somehow turned into a marriage for her. The poor thing was being attacked by the cancer at such an alarming rate that the drugs she was being given were really affecting her mind. She was not the clear, rational and logical thinker she had always been. It was during our time staying with her that one "funny" incident occurred that is worth recounting.

Donna had undergone some surgery to the leg she damaged in her accident, so she was hobbling around on crutches, and my sister by now was almost permanently confined to a wheelchair, the cancer having penetrated her bones and hips making it incredibly painful for her to stand.

As was the morning ritual, we walked the dogs. My sister was the quintessential animal lover. Given that she had had no children of her own, her kids were her animals, especially her beloved Labradors, which she bred. On this morning, our own dog, whose name was Noddy and who had been gifted to Donna and me by Viv, was up and about but I didn't know that at the time. I let Paddy out – the pack leader, the Alpha male, the man! He and Noddy didn't get on at all, Noddy was jealous because Paddy was a stud dog and well, you know, got "it" much more than Noddy!

So anyway, Paddy and Noddy met, and all hell broke loose. Unfortunately, I got in the middle of the fight, which was clearly the wrong thing to do and my sister told me off.

As I was about to lock Paddy in a paddock, along came Noddy behind me, blind in one eye. He decided to have a last go at Paddy but missed and got me instead, sinking his strong jaws into my leg! I managed to hobble back to the house and call for Donna who came out on her crutches to see pools of blood all over the patio.

An ambulance was called, and when they arrived there was me lying on the floor with my leg elevated on some raised flower beds, there was Donna on her crutches and there was my sister in her wheelchair. The ambulance staff looked at each other and one said: "We don't have room for you all!" It was such a funny comment and defused a tense morning.

I was trolleyed off to a small local hospital with Donna in tow. When we arrived, it was quickly decided that given my heart condition and the risk of infection from a dog bite, I needed to be sent to the main hospital on the island.

Before being transported away the ambulance crew decided what I really needed was some iodine in the wound. Holy mother of God! I just about broke Donna's hand as I grasped it when the iodine hit.

To that point in my life, even with all the surgeries and procedures I had been through, that was without doubt the most painful thing I had ever endured. Not the dog bite, that didn't really hurt much. No. The ramming of iodine-soaked dressings into my gaping wound was horrendous!

Because of my condition, the doctors at the main hospital decided to leave the wounds open so as not to trap any bacteria inside my body. The result, because no stitches were ever given, is that today I have two quite impressive scars at the front and rear of my left leg, just below the knee at the top of my calf. But it was the comment of the paramedic that will stay with me forever. It really must have looked like a bit of a war zone!

Our journey to New Zealand began the morning after my sister's birthday gathering. We were off. I waved goodbye to my family, thinking I would see them all again in a year or so, perhaps after we had completed our adventures and had come home to continue our lives back on the Isle of Man.

There are two ways to get to the island, sea or air, ship or plane, that is of course unless you have your own boat!

We opted for ship, well SeaCat in fact, as it was much cheaper than flying and we were on a tight budget. Donna, being a banker, was our financial controller; she was much better at managing money than me. In Liverpool, my home from home, we caught a train to London and had a night there before flying out the next day to Kuala Lumpur. We had decided to have a bit of a last holiday with a little touch of comfort on the way to NZ.

Our first stop was the small island of Langkawi, on the west side of the Malaysian peninsula. The island was amazing and our 10 days there were just what we had needed after what had been an incredibly busy, but also emotionally draining, year.

I believe it was because of the frenetic nature of that year, the transfer of my business to new owners, my sister being ill, the tension between Donna and my mum, and the general planning of this huge trip, that somewhere along the way Donna and I forgot to ask each other what we wanted from NZ and what it was we were seeking for our future life there.

I have recounted many times to people when they asked how I ended up in the Antipodes, that I was actually quite happy on the Isle of Man.

Sure, I had frustrations with the place, but until I met Donna, I would never have even begun to think about crossing to the other side of the world to begin a new life.

Was it fate that I met Donna and this journey happened? Perhaps. I am certainly a believer in fate, right place, right time and vice versa. As it would turn out, the one person who wanted so badly to move to NZ ended up returning to the UK a few months later, without me. And the other person who didn't much care about going has now spent almost 20 years living Down Under.

However, when I reflect I know why I left the Isle of Man. It was, without doubt, 100 per cent escapism. Too much was going badly, and I needed to get away from it all, even for a short time. Is 20 years a short time?

It became clear then that our pathways of life, what we wanted and how we wanted it were different.

Donna, I believe, had quite a romantic vision of us buying a nice farmhouse-style property maybe in Taupo or Rotorua, or even perhaps somewhere on the South Island, and being bed-and-breakfast hosts.

I, on the other hand, knew that at 33 years old I wanted to extend my career, and while I had run my own business it wasn't that successful really and I knew I had much to learn. I needed to join a larger organisation, one that I could grow and develop in and the only place I could do that, in NZ anyway, was Auckland. That's where I needed to be. With our pathways on different tangents our relationship ended around March of 2004, after having been in NZ for only six months or so. I was lost. She was gone and I didn't want to be there either, not on my own at any rate.

I wasn't going to stay, but I also wasn't going home. I wasn't going to fail. This wasn't going to beat me, and I knew that if I returned home, I would miss out on ever having the chance to develop my career to the same extent.

So, I decided that for now I needed to be somewhere else. NZ had not worked out and while I had met someone, someone I liked for sure, I needed to explore other options. That option came one night by way of a job advertisement for a role in Papua New Guinea, where the grass was always green, literally if not metaphorically.

It's funny, me using the word career, because in many respects I don't feel that I have had one, not in the true sense. Career advice at school was basically non-existent. The school was trying to breed academic students, ones that would go on to well-known universities, perhaps Oxford or Cambridge for subjects such as law and accountancy.

I didn't fit into this mould and any desires I had of being a "high achiever" were usually scuppered in one of two ways. The first was that while there were jobs that interested me, almost all of them had a degree of risk attached and/or you definitely needed to be physically fit and able. The second issue was I never believed in myself academically. I just didn't think I could have a career as say a doctor, which is a career I would loved to have pursued.

The other couple of jobs that I had properly thought about were joining the Police and being an airline pilot, although this came a bit later.

I actually applied for the police and passed the entrance exam. I went for my interview only to have my hopes dashed, not for the reason you may think, but because I wore glasses, still do.

And while these days the Police will accept candidates who need glasses, back then, certainly on the Isle of Man, they didn't. I had really wanted to be a traffic "copper", driving fast cars and riding motorbikes really appealed to me. But it wasn't to be.

As I found out later when I decided to learn how to fly, there was no way I would ever be granted a commercial license because of my heart condition. So that was out too.

I returned from London after working at the Harrods department store and deciding that retail wasn't for me, albeit in the most famous department store in the world! It was fun and they certainly did promise me a career, which maybe I should have pursued, who knows?!

I had started to miss the island, especially riding my bikes. Not much chance of that happening in central London, so I went home.

Certainly my time in London did me good, taught me a few things, lessons I have remembered to this day, most especially how to speak and position myself to a customer. Back on the island I needed something to do (other than ride bikes all day), so it was then that I fell into the chemical world and there I stayed, primarily in the areas of cleaning and sanitising products in the food, beverage, transport, hospitality, medical and numerous other industries. I guess on reflection it's been OK, I have on balance done quite well, but I have never seen it as a "proper" job, I don't know why.

Anyway, back to Papua New Guinea. Being totally honest, I had hardly heard of PNG, much less its purported dangers. Where even was it?!

This may sound very ignorant and no doubt it was, but I think it was a blessing in disguise that I didn't know too much (nothing really!) about the place. Had I done, I don't think I would have gone! And who could have blamed me? The place is crazy.

After landing the role after a fairly extensive interview process which involved a trip to Brisbane and a separate one to Cairns, I packed up my fairly simple life in NZ and headed north courtesy of a business class ride on a Boeing 747.

This was my first ever trip sitting in the posh seats and what a treat it was! First there was the experience of being treated like royalty, then there was the seat and in-flight entertainment, not to mention the food!

I suppose the only disappointment was that it was a fairly short flight, around four hours, so I didn't get to take full advantage of the business class experience.

We soared high over the Tasman Sea towards Brisbane where I had to change planes and I looked out the window and felt lonely. This wasn't how our adventure to the other side of the world was supposed to have played out.

Here I was, on my own, on the opposite side of the world from those that loved me the most, making my way to yet another new land. Really, on reflection, I had little to no idea of what I was doing, or what was in store.

What was wrong with me? Why and how had I found myself in this position?

I was unsettled and had been since I left the Isle of Man, but in an act of defiance I wasn't throwing the towel in, not yet anyway.

I always wanted to make a success of my life. This was a life that had been fought hard for, that by no means had come easy and its owner had long felt he needed to compensate for that and prove if not to others, certainly to himself, that he wasn't going to let some poxy medical condition slow him down.

It had been the same through my school years, proving that I could be like my friends, joining in with physical activities and other attention-seeking activities, such as being a bit of a smart

Alec at school, always wanting my peers to look at me positively. Of course, more often than not this landed me in some kind of trouble with the teachers!

It was the same through my motorcycle escapades, wanting to win, being the best and be well recognised and respected in that community. It was something I was actually good at, something that did win the notice of others, something that all of my friends, other than one, couldn't do as well as me. Even the reckless driving and other slightly crazy activities I had done, they were all because of one reason. I needed to show the world that just because I had been dealt a rough hand in life, it wasn't going to stop me from succeeding, from being noticed.

The runway at Jackson Airport at Port Moresby, the capital, runs north to south (and vice versa obviously). The day I arrived the southern runway was in use, number 14L (left), denoted by the direction it follows on the compass. The northern runway was 34R (right). This meant for a longer approach as we had arrived from the south and had to essentially turn back on ourselves for the final approach.

In turn this meant that I got my first glimpse of my new home.

To say I was shocked was an understatement! It suddenly dawned on me that I had come to live in a Third World country. As the next year or so would show me, PNG is both beautiful and dangerous. The style of living was going to be unlike anything I had previously experienced and certainly a lifestyle for which I was in no way prepared.

After being collected by my new colleague, Paul, who was also the incumbent in my new position, we made the journey back to the centre of the Moresby, as it is known locally. What hit me almost immediately, aside from the heat and intense humidity, was how dirty the place was. There were basically shanty towns, with wooden huts perched in the main high up on stilts, as homes. The place was filthy, with general rubbish everywhere and what would, to me, become a well-recognised trademark of the country, the stains of Betel Nut everywhere! Known locally as "Buai", the nut is chewed and the remnants spat out on the ground, hence the staining of the road/pathway etc. everywhere you go. The blood-coloured stains could easily be thought of as left over from a brutal war. I certainly never tried it while I was there, but it was easy to see those that chewed it, as it left similar staining on teeth, the chewer resembling a boxer who may have received one too many punches! Apparently the chewing gave the user a slightly euphoric and more alert state of being.

I arrived in PNG on a Friday. I had the weekend to settle in to my new digs and try to acclimatise to the oppressive heat. This was, without doubt the hottest and most humid place I had ever been to, and it was going to take a bit of getting used to.

I was staying with Paul, the person I was replacing in a month's time. Between now and then he would be showing me the ropes and eventually I would inherit the very well-appointed and fabulously located three-bedroom apartment which sat up on the hill and overlooked the harbour and CBD. Paul was being relocated back to Australia, where he lived, although he was a Kiwi by nationality. Certainly an interesting character, it seemed to me as if he had lived quite hard during his time in PNG, taking full advantage of the ex-pat lifestyle! I am not sure he actually wanted to leave, but I got the feeling his wife did want him to leave!

Saturday was spent just settling in, swimming in the pool and getting to general grips with the place. Similarly on Sunday but for one outing; Paul took me with one of the local ladies he was "friendly" with to an open air market. Amongst the fresh and exotic fruit and vegetables was a trader selling fish. Full yellowfin tuna, massive lobsters and crab and many other species of the deep ocean that were new to my eyes. All of a sudden a bang.

"What the ^&*$ was that?" I asked.

"Oh don't worry it was just someone shooting a gun," Paul replied. Jesus! What the hell was this place? As this and many other "fun" future incidents would testify over the coming year or so, this really was the Bronx of the South West Pacific!

There truly were many memorable events during my time in that remarkable country, not always memorable for the right reasons; like the time I headed over to our main offices in Lae, the main business hub of the country. Nadzap airport is around 10km outside of Lae and transport from the airport into the centre of town was by bus. If ever you have seen the buses they use to transport prisoners, with metal mesh grills on each window and a couple of guards aboard, that was the bus! Except the guards were there to protect us and the grills were there to keep people out as opposed to in.

On my first trip to Lae when I enquired why the security was necessary, those in the know explained that the route from the airport to the town centre was fraught with danger. Episodes of ambush were commonplace, the local villagers knowing that the white man no doubt had possessions, money, jewellery, clothes even, that could be used, sold or bartered. They would put logs across the road, making the bus stop and then climb aboard, hence the use of the armed guards.

On one of the first trips I did to Lae, I was on the bus with my fellow travellers, when all of a sudden there were multiple tin sounds against the side of the bus. We were being shot at! These were generally from home-made guns, which in fact, more often than not would backfire and blow up in the user's face. We call that poetic justice!

Not long into my stay I had to travel to East New Britain, a trip that required a plane ride. I was there to meet and work with the local sales rep, one of several on my team across the country.

One day, we visited a dive resort. It was a customer of ours and I was being introduced to the owner who asked where I was from. By default, when asked this question, I usually just say the UK, it's easier and easily recognised, as opposed to saying where I actually was from. Max, the owner said, yes I know you are from the UK, but where exactly? The Isle of Man I answered. "Stay there!" he instructed. I did so and several minutes later he returned with a beautiful, long legged, beautifully toned, blonde girl. It took a moment to register, but almost immediately I recognised her as a girl called Pippa that I went to school with! She was out there working as a dive instructor. What were the chances?!

We started seeing each other and she would come over to stay with me most weekends. I bought a boat, nothing flashy, just something to while away the weekends as the full ex-pat lifestyle of beer, beer and more beer with a lot of Chinese food thrown in wasn't really my thing.

Pippa and I had lots of fun together during the time I was in PNG, but eventually a decision had to be made as to what I felt was going to be a long-term and sustainable place to live and realised that this lifestyle was eventually going to catch up with me.

In mid-2005 I returned to NZ, a good job I did as it turned out.

THIS ISN'T WORKING

"This isn't working," I remember the doctor in the emergency department saying as I was dropping in and out of consciousness or at least dropping in and out of lucidity.

"I don't want to die," I recall saying and holding tight the hand of a nurse. Rather than words of reassurance coming back, such as "you won't die", the words were: "We are doing everything we can to make sure that doesn't happen." I knew then that I was in trouble. Not that I hadn't known it two hours earlier, but two hours earlier I really had no clue what was happening inside my body, just that I was very sick.

I had been in Auckland for work. Donna and I made the move to NZ in the northern autumn of 2003. However, by this day, December 9, 2005, Donna and I had parted ways, our dream of a new start and a new life in NZ had not worked out, for many reasons.

The Christmas function had been one of those outdoor pursuit days, you know the type.

More typically seen as a team building/bonding day, but for us it was our thanks from the business to acknowledge hard work throughout the year. I had joined the business a few months earlier after working in Papua New Guinea, after Donna and I had split up, trying to find myself. PNG was an incredible experience but not one for me long term.

I applied for a role back in NZ with a large chemical company and got the gig. I was to be based in Christchurch. I had been looking forward to it and for a short time I had enjoyed it.

My first task of the day was to ride a mountain bike around

a course as fast as I could. I remember thinking, well, this is right in my wheelhouse, I've got this. And I did have it, I set the fastest time of the day, but I also set the record of being the only person needing urgent medical care that day, too.

As I pedalled hard up the final part of the course, a short incline, I could feel myself becoming out of breath. At the top, once off the bike, I couldn't get my breath back and became really aware of my heart beating very quickly. I sought some shade from the heat of the day and had some cold water. But it was still there, this awful feeling, and by now I was starting to feel very unwell.

Much of the next 24 to 48 hours is vague, sketchy at best, but I know an ambulance was called after I had alerted one of my colleagues to my plight. I can remember while waiting for the ambulance feeling so hot, hotter than I had ever been, with sweat flooding from me as I became more and more increasingly short of breath. The energy it was taking just to make my lungs work was like I imagined a marathon runner might endure. I had to keep breathing. I wasn't dying, no fucking way!

The event was being held north of Auckland near an area called Dairy Flat, which is around 50 kilometres from Auckland as the crow flies. By the time the ambulance arrived, which seemed indeterminably long, I was very sick. I can't recall with accuracy how I got into the ambulance, but I do remember thinking: "Oh, my god, they have only sent one paramedic!"

The paramedic, Chris, who also came to see me later during my recovery, was shitting his pants at the situation he had been sent to. The communication evidently hadn't been great and there was a misunderstanding about the seriousness of my situation.

He did his best, absolutely he did, but he was both trying to get me to hospital, which was almost an hour away because of the rural location and at the same time he was having to pull over every few kilometres as I started to go downhill again.

The main issue I was having was that I had developed a pulmonary oedema. Essentially, fluid was building up in my lungs because my heart was beating so fast that it couldn't effectively pump blood to my lungs.

I started to cough up blood and I don't mind admitting at that point I was scared, really scared. I remember looking out of the window of the ambulance as the countryside went past, almost coming to accept that this would be my last trip.

I was exhausted, I just closed my eyes and started to drift away.

"Victor!" came the cry from the front of the ambulance. "Stay awake for me, we're almost there". He was lying, we were nowhere near the hospital, but he clearly wanted to reassure me that the help and security of a full trauma team was almost at hand. I did my best to stay awake. In some ways I was too scared to close my eyes, I knew if I did, I wouldn't be opening them again, at least that's how I felt.

My heart rate by then was hovering around 220 beats per minute. In a normal heart that is very fast and usually the maximum heart rate in a very fit and healthy person is around 220, less their age. So as I was 35 at the time the maximum should have been 185. But it wasn't just the speed of my heart, it was, as I would later come to understand, how it was beating. Added to that, as my heart was anatomically not normal, it literally couldn't cope with beating at that speed.

We pulled over again, this time Chris came into the back via the sliding door on the side of the ambulance. "I have organised for another crew to meet us," he said. Another paramedic jumped in and started the medical management. The other crew met us at a large intersection which connected the rural road to the main northern motorway in Auckland. We were soon on our way, and I recall the sirens and feeling the speed of the vehicle as it charged towards the North Shore Hospital in Auckland's northern suburbs. Other than remembering one incident of very heavy braking, where maybe a car had pulled out in front of the ambulance, we arrived at hospital perhaps 15 minutes later. (To this day, I can't understand how general road users can't see or react to emergency vehicles; to me it beggars belief!)

At the hospital I was taken into a resuscitation room, there was a cavalry of medical staff and for a moment I felt much better about the whole situation. One of the doctors, I presume he was a consultant, explained to me what was happening with my heart and more importantly what they were going to do to make me better.

My heart had gone into an abnormal rhythm called a supra ventricular tachycardia, or SVT for short. As soon as I heard those words I remember thinking, geez there isn't much super about this! As I came to understand later, supra means above, ventricular means the ventricles and tachycardia means fast.

So, this rhythm meant a fast heart rate emanating from above the ventricles, in other words, the atriums. Anything above 100 beats per minute is considered tachycardic in medical terms. I was chugging along at more than double that rate.

In a normal heart a fast and irregular heartbeat while usually needing medical attention, isn't typically a case of life or death. An anatomically normal person who is generally healthy can withstand their heart being in this rhythm and beating very quickly for a period. Unfortunately, my heart was structurally far from normal, and my right ventricle was now under huge stress. There was a significant risk that I could have suffered a stroke, a heart attack or worse! I really admire medical staff, not just for their incredible capacity to retain and implement the knowledge they have all studied so hard to gain, but also for their ability to perform under pressure.

By no means would I have been the sickest patient the people working on me had seen, maybe even that day, but I was unusual, simply because I wasn't built the same as 99 per cent of the remaining population. The air of calmness is reassuring, but as treatments that would normally be textbook, bread-and-butter procedures, were failing on me, I could sense a more tense and worried medical team. I think this is why the nurse had offered her partial assurance that they were doing everything they could to try to save me.

The normal drug that is used to correct a rhythm like this is called Adenosine. The drug works by chemically stopping the heart for a moment and the hope is that as it fires up again a normal rhythm is restored. The really interesting thing about this drug, though, is that as it's pumped into the veins the patient quite literally feel as if they are dying. Everything stops. Everything. The medical staff warn about this most bizarre feeling, but nothing quite prepares a patient for it.

I remember, though, that before administering the drug, they moved me to another part of the ER, presumably with more space and better equipment; I am not totally sure why, but that's my assumption.

Unfortunately for me the first dose of this drug did nothing, except make me feel like I was departing. So, another larger dose was given. Again, nothing positive, just another near-death experience!

The next tool out of the toolkit was a drug called Sotalol, which I take twice a day. It was going to be given intravenously, as was the previous drug. If the Adenosine had been a hammer, this stuff was a mallet, although it didn't have the same side-effect of making me feel totally weird.

Unfortunately, as I would discover much later, at that time my blood pressure was already very low as my heart was struggling to pump blood effectively to my vital organs and this drug exacerbated that situation.

Almost as soon as it was given, I started to feel even more terrible. I lost a huge amount of blood pressure and my heart went into heart failure. Heart failure doesn't mean your heart isn't beating, that's called cardiac arrest. Heart failure is when the heart is unable to beat effectively, which has some significant repercussions. One of them is the retention of fluid. So, before they could try anything else, I needed a healthy dose of a drug called Frusemide, which is a fast-acting diuretic. In short, it makes you pee! But I wasn't in any fit shape to be popping up off the bed to have a number one.

They say that you need to leave your vanity at the door of a hospital and certainly vanity was the last thing I was bothered about, so when a catheter was placed up my old chap, I kind of just went.

Whatever, do what you need to do. It's not like I hadn't had them before, albeit many years had passed since the last one!

I recall there was a bit of head scratching going on and then an ultrasound machine was wheeled in, and a cardiologist was beeped to come and help.

The cardiologist prescribed a drug called Amiodarone. If Adenosine was the infantry, this drug was the missiles and bombs. It's a super-strong drug, but its long-term use can cause some irreversible and unwanted side-effects.

Unlike the other two drugs they had used with no success, at least this one didn't have any weird side-effects; well that's if you don't include thyroid, liver, kidney and eye damage, not to mention sun sensitivity! Gradually, my heart rate came down, it was still over 100 beats per minute, but I started to feel a little better and began to think that I might actually survive.

The doctors decided that I needed an urgent CT scan to determine if there had been any issues with the pulmonary oedema. For the uninitiated, a CT scanner is a large X-ray machine, shaped like a doughnut that the body slides through, forwards and back, while pictures are taken. It's similar to an MRI machine, but the images aren't as detailed as an MRI. I think it's a cheaper option!

One of the aspects of a CT scanner is that a dye is injected into the veins; this is called contrast. It allows medical staff to see more clearly the blood vessels and so on.

To this day I have had numerous CT scans and I must confess it's probably one of the things I least look forward to as far as regular follow-up appointments are concerned, and I think I know why.

As the contrast was injected into my arm, I felt an intense heat come over my body almost immediately and the sensation that I had wet myself, which, given I had a catheter in my wotsit, was unlikely. I have since come to learn that this is normal.

A number of years later, while having a CT for a heart study, I remember discussing the sensation with a nurse and she told me that she had one patient tell her it was better than having an orgasm. I am not sure what type of orgasms he was having but trust me when I say it was nothing at all like any orgasm I have ever had! Maybe I have been missing out?

Anyway, just as the flush of heat and odd accompanying sensation was leaving me, I heard the voice over the speaker say: "We are coming Victor". I suddenly felt unwell and short of breath again. The fluttering sensation in my chest came back and I became panicked and agitated. My heart rate had shot straight back up to 180-plus BPM, I was back where we had started, except this time I was already in hospital.

More Amiodarone was delivered via what was now becoming a

very well-used cannula. The heart responded as it had the previous time with a reduction in heart rate and my ability to breathe more normally returned.

I had stepped off the bike at about 11am that morning, it was now late afternoon. What a day it had been. I had no clue that any of this could happen to me. I had, in the space of a few hours, gone from being a normal guy enjoying his mid-30s to someone who would become, in every sense of the word, a shadow of his former self.

STAND CLEAR

The weather had turned during the day, not that I would have known! It was typical of New Zealand and particularly Auckland with its microclimate, given that the city is encased by two oceans, the Pacific on the east and the Tasman Sea to the west.

Some of the best storms I have ever seen were there, spectacular lightning shows with monsoon-style rain. Such rain that, until I had lived there, I had never seen, except for once being in Hong Kong and being caught in a downpour there. The thing with Auckland, though, was that often the rain came and went quite quickly because of the ocean effects. However, this day was an exception to that rule.

My then partner had been told of the news of me being ill via a phone call from the hospital earlier in the day. Jill lived in New Plymouth on New Zealand's west coast, halfway down the North Island.

Nestled under the imposing Mount Taranaki, New Plymouth, an isolated town even by NZ standards, is an agricultural hub. Agriculture, especially dairy farming, is extremely popular and Jill's parents were some of those who had built up a decent head of cattle and had grown their farm over the years to become a successful family business.

Jill had left school and studied hospitality, and it was in this capacity that she had been working when I met her before my tenure in PNG. We met in Auckland but during the time I was overseas she had returned to New Plymouth to run a family motel. We had had plans for her to come and join me in the early part of

2006 in Christchurch, where I was now based.

I am sure the drive to Auckland from New Plymouth was not easy. The weather was terrible, and I am sure she was worried about me and probably wasn't quite sure of what she might find when she arrived at the hospital.

It was good to see her. I think it's natural in times of trauma and when one is facing adversity that you want to be with people you care about and who care about you in return. The comfort that brings is important and I certainly felt more at ease with the world when she arrived.

But that ease didn't last long. As I was getting ready for bed that night and in the bathroom using the toilet, I heard a loud knock on the door in concert with feeling my heart starting to race once again.

I had been "wired up" with what is called telepathy monitoring. The medical staff could watch my heart rate and rhythm and respond to any issues. The medical staff, two nurses from memory, came into the bathroom and told me I needed to lie down. Almost immediately a wheelchair came, and I was transported back to bed. The registrar came to see me and while he didn't really need to explain that my heart had re-entered this SVT rhythm, he told me that was the case. Further, given the amount of Amiodarone I had been given and that all the cells in my body would now be flooded with it and given its extremely toxic nature, they really didn't want me to have anymore.

I asked, while trying to grab some air as I was again very short of breath, what they planned to do. The doctor explained that the best and safest thing to do was to pop me off to sleep and electrically restart my heart!

"Jesus!" was my initial reaction. This really is not how I had planned my day. Of course, I didn't really have a choice, and I also didn't really have time to process this news. Probably a good thing in hindsight.

I agreed to the procedure and almost before I could say or do anything else a decent amount of sedating anaesthetic was given to me via the cannula, which had already seen a reasonable amount of activity for one day. I can't really recall much after I was popped off to sleep, but I know what they did.

A cardioversion procedure is fast but needs precision. It's vital that the electric shock is delivered at exactly the right time during the cardiac cycle. Failure to do so can be fatal, so again this wasn't necessarily a check-up at the dentist but something a little more serious. The shock was delivered and luckily for me my heart reverted to normal rhythm immediately. I began to wonder why they hadn't done this in the very first place! Gosh, I wish they had, even to this day.

When I woke up, I asked the doctor if Jill was there. She was. The doctor checked with her that she was, in fact, called Jill! Could have been an awkward moment had she not been!

"Cup of tea?" came the voice the following morning around 10am. "You have missed breakfast, love." I recognised the voice, well the accent, not the person. Barbara, as she introduced herself, was from Lancashire in the UK and I felt a strange, distant but actually vital, connection. I had been on my own for the past 24 hours apart from having Jill there for a short time before the cardioversion. I had been lonely, I had been scared and oddly I had felt guilty about living on the other side of the world.

During the previous day, I had thought several times about my parents, who had not long since buried one of their daughters as she was taken far too early, aged 43. Here I was 10 years younger on the other side of the planet, having gone through a fairly traumatic and serious medical event which at times had become very close to being, if not fatal, something such as a stroke that could have had some devastating life-long consequences.

I spoke to my sister, Ninee, first. She had called the hospital and she must have been put through to the ward. She asked how I was and of course I said "fine" because that's what we had been brought up to say. While our family had always been close, we had never been a family that wore our hearts on our sleeves. We didn't talk much about our feelings, just superficially perhaps. I don't think we knew how to, really. Certainly, even in 2005, one didn't become micro in how we conveyed how we were feeling to one another, it was all very macro.

Feelings were having a stomach-ache or a headache or just not being "on form." The only person in our family I had ever got close to talking about emotional feelings with was Viv and she was gone. Ninee and I chatted about what had happened, and I remember her asking what was next and how long I might be in hospital. Her answer when I asked how Mum and Dad were: "They are worried about you."

Again, this was pre-fatherhood for me, so while I did understand that they were worried I didn't and couldn't have understood the depth of that worry, especially as I was sitting in a hospital bed on the other side of the world. I can appreciate now they would have been beside themselves with fear and worry that their son was sick.

For some time after the event, I wondered why my parents didn't tell me that what happened to me that day was likely someday to happen. Why had they kept it from me?

Was it so I wouldn't worry myself, or was it a denial thing? I had seen their denial when my sister Viv was sick. Even after the diagnosis that her cancer was terminal and right up to her death, they both thought, my dad more so I believe, that she would somehow pull through, that she would beat this ghastly disease and that she would in some way and somehow be OK. She wasn't and it shattered them.

So, why would they not have told me of my certain plight? It troubled me for a long time, months certainly, until it dawned upon me that they themselves had no idea that this could happen to me.

I had always been a little ambivalent about my condition. As a young boy I obviously didn't know much about anything, I can't really recall thinking too much about it, which I think is normal and probably a good thing.

My parents, Mum mostly but sometimes Dad too, would take me to all the regular check-ups and so on, but I viewed it as quite fun really. I got to go to Liverpool for a day or sometimes two. As a treat I would often be taken to the restaurant inside the Liverpool Tower, which I think was also home to a radio station. We would almost always go to the John Lewis department store; I remember getting locked in one of the changing rooms once and having a real panic that I would never see my mum ever again!

Then came that second operation. I was by then old enough to start understanding that the condition I had was serious, life-threateningly so.

Through my adolescent years as I transitioned into becoming a young adult, I was still diligent in attending my appointments, albeit on my own mostly.

As I look back now, I never really asked about the future except in a broad sense; I would ask the consultant cardiologist how long I would live, which is like asking someone if I will win the lottery next week. "We don't have a crystal ball, Victor," would be the standard reply.

As my 20s went by, except for my trip to Australia, I attended the appointments, in fact right up to leaving the Isle of Man to head to New Zealand. The point is, that all through those years, no one, at any time, had given even a hint that what I had just been through this time was a possibility.

Unlike the how-long-will-I-live question, the medical staff did know that these events were not just a possibility, they were likely to happen, they just didn't know when or what form they might take.

The fact that they had known though, initially made me angry. I lay in my hospital bed wondering how on earth this had occurred. I asked one of the nurses a couple of days later, as I recovered on the cardiology ward, that very question. Bearing in mind that cardiology wards are more typically dealing with people that have had heart attacks and so on and given the relative rarity of my condition, I understand now why she gave the answer she gave to the question about what caused this to happen to me?

Heart rhythm disturbances can be triggered by numerous factors. Leaving my condition aside for a second, factors such as age, smoking, drug use, alcohol and caffeine can all cause problems.

As soon as the cardiologist said the last two I made my mind up there and then that it was these two that had caused the problem. I had never been a big drinker, aware of my condition and feeling the effects of a big night out more than someone of the same age with a normal heart might do. That said, I did like a beer or two and probably even though I thought I didn't drink much, I still probably drank too much. Then there was the coffee. I loved coffee! I liked tea too, but during the working week I quite enjoyed the odd cuppa.

I then started to try to rationalise what had happened and make conclusions as to what had caused my heart to go into this frenzy. It was obvious! I had been away from Christchurch for the week working, I had been having a few late nights, staying in a hotel all week, not eating as well as I should have and would normally do, drinking a few more beers than I would normally do, and vitally, as I had been living on the dreadful coffee out of the machine at work all week, my body would have been flooded with caffeine. So, it was a simple solution, cut out coffee and alcohol and this won't happen again! Great theory, crap in practice!

WHAT THE HELL JUST HAPPENED?

I spent the next week recovering in hospital. My heart settled down and there were no more major arrhythmias. I have often likened a major arrhythmia to an earthquake. There is no warning, it just happens and causes devastation. After it there can be many aftershocks and that's what I was about to experience.

Jill drove me to New Plymouth to have Christmas with her family. I started to notice subtle changes in my body. Almost immediately I began to lose weight. I had been close to 88kg when the SVT happened, and within two months I would be 10kg lighter. Perhaps it was the cessation of the alcohol or the reduction of any rubbish food or maybe it was the anxiety which had already kicked in.

It wasn't just the weight though; I had become aware of my heart beating in my chest all of a sudden. I could feel it speed up whenever I did anything such as walking up some stairs or up a hill, for example, so I didn't! I hated the sensation, it just brought back memories of the day a week or so earlier when I thought I was going to die.

Another thing that had changed was my taste. I did give up alcohol almost immediately after the SVT. Jill's dad offered me a glass of red wine one afternoon a few days before Christmas. I accepted as I had previously been a red wine drinker and enjoyed a nice glass from time to time. I took one sip and almost spat it out, but not in a sommelier kind of fashion. No this was in a "My god, what is this poison?" way. I couldn't bear it. The taste was putrid, the small amount I had swallowed burnt my throat and we weren't drinking any old $10 cheap crap, this was top-shelf stuff, Penfolds or something along those lines.

I had to apologise and say I wasn't up to it just yet. I would never be up to it ever again, but at the time I thought that maybe the drugs I had been sent home with had affected my tastebuds. I had been prescribed with a tablet version of the medicine that had finally stopped my heart from going at a gazillion miles an hour to a more sensible and acceptable speed. The only thing was that this stuff was very toxic to the body long term, so I was only prescribed a month's worth.

Christmas came and went; I was lonely even though I was being well looked after by Jill and her family. But I was also scared of my heart flipping itself back into an abnormal rhythm. My first true test came sometime between Christmas and New Year when Jill and I left New Plymouth and headed south back to Christchurch. I had not been looking forward to the flight, not for any reason other than if my heart decided to go bonkers on a plane what could I do? What could anyone do?

We sat at the end of the runway, waiting to take off. My heart racing, my hands sweaty, in fact my whole body hot and shaking. Jill was trying her best to calm me down, but I needed to get off that plane, there was no way I could fly, plus, I knew that it was going to be a turbulent flight and what's more we were flying via Wellington, a city and an airport well known for bumpy landings! This was my first taste of a panic attack. There would be many more to come but I felt almost as terrible at that moment as I did when the SVT happened just a few weeks before.

It wasn't the flight as such that I was worried about, it was the fact that if something did happen to my heart how could I be looked after? In fact, winding back the clock back to when I returned from PNG, I had decided, for a few reasons, that I needed to learn to fly.

I have always been someone who likes to be in control of a situation, be it the loss of faculties from drinking too much or being a passenger in a car, with some notable exceptions. I didn't ever like the feeling of being out of control. It was similar with flying, not quite the same, but it had most definitely been firmly etched in my brain during my time in PNG. I had many flights for work while living there, most would involve some turbulence of one degree or another, but two flights stood out when I thought we wouldn't make it.

Once, I was on the way back from the Solomon Islands to Port Moresby in a Fokker 100, a very outdated jet, noisy and compared to something like an Airbus or Boeing, a much more primitive aircraft. The engines on the Fokker were at the back, level to the cabin, so the noise was deafening. I heard the engines spooling up and down as the pilots tried to speed up and slow down the plane to help guide it on to the runway in a storm that would in most places around the world be a definite no-land situation!

We tried not once, not twice but three times to land, the last time as I looked out the window to see driving rain, lightning and mist, the ground came right up to us and I thought, yes, this time! But within a height that felt like I could jump safely from the plane, we pulled up yet again and powered up through the clouds, which were full of water and electricity.

The pilot came on the speaker to say we were going to divert to Lae, refuel and wait for the storm to pass. When we arrived in Lae there were several other planes there. When we talked to other passengers from them it became clear that their pilots hadn't even tried to land in Port Moresby but had diverted to Lae instead! I was furious! We eventually got going again later that evening and arrived in Port Moresby around 9pm.

The second time was on a small plane ride from East New Britain back to the mainland. The pilot, an ex-pat who had lived there for years, was a real bush pilot. He was doing a bus-route trip, picking up people along the way to deliver them to a hub for an onward journey. Before we left though he declared there was a problem with the plane. Not ideal, I thought! "Can you hang on for 30 minutes?" he asked, "I need to nip home and get a spanner." Jesus, I thought, really? He returned within about 10 minutes and proceeded to take off a part of the plane that covered the wheels up once they were safely nestled in the body of the fuselage after take-off. "We don't need that," he said, cheerfully.

We set off on our journey and the next port of call was a remote village just off the coast on the far eastern corner of the island. The cloud and rain were enveloping the plane and it was bloody bumpy. I was sitting directly behind what is known as the co-pilot's seat, the co-pilot being a local who was fresh out of flight school, it seemed to me. You could see the whole cockpit and easily see through the front window, except there wasn't much to see. This was a 10-seater small commuter plane that was being thrown around like a rag doll through the turbulence caused by the convection currents from the heat of the day and the clouds.

When it came time to land, I was thinking, where the hell are you landing and I asked the question. "Oh, just down there," the captain said. "Christ," I thought, I can't even see what you are pointing at. We were pretty low by now, maybe 1,000 feet, when the captain asked me to pass the rag that was on the floor in front of me. I did so and he started wiping the inside of the window which had fogged up, probably from my heavy breathing!

I was terrified, this wasn't good, I was surely going to die, we would plunge straight into the ground and burst into flames, I was sure of it.

At last, though, I saw the "runway", a rough dirt strip of land that, as I would later discover when I talked to the maverick pilot, was their bread and butter and what they loved about flying. We landed without incident and the next couple of pick-ups were fine. We had broken free of the local weather, and I managed to divert my attention by looking out of the window at the stunning scenery. But it was there and then I said to myself, Victor, you need to learn how to fly.

YOU HAVE CONTROL

I first met Blair at the Christchurch aerodrome when I got back from Papua New Guinea in the late winter of 2005 and had taken up my new role.

An awesome guy, Blair was a young, smart and clearly very intelligent man who had just finished all his commercial flying training.

He was, like many others in his shoes, looking for work at an airline, which in NZ was basically Air New Zealand or Jetstar. To help keep his hours up and to keep himself current he had become a flight instructor, teaching the likes of me, people generally older than himself who had always wanted to give flying a go. He was a typical Kiwi, laid back but professional and meticulous in everything he did.

My first taste of flying a plane had been a few years earlier, back on the Isle of Man. I had been given a pleasure flight, which really just entailed a 30-minute introduction. I didn't do much, I think I held the yoke for a short while and did some turns, but that was about all. The real stuff, the fun stuff, was all done by the instructor.

But this time it was me who would be learning how to take off, fly and land under Blair's watchful eye. On our first trip together, I thought it would be me watching him, but no, he had other plans.

After the pre-flight checks, ranging from checking the fuel to inspecting the engine, we taxied out to the grass strip, which in Christchurch ran parallel to the main runways. This was one of the most amazing things about learning at this airport, you were sharing the space with large heavy jets, listening to their radio chatter and having to be aware of what was happening around you.

As we powered up and headed off for our first flight, Blair was talking me through what to do. He had his feet on the pedals, as did I, so that I could feel his input, similarly with hands on the yokes. The feeling of the plane leaving the ground and becoming airborne was something I will never forget, it was incredible. The plane became light and felt nothing at all like it did on the ground.

Shortly after take-off, and once we had flown out of the immediate airspace, Blair asked for clearance to head over towards Port Hills in Christchurch. This was deemed a non-controlled zone, meaning it was free air space where as long as you were aware of the other aircraft around you, via radio and visually, you could be in a space in which it was safe to learn. Cleared for the Port Hills, Blair spoke those three words in common with pilots around the world: "You have control." The reply to this is "I have control", which I said back to him. I was now flying a plane all by myself above Christchurch in NZ. This was amazing, this was exactly what I had always wanted to do.

We flew for about 30 minutes then it was time to head back to the airport. "Do you want to try landing?" Blair asked. "What? Really? I can?" I asked in utter disbelief that he was going to trust me with this plane on my first real flight. "Well, you fly well and have a natural style and anyway I am right here if you need help," he reassured me. The adrenalin was surging through my body, just like it used to when I was riding motorbikes. The excitement was palpable, I was grinning like a Cheshire cat!

As we approached the airfield, he talked me through what was happening and why. This was exactly what I needed; my entire make-up runs on not just what is happening but why is it happening. He had me dialled in perfectly.

Easing the plane into the final set-up, he told me how to keep my line of sight relative to the runway, while checking air speed, pitch and trim. About 10 feet from the floor, he told me to pull back gently on the control column and allow the plane to float to the ground. He was there, helping and I could feel his input to make minor corrections to my flying. As we touched down, I pulled back the throttle and kept the nose-wheel light, with my feet taking over the steering. The plane immediately transformed into a more sluggish vehicle, almost rebelling about being back on the ground, not in its natural environment. Singularly, this had been the very best thing I had ever done and it was only going to get better from here.

After a few flights together and with my skill and confidence gaining, it was time to decide whether I wanted to get serious about flying, so I needed a medical to be able to proceed any further. Obviously, I always had in the back of my mind that maybe because of my heart condition I wouldn't be allowed to get a licence.

Blair told me to go and see a particular doctor who was CAA approved. He was a great doctor; in fact, he became my GP. He fired me off to see a cardiologist who was very interested in seeing me. I had also asked if I could see him for a general check-up.

I was granted a licence, but it came with a condition, a significant one, being that I would never be allowed to fly a plane on my own. I was so upset, there seemed no point in having a solo pilot's license if I couldn't fly on my own. It would mean that when I qualified, I would always need another fully qualified pilot with me. I discussed it with Blair and while he very much understood how I felt, he did say that it wasn't too uncommon and that there were always other people around that would be happy to fly with those who had this caveat on their licence. It gave me hope and I agreed to continue.

Not long after being granted a licence and deciding that learning to fly and qualify as a private pilot was my goal, the trip to Auckland that saw me being resuscitated in North Shore Hospital pretty much put an end to any dreams I had of flying.

In theory, I could have carried on flying, but the practicality was different. After I returned to Christchurch with Jill, in time for New Year's Eve of 2005-06, we settled into living together.

But I was now a very different person, in mind at least and physically too in some respects, to the one who just weeks earlier had been loving life, enjoying a new job, and looking forward to his girlfriend joining him.

The house had been bought a month or so earlier; the deposit was gifted to me by my late sister in her will. Things had all been coming together; it had seemed that life was working out fine, that I had control.

But now, suddenly and without warning, I had lost control. I was a passenger and I had no idea where I was headed. It wasn't a good feeling at all.

There were so many impacts of this major health event that I hadn't even considered, but they became apparent very quickly. The first was a physical symptom. I likened what happened to me to an earthquake. Now, a month on, and after being taken off the strong beta blocker, I was starting to get the aftershocks. My heart would skip a beat, or maybe two, and it became very disconcerting. My anxiety levels began to rise and I felt terrible.

By now, I had been referred to a congenital cardiologist in Christchurch, a man by the name of John Lainchbury. A super man, incredibly funny and smart (aren't they all?) and someone I thought was going to be my salvation.

I thought back to the time when I had first mentioned to my cardiologist in Liverpool that I wanted to live overseas, specifically in NZ. He said to me that if I was going anywhere in the world NZ was a great choice as the cardiac care, particularly in Auckland, was excellent. Adult congenital heart disease is a close-knit network, for two reasons; one, because the conditions are rare and two, because many children born with these conditions sadly don't make it to adulthood.

The consultants all know each other from conferences and before I left, my then cardiologist wrote the name and number of a man he wanted me to seek out once I got to NZ. I didn't, and while it is likely that wouldn't have changed the course of events in terms of my SVT, what it would have done was place me in the system with notes for referral. Another regret, but that's life, I guess.

John saw me at Christchurch hospital a few weeks after I returned from Auckland, via New Plymouth, the awful flight! We had spoken briefly on the phone before meeting.

With a relaxed and laid-back, typical Kiwi approach and demeanor, he quickly made me feel less anxious. He reassured me that while what I had been through was traumatic and awful for me, it had been the first time it had happened and there was no reason to start pumping me full of drugs just yet.

In some ways I was happy with that, but I knew that these aftershocks were not right. I felt every one of them, having become hyper-vigilant of my heartbeat almost overnight. He asked me to try to persevere and I did.

The next impact was on my job. My role at the time was working for a global chemical company called Johnson Diversey, these days just called Diversey. They manufactured cleaning and hygiene products used in all manner of industrial and commercial settings. From products to clean food-processing plants, to products used in hospitals and care homes, the range was vast. I was in charge of sales for the South Island. I had a small team of sales reps who reported to me; they were dotted around the island from the northern tip in Blenheim to Queenstown. There were six reps and me to cover the work, it was a busy role and up until December 9, I had been enjoying it immensely. But suddenly, after a bit of sick leave and the Christmas/New Year break, it was time to go back to work and get back into it.

As their manager, it was important that I visited each of the reps regularly to work with them in the field and guide and support them. The role obviously required a fair amount of travel. Then came the first problem, as I returned to work.

I set off from my home on the outskirts of Christchurch in a suburb called Somerfield, directly south of the city centre. I made my way towards Highway 1, which runs from the tip of the North Island to Invercargill at the bottom of the South Island. I was on my way to Dunedin, which was about four hours' drive from Christchurch, to visit my sales rep, Warren, and work with him for a couple of days.

Being in Christchurch had certainly been an attraction, at least at the outset. A city designed by Captain Joseph Thomson in the mid-1800s, it followed a simple, yet effective grid system, which allowed for easy navigation. That was, until the powers-that-be got carried away with one-way systems! Truly, I don't think I have ever seen as many.

Christchurch, the so-called Garden City, was a beautiful place. Glorious in the summer months with its Avon River dissecting Hagley Park, nestled on the fringe of the city, the destination for many tourists either as a port of call while touring NZ or as a single stopping place to visit.

Winter though, and especially the first winter I was there, was brutal. People used to say all the time, as I complained about how cold it was, that I should be used to it coming from the UK.

The main difference, though, is that in the UK our homes and infrastructure were built to face these elements, whereas here they seemed not to be in NZ.

A typical "Kiwi" home was made of wood, had little to no insulation, single-glazed windows and was almost colder inside than out! In fact, I recall the ice on the inside of the windows in my spare room during that winter. It was ridiculous. During the winter months the smog that lay over the city and suburbs from people burning through what would once have been acres of woodland was very reminiscent of a northern town or city in the UK, except there it was coal they were burning.

What I did love about Christchurch, though, was how flat it was. Great for walking and bike riding, but you could then take a drive over the Port Hills into Lyttleton and experience some incredible views. And, of course, I had loved learning to fly there.

It wasn't long into my journey that a wave of anxiety came over me, and with it all the usual accompanying symptoms, sweating palms, racing heart, fast breathing etc. I pulled over to the side of the road and began to weep.

I had known that my life was no longer going to be as it had been, but the harsh reality of this was starting to show its ugly hand.

After maybe 10 minutes, a police patrol car pulled up behind and an officer got out of the driver's side. The usual exchanges took place, him introducing himself and asking where I was going, what I was doing and if I was OK. "Not really," came my reply as I started to give him a brief rundown.

I think back to this moment now and maybe he thought I might have been going to do something silly. He was obviously concerned and asked if I needed an ambulance or anything. I explained that I only lived a few kilometres back towards Christchurch, perhaps 30 or so, and that I would drive home and call my doctor. I had called Jill from the car on my way home. I felt weak, I felt a failure and above all I felt a total lack of hope that I could have anywhere close to the life I had been enjoying just a few weeks earlier.

I now needed to call my boss in Auckland to explain why I wasn't going to be where I had planned to be. Also, I needed to call Warren who was waiting for me in Dunedin, to tell him I wouldn't be joining him. I made up some excuse, I can't remember what it was, but no way in hell was I telling him the truth at this point. That kind of truth would go through the business like a wildfire tearing up bushland on a hot Australian summer's day and I wasn't having that. No, for now I needed to lie.

Jill was waiting for me with a hug and a smile as I got out of my car and I told her I didn't think I could do this anymore. I am not sure what I meant, did I mean I couldn't do my job, I couldn't do living in Christchurch, or I couldn't do this life anymore? I wasn't sure what I meant but I knew something had to change. I was no longer in control.

I CAN'T DO THIS

I made an appointment to see my GP, Robert. The man who only a few months earlier had said I was fit to fly, was now going to see a person who could barely drive 30 kilometres down the road before having a panic attack.

Robert's practice was on the east side of the city, and he invited me to come and see him the next day. He was a prominent brass-band member, and his practice was full of memorabilia from concerts he had played at all over New Zealand and further afield.

What I hadn't realised though was that he was also a keen pilot. Most of the appointment was taken up with him telling me how he had started flying and how that led him to combine his medical training with an interest in aviation medicine. He told me I needed to get back on the horse, so to speak, and encouraged me to get myself out to the airfield and go flying with Blair.

Honestly, this was something I hadn't even thought about. I could barely drive a car without having a panic attack, never mind be up in the air three or four thousand feet and have one. Nevertheless, I made a booking with Blair for the following weekend.

What I was fast coming to understand was that I had huge amounts of anxiety around being in situations that I had no control over. Whether that was being in a remote location with no access to phone coverage, as was very common on the South Island, or, as I would soon find out, even in some business meetings, my heightened level of awareness regarding my heart and my heart beat was about to bring me down.

I met Blair next Saturday morning, the drive out to the airport took about 20 minutes from my house and all the way I was ruminating and catastrophising about what was going to happen.

Blair was his usual chirpy self, very welcoming and offered his support and care and told me not to worry. Easier said than done, I thought, but I appreciated the sentiment.

We did the pre-flight checks together. It was quite a warm January day, clear skies, perfect for flying. "We aren't going to do anything too silly today," he said. "Just a nice flight over to Lyttleton and back, maybe head down the coast a little way, see how you feel."

As we taxied out, I could already feel my heart pounding. Maybe it had in the past. I doubt it though; previously this had been fun, so much fun, now it was a tense and honestly unpleasant experience. I pushed on though, thinking that maybe once we were airborne that I would settle, distracted by the stunning views that this summer's day had planned for us.

We increased the revs in the engine as we were cleared to take off by Christchurch control. Again, the feeling of sharing this area with some of the biggest aircraft and the world's best-known airlines, such as Emirates, was almost too much to take in.

"You have control," came over my headphones from Blair, "I have control," I replied, and we were "rolling". I pulled back on the control column at around 90 knots and our Piper lifted effortlessly off the ground. I looked at Blair with a huge grin on my face.

"Yeah!" I thought. I am back! We levelled off at about 3,000 feet (around three minutes of flying) and made our way over to Port Hills. It was a warm day and inside the cockpit could get a bit toasty on these days. With the sun streaming into the cabin, sweat began to bead on my forehead.

As is common on a warm day, convection currents form and cause the air to become more disturbed. If you have ever flown and encountered turbulence, looked out the window and wondered why it was bumpy when there were no clouds, it's often being caused by winds or convection currents. Pilots call it clear-air turbulence, for obvious reasons, and it can be quite violent. Today was one of those days.

As we approached Port Hills, which lies south of Christchurch, our little plane started to get thrown about a fair bit. No matter how much of a seasoned pilot someone might be, it's natural for your heart rate to rise a little. Mine started to rise a lot and suddenly I started to feel the surge of adrenalin flood my body as its fight-or-flight mechanisms became activated.

I asked Blair to take control while I started to take my pulse. It was probably the first time, but certainly wouldn't be the last, that a real fear like that of December 9 came over me. It was most definitely the environment I was in, in the air in a small plane. What if I collapsed? How could Blair help me?

I calmed down after a few minutes and my pulse returned to a more normal state, but I needed to be on the ground, so we turned the little Piper around and headed back to the airport.

Blair asked if he needed the airport to call for an ambulance, or anything. I didn't need one. Blair flew us all the way back, a perfect landing onto the grass strip. After shutting the engine down, not much was said really, except Blair asking if I was OK. I didn't say anything, but I knew that at least for now, that would be my last flight.

I was gutted. I had hoped so much that this flight would give me the confidence I was looking for to start returning to a normal life. I had failed, the worry had got the better of me and I felt another piece of my life slipping away.

When I think back now it was that day that really bookmarked the beginning of the end for me, at least psychologically. Sure,

December 9 was a physical bookmark, but I had been optimistic that I would start to regain my confidence and life would eventually return to normal. Now, two things had occurred within a short time to contradict that opinion or wish.

Life continued, I went on a few work trips and they were harrowing for me. I hated it. Each time, I couldn't wait to get home to my safe place. Once, I had to be driven back from Dunedin after being at a sales conference after lying awake all night worrying about my heart.

It was becoming ridiculous. Fortunately, or unfortunately for me, my boss was beginning to feel the same way, frustrated no doubt with all the time I was having off or work tasks I couldn't complete.

Eventually the inevitable day came, and a conversation was had about the fact that I needed to up my game if I was to stay there. I knew though that if they wanted me gone, which was obvious to me, that there would be a process to go through. They couldn't just kick me out. So, I put a proposal to my boss that basically saw me get three months' salary in lieu of a notice period. He accepted it, and by the following week I was unemployed.

Christchurch, by comparison to Auckland, is tiny.

Certainly, from a commercial perspective, it's a fraction of the size. Most of the businesses in the industry I was involved with were based in Auckland, or even in Australia, so I wasn't hopeful of finding a job within the industry there.

One thing I have always managed to do in life is make connections with people. In sales generally, but especially in tight-knit industries, you meet plenty of people; colleagues, competitors and clients and it's good to keep the doors open.

The phone rang a few days after I left the business, and it was a sales rep from one of my customer's businesses, a large food service business that was very well known in NZ, called Trents. It was the wholesale arm of the foodstuffs business and needed a sales manager. After a few calls and a few days, I was in front of Mel Phillips, a very charismatic, full of energy and driven individual, who was well on his way to having an illustrious career with the organisation. He was the general manager of Trents. His previous sales manager, also a company man, had been transferred into a different part of the business.

Trents sold everything you can imagine, from food to dry goods, consumables, even cigarettes and alcohol – and cleaning chemicals, my specialty. Mel and I got along fine, although how I quite managed to bluff my way into a job with them I have no idea. Even at the interviews I was there with my index and middle fingers of one hand resting on the wrist of my opposite arm taking my pulse, under the table as he spoke to me. I don't know why I did it, I guess it became my security blanket.

Like all things if you do them enough, they become habitual, and that practice of mine became just that. It also became something that was a huge distraction from what I was supposed to be focused on and this again started to impact on how I listened and understood.

By some stroke of luck and good fortune I was offered the job at Trents. I guess they couldn't find anyone else. It's perhaps the shortest "real" job I have ever had, aside from being a bar tender and working on a building site one summer, I think it probably held the record. Three months, I think, is all I lasted, for a few reasons.

By now, my heart was becoming an ever-present factor in my daily life and not in a good way. Generally, I felt terrible for much of the time. I would call John, the cardiologist, on an almost bi-daily basis telling him how terrible I felt. At this point, I wasn't on any anti-arrhythmia medication, just a tablet generally used to reduce blood pressure; for me it was used to help my right ventricle pump blood more effectively. I had been on it for years. Like my previous role, I was expected to travel, although not as much.

There was one occasion, while in Nelson with Mel and some other colleagues for the night, we went to a customer's restaurant. It was late when we got home, and I had eaten too much food. I couldn't sleep, my heart was pounding and at last I couldn't take anymore and called an ambulance. They woke Mel up, too, which didn't go down well, and he saw me off to the hospital. The usual tests were done, ECG, bloods etc. and nothing showed up as being out of the ordinary. The following morning, I was discharged, but with no sleep I was absolutely exhausted. I couldn't drive, so Mel had to drive my car and I was the passenger, not a good look.

I think it's worth mentioning that now I always made employers and prospective employers aware of my cardiac condition. I think that's only right and fair. Do I think I have been overlooked for roles because of it? Absolutely. Do I blame them? No. It's asking a lot of people to employ a person with a cardiac condition, not just for the issue of irregular attendance at work, but also the added responsibility that the employer may feel, rightly or wrongly.

However, what I definitely didn't do with Trents, was fully disclose how I was feeling, mentally more than physically. There was no issue with my physical being to do this role. Sure, I would get tired after a long day, but then doesn't everyone? No. What I didn't disclose and mostly because I didn't know what to disclose, or indeed how to disclose it, was my mental health.

Trents was a large corporate organisation; they had employee healthcare benefits, and within that, access to psychology support. My boss suggested that I should take advantage of that, and he organised a couple of sessions for me.

I had never been to see a "shrink" before, and technically a shrink is a psychiatrist, not a psychologist, but I am sure you get my drift. I didn't really know what to expect. I had visions of laying on a chaise longue, while revealing my innermost darkest thoughts.

Clearly, I had watched too much *Frasier*. Of course, it wasn't like that at all. I did sit down but just on a regular chair. The woman, whose name I can't recall, wanted to know about my background and a little about what had led to me needing to come and see her.

I have always been a very open person, not one to shy away from saying how I feel and telling my life story to anyone that would listen. But I must confess, I struggled to open up to her. Maybe it was a personality thing, I am not sure, but I wasn't getting what I thought I would get, to help me cope with the almost constant state of anxiety I was in.

I didn't really get anywhere with her, and my anxiety rolled on, gathering in size and pace.

Several incidents occurred until I finally said to Jill that I couldn't do it anymore. I couldn't do my job and I couldn't do life generally, at least not in its current form.

When I had originally returned to NZ from PNG, I had asked Jill to marry me – this was before any of the heart troubles began. So now, as well as all this medical stuff I had going on, we were trying to organise a wedding.

NORTH BOUND

The relationship I had with Jill had been a huge rebound for me. This sounds callous and mean, it's not intended to be. When I knew that PNG wasn't going to be a long-term option and having already met before I left, we had kept in touch, mostly via email and a weekly call.

She even flew up to PNG for a long weekend and met some of the friends I had made there. Donna had left a huge void in my life, and I was still a bit perplexed about what had happened. I mean, I knew what had happened, but maybe we had both allowed things to get the better of us and our relationship.

If hot is opposite to cold, then it was almost as far opposite to Donna that Jill could be. She was nine years younger than me, very much a girly girl, liked partying, had a double persona really. On the one hand she was the good Catholic girl, whose parents thought she was towing the line in everything that she would have promised during her confirmation. On the other, when her parents weren't with her, which was most of the time as they were back in New Plymouth, she was different.

I had met her while working in Auckland where she worked for a client of ours. It had been a light-hearted romance from my perspective, I think she liked a slightly older, well-travelled guy, who had seen a bit and done a bit with a good education and background.

I liked that she was uncomplicated. What I mean by that, is she came from a good family, understood that there was a time and a place for everything and that she clearly wanted to go places in life.

We enjoyed dining out and the other usual stuff that couples do in the infancy of their romance, but it never did zing, there never was that je ne sais quoi, that you know when you know.

It had been a very impromptu proposal. Geez, I had thought, I am nearly mid-30s, it would be good to have a family. Also, I was no doubt flattered that an attractive girl, almost a decade younger, would even look at me!

Unfortunately for our relationship, things started to go wrong long before we tied the knot, which was December 29, 2006 – ironically, Donna's birthday. It wasn't Jill's fault, and neither was it directly mine.

It was just that my heart condition started to make an appearance, almost as the third wheel of the relationship. Our physical relationship had turned, I was too afraid to have sex with her, for example. Heck, I was too afraid to even walk up a flight of stairs for fear that my heart rate would increase and go off into some dreadful abnormal rhythm.

I was avoiding doing other things too, things that we once did together, such as going out for a glass of wine or going for a decent walk. Jill loved her wine and would sit at home in Christchurch pouring herself glass after glass most evenings.

I began to feel that instead of me being attractive to her, she now saw herself as a carer for me, as someone that would be stuck with me forever. I believe she really resented that. I got it though. I understood why she would feel that way, she was 27; she didn't need to have me as a millstone around her neck.

With all that had gone on in Christchurch, from not feeling that I could work, to not feeling that I was getting the proper care I needed, I began to feel as I had done when I left the Isle of Man three years earlier, the sense of needing to escape.

A chance conversation had led to an opportunity in Auckland, and so we decided to sell the house in Christchurch and make a new start back in New Zealand's largest city. I was excited, I felt like I was going home in some ways. First, though, we had a wedding to attend. Ours!

My parents had visited NZ once before. It had been talked about after my sister died, when we went back for her funeral they promised to come out and see us.

However, as it turned out they arrived a week or so before I took off to PNG. It was terrible timing; they had come all this way and only got to see me for a short time. I hadn't seen them for over a year and so much heartache had been absorbed by them. Regret number three: not delaying my relocation to PNG until after they left. That time would have been precious. It was precious, all time is, but I didn't use that time as I should have done.

So, this time they were coming for a wedding, my sister too with her husband and two of my nephews, Tom and Sam, who were still quite young back then, no doubt excited about the prospect of a big trip to the other side of the world.

My sister had chosen to arrive earlier with her husband, Tony, a class act of a man, the man that made my sister happy. It's all you want for your family, isn't it? Health and happiness. I am glad she had both. They touched down in Christchurch before Jill and I left. They stayed with us, and we had a few lovely days with them as they recovered from jet lag. Tom and Sam were coming out with my parents – their grandparents – a few days later, giving Ninee and Tony some adult time to explore NZ a bit.

As much as it was amazing to see them, and it truly was, they hadn't seen me since my other sister's funeral, and I knew that they could see an immediate change in me.

There was, of course, the physical change. There was 10

kilograms less of me now than there had been. I hadn't ever tried to lose weight; it just fell off me when I stopped drinking alcohol. I am sure a healthy dose of anxiety was helping, too.

Then there was the mental change. No longer was I the fun-loving, happy, carefree younger brother my sister had helped raise. Now I was nervous, anxious, on edge and unable to relax.

One night we headed out for dinner, the four of us. The other three were relaxed, drinking wine, enjoying the amazing NZ culinary fair that is so plentiful.

I was taking my pulse out of sight as I almost always did. By now, it was more than my safety blanket, it was an extension of me. Standing, sitting or lying I would covertly be taking it. If standing, my hands were behind my back or at my front. If sitting, they were under a table, and if lying down, I would have my hands clasped across my stomach.

They say addicts find a way to deceive and cover the truth or their real actions. I had joined this club with ease and I needed to be counting my heart rate in my head, constantly. I would count to 10 with each beat, then start again if I was interrupted by a missed beat or pause in the rhythm, which so often occurred. If my counting sped up, then that meant so had my heart, and if I couldn't figure out why then I would start panicking. That is what happened during the evening.

We had returned home after dinner, and I felt all manner of palpitations. Next thing, Jill was driving me to hospital at 9pm. After another round of tests, I was given the all-clear and told to eat a banana as my potassium was a little low!

But it was this constant feeling of impending doom that was causing my life to be on hold. The feeling of knowing something bad will happen, buy just not knowing what it will be, or when.

I felt very sorry for Jill on our wedding day for several

Snuggling into my dear mum at a few months old with oxygen supply taped on my nose before my first heart surgery. Royal Liverpool Children's Hospital.

Home after the first nine months of my life in hospital. A day out at the beach with my dad and my beautiful sister Viv. Summer 1971.

Above: Nine years old. Trials riding was my saviour. It was a sport I could do from a young age. My dad (on the right) looks on making sure I'm doing it right!

Above right: Messing around after an event in 1985. I'd finally started to grow after my surgery the year before.

Right: One month before my next big operation, I attended the 1983 annual motorcycle awards (pictured here with British motocross champion, David Thorpe). I wore the same velvet jacket to my sister Jacqui's wedding three years prior. Mum was obviously trying to get more wear out of it as I wasn't growing much!

Above left: Our take on Burns night trying to uphold the Scottish side of the family. My dad and then brother-in-law looking much better then than we all did later!

Above right: Around 1987, trying my hand at motocross. I loved it but my heart struggled to keep up. I came off later this day and chipped a vertebrae. My mum didn't come to watch me for a while again after this!

Left: Halfway up Ben Nevis competing in the 1991 Scottish Six Day Trial. It was a long week!

Left: I'd promised my mum that if they bought a trials bike, I would never ride a motorbike on the road. But I made that pact when I was eight. She must've known it wouldn't last forever. I lived on the Isle of Man for goodness sake, what else was I supposed to do?

Below: The night before Donna and I left for New Zealand in 2003. We were only going for a year, two plus decades later. My dear mum, my wonderful sisters and Tony my brother-in-law. My sister Viv passed away two months later. My world caved in.

The day we said I do to one another! Our wedding day on the shores of New Zealands Bethells Beach. A wonderful day.

This little guy arrived and everything changed. All my efforts to stay well, stay alive and make it were motivated by Fergus. He and I went on a boys trip to the Gold Coast. Here we are at Sea World hoping that the whale would soak us.

In 2019 we headed to Belgium for Fergus to race in the BMX World Championships. BMX racing demanded a lot of time, dedication and money, but it was all worth it to see the joy that racing brought him.

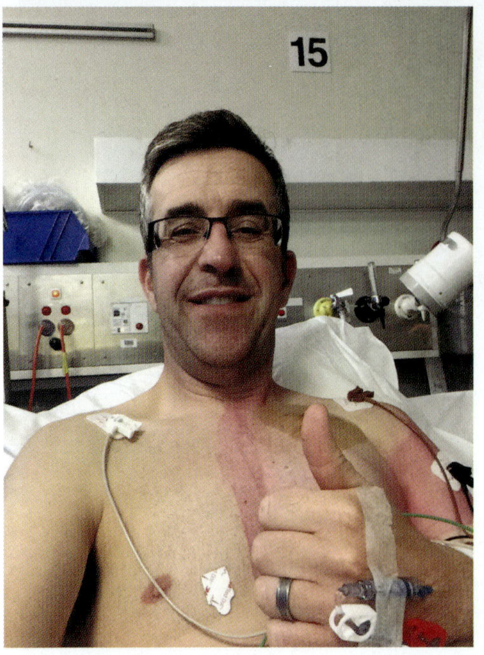

By late 2022 my health had really started to go south. I am smiling because after many long hours of being in an arrhythmia and feeling dreadful, I was finally back in a normal rhythm.

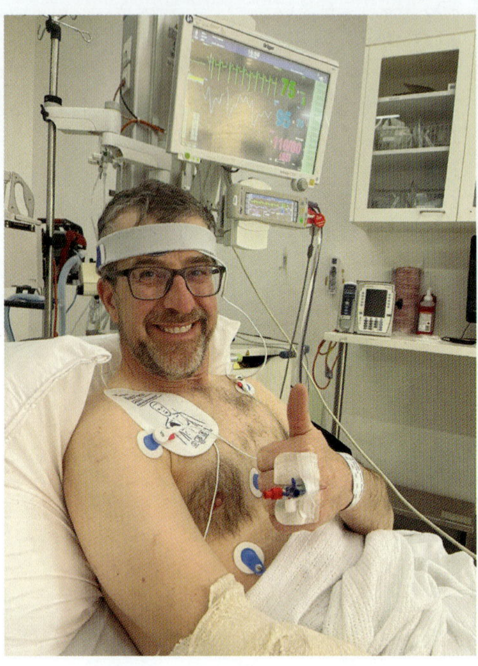

Recovering after my "upgrade" to an ICD-type pacemaker. Now I had a defibrillator with me 24/7.

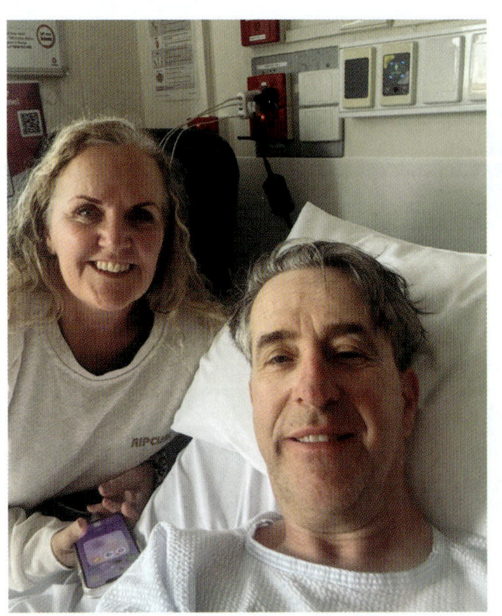

I had got the call for a new heart the night before. Here we are waiting for me to go to theatre. Even though she is smiling I can see the worry on her face.

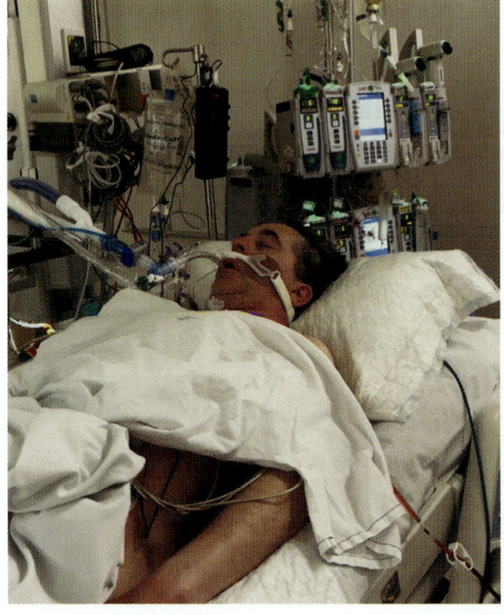

The operation went well. This was taken about 24 hours after it. I am about to be woken up.

Two weeks after my operation I was allowed out of hospital; two days later I was in the cardiac rehab gym, which is when the hard work really began!

Several weeks after I left the hospital I was very fortunate to meet my surgeon. What a day that was.

May 2025: We are all back together and we are all smiling and I am fighting fit. Mission accomplished!

First ride back with Fergus April 1st 2025.

For me this is what it was all about. This is why I fought to live. To be able to go riding again, but most especially to be able to ride with Fergus, is an absolute dream come true.

reasons. The first was that I was in no way present. I mean I was there, obviously, in the physical sense but not in an emotional or connected one. This was her big day, a day she had planned down to the last detail, a day we should both have been absorbed in, but the truth was that I wanted to be anywhere but where I was.

As I waited for her to come down the aisle in all her regalia, the beautiful white dress, the fairy-tale picture, I was taking my pulse, inconspicuously of course! I made eye contact with my parents who smiled at me and then at her mum who was waiting for her husband to guide their only daughter and place her into my care.

Her mum later took me to one side quietly and told me how important it was to have sex. I was dumbfounded. Here I was, being lectured by a devout Catholic, who, had she known that her daughter and I had been at it well before I left for PNG, would no doubt have been mortified. But then, I think out of sight was definitely out of mind with Jill's parents.

The wedding itself was lovely, but in all reality we should never have got married. I wasn't in any fit state to do so, I was so disconnected from life, living mostly in my own world, a world full of anxiety and fear. I was absolutely terrified from when I woke up to when I went to sleep most days. Terrified of something terrible happening and I knew it would, terrified of my parents having to bury another child, terrified of being viewed as a liability and a failure.

Less than 12 months later, while living in Auckland, Jill left.

SUNNY DAYS, RAINY DAYS

We had arrived in Auckland early in 2007, following the wedding. We rented a house while we looked around for one to buy, which eventually we did, in the suburb of One Tree Hill.

The house was modest in size, quite new. It had been built on the rear section of the front property but with its own driveway. It was the first open-plan home I had lived in, with all the rooms radiating from the kitchen, lounge and dining areas which comprised the hub of the property. Easy maintenance with just a bit of garden to mow in summer and some leaves to sweep up in autumn and winter. The thought was that it would allow us to get stuck into our jobs and, who knows, maybe a baby would arrive sometime.

Jill had been transferred from her job in Christchurch working for a very well-known beverage company, you probably know the one; shiny red can with some fancy writing on it. I was working for a national supplies business helping to set up their cleaning and hygiene chemicals division.

The absolute best thing about moving back to Auckland for me, though, was that I had been referred to the adult congenital heart disease centre at Auckland City Hospital.

What was about to happen was life-changing for me. Until being seen by the team in Auckland, I had no medication for all the nasty and irregular heartbeats I had been getting from December 9, 2005. It was now 2007. That's a very long time to carry on feeling like crap. Those "aftershocks" as I have called them, where my heart would start beating erratically for a few seconds, or be thudding in my chest when I lay down, or skipping beats were all things I had become used to, but hated just the same.

The first meeting with Dr Tim Hornung was so reassuring. A Pom like myself, he hailed from the north of England, so we could understand each other just fine! A relaxed but highly intelligent man (I guess you have to be in that job) he immediately wanted to know about my life and showed a real interest in helping me as a person, as opposed to me being just another patient. There was commonality too. Tim had done most of his training at London's Brompton Hospital, he knew Alder Hey and he also knew my old cardiologist, Mr Wilkinson.

Tim explained that what I needed was a beta blocker, but because my heartbeat was already slow they could only give me a baby dose, as one of the effects of beta blockers is that they further suppress the heart rate. If it went too slow, I might faint or pass out. Not the best look!

So, I was sent on my way with a small dose of the medication, but I could feel the effects of it quickly. It evened me out, and I experienced less of these nasty heartbeats that had so troubled me. My confidence levels rose, and I felt myself being able to do a bit more by way of activity and so on.

Sadly, though, on the home front Jill had had enough. She left one Sunday to stay at her friend's house for a few days of space and never came back. I didn't blame her, and I got it. Living with someone who has a chronic medical condition, no matter what it is, must be hard. I think even though she knew I had the heart condition long before we got married, things had changed with me. I was not the man she met.

My only regret is that I went through with the marriage. On reflection, I knew it was the wrong decision. Not even a year after we were married, we had split up. She went on to find a new partner and had a child. I wish her and her family all the best.

BACK ON THE SHELF

With a mortgage to pay, I needed a lodger. That came in the shape of Kate. She moved in and we seemed to get along well. A free spirit is how I would describe her, oh, and tall too, very tall! After a while of us co-habiting and having got to know each other a bit, she asked me one day when I was going to get back out there, referring to finding a new partner.

At first, I wasn't really interested. I mean I was happy to go on a date or two and maybe have a bit of fun, I was still only in my 30s and if the last few years had taught me anything it was that this was one lap and you didn't know when that lap might end, when your own personal chequered flag awaited.

I ended up joining the many others on the internet looking for whatever it was they were looking for, something casual, something fun or maybe something more serious.

I think I had messaged her first, not realising at the time that she lived in Invercargill, which was just about as far away as one could get from Auckland and still be in the same country.

But we struck up a good relationship by way of messages backwards and forwards for a few weeks. Finally, we decided to meet, and she flew up to see me.

She was from the UK, had moved out here with her then husband, a Kiwi. She had two young kids, which I wasn't particularly fussed about either way. It certainly wasn't a deal breaker for me. Time wore on, and once again I thought, this could be it.

A few months passed, then one day she said she could get a work transfer to Hamilton, a couple of hours south of Auckland.

This meant we would be able to see and spend more time together. It all looked good.

Meanwhile though, the world was having a tough time of it, NZ included. The great financial crisis meant property prices had dropped, not ideal with me buying at the top of the market.

They say, don't they, that so as long as you buy and sell in at least the same market or a comparably better market, then all will be well.

That is all fine and dandy, but the mortgage had to be paid. Kate by now had moved on and my money woes were real.

All through this journey, while I had felt a little better with my heart, it still caused me a great deal of anxiety. The same old traits of me avoiding certain things, taking my pulse at every opportunity, making excuses and so on, they were all still a big part of my daily life and honestly, it was pretty shit!

On the plus side, though, things were going well with my new beau. She seemed ever more increasingly to be the one. I had paused my internet dating membership, and I was happy on that front.

A few more weeks passed, maybe a month or two, when she told me she was pregnant. I was overjoyed. I had always wanted a family of my own and, yes, while she already had some offspring, I could see that this new blended family could work.

Naturally we made plans, and we decided that because she would be out of action work-wise for some time, and that I was the major bread winner anyway, she needed to move to Auckland for us to set up home.

At first, we discussed all living in my house, but there just wasn't going to be room, plus she really didn't want to be in a major city. Very much a country girl, Auckland wasn't really on her list of places to live.

At the same time, I was really struggling to keep up with the mortgage payments and once I crunched the numbers it was clear that renting my house out and moving to another rental property of our own, further out of the city on neutral ground, big enough for the soon-to-be five of us, it would be financially better, too. So, we looked for a house, found one and committed.

The day of the move came, and I was excited, as was she or so I thought. I had organised a removal truck and packed. I was meeting her and her two kids at 2pm after picking up the keys to our new home. I arrived around 1.30pm with a huge bouquet of flowers and some chocolates for her kids.

By 4pm that day I was starting to worry, and finally when my phone pinged, I read the text, it went something like this:

"I am sorry I can't do this. I can't have a child with you, I am going to terminate the pregnancy. I don't want to move from Hamilton, and I don't want to live with you."

So, no phone call, just a text! I was gutted, upset, not just for the fact that she had decided to deny me the chance of being a father, but also that she had lured me into a false sense that everything was fine and wonderful, only to be jilted at the metaphorical altar!

Luckily for me, the houses in the area we had chosen to live were going like hotcakes, so I was able to get out of the lease and spent a week or so in a hotel while I decided what I was going to do and how I was going to do it. With the house I owned now rented out, the only choice I had was to find a small apartment back towards the city. I did this and moved myself into a nice little two-bed unit in a suburb called Ellerslie. When my head stopped spinning from the past few weeks of emotional and physical upheaval, I sat back one night and reflected that I had most definitely dodged a bullet and that everything happens for a reason, I just didn't know what the reason was... yet.

REPENT AT LEISURE

The dictionary entry of the word spontaneous is: "Performed or occurring as a result of a sudden impulse or inclination and without premeditation or external stimulus." It also says this: "Having an open, natural, and uninhibited manner."

When describing me, I personally prefer the second offering, but if I was to ask my dad, he would no doubt offer the first one as a closer description. My dear dad would often use the phrase "Victor, you buy in haste, and you will repent at leisure."

Of course, this means that unless you take your time to weigh up the pros and cons of a particular circumstance, opportunity or situation, you may find yourself regretting the decision you made.

I could never understand or see this as a young man and even into adult years. Some of my relationships that I have reflected on previously, for example, have reflected this, no doubt. However, now, I see this trait of my personality as clear as day. I am impetuous, I do act on impulse, but I think I also have an open and uninhibited personality, those that know me best may disagree.

It's taken quite a while to understand and reflect on why this would be, but these days I know why it is so. It's simple really, I want to do things while I have a chance to do them. I don't wish to get all gloomy here, but the reality is I just had no clue how much time I had to live because of my heart condition. There is another aspect of my personality which I dislike more, but it's very much linked to my spontaneity and that is I am probably the most impatient person I know. I could recount many examples of my impatience; they range from everything from driving a car to making a business decision or even something as simple as waiting for a train or whatever.

Simply put, I hate waiting for anything. Again, in my mind, this is aligned to the fact that I might not be here to do or enjoy the very thing I am waiting to do. I know that impatience adds fuel to my anxiety, and I have tried to talk about it with various psychologists over the years, none of whom have been of any damn help, by the way!

An example could be that I might be doing something exciting at the weekend, and I will worry that something bad will occur before then (it could be Friday). So, the impatience, while not in any way rational, is driven by the fear of death or at least of being incapacitated and therefore not experiencing whatever it is I am waiting to experience.

Over the years, I have made decisions based on the here and now. I have always been terrible at planning, be it financially, career or whatever. I struggle to play the long game, because I can't see the long game.

I once planned a trip back home to the UK about a year in advance of leaving and for the whole year, right up until the morning of the trip, I couldn't fully relax and look forward to it because I was worried I wouldn't get to do it. And then as the various stages of a trip such as that unfold, for example the plane journey, I would again worry that I wouldn't get there or see my family.

In the same vein, I have always found it very difficult to relax fully. I have always been on the go and wanting to fit in as much as I can. While this may seem a virtuous quality to have, trust me, it's not! Being like that means it's very hard to be fully immersed in an experience, because you always want to move on to the next thing.

I suppose these personality traits became clear at around the age of 12, at about the time that I was told I would need that second operation. I didn't connect the dots at the time; there weren't many dots to connect, and my mind was nowhere mature enough to understand my behaviour – I'm not sure many boys that age would.

My schoolwork was never that brilliant. I could hold my own, but I was always wanting to move on to the next thing. My concentration span was very short, it still is. It's a miracle I have managed to write this book to be honest!

You might think this is just typical of a kid at that age and so did I. Until one day, maybe about 10 years ago I went to a presentation in Auckland by a select group of doctors. Among them was a clinical psychologist who specialised in congenital heart defects. I sat there with my mouth open for the entire talk. Almost everything that I had ever experienced in terms of how I thought and the actions I had taken, clicked into place.

What this specialist said specifically was that children born with serious heart defects were much more likely to have been starved of oxygen for a significant time. I immediately thought about the operation notes I had copies of, which detailed that on arrival at hospital way back on October 8, 1970, my oxygen levels were 65 per cent. This was a massive reduction in the oxygen required to sustain life.

During the post-talk tea and biscuits, (these events are always so civilised) where the doctors hung around, I managed to sneak a word or two with the psychologist. I explained that what she had described was a lightbulb moment and she kindly spent a few minutes talking to me about my history which I recited to her.

The long and the short of it, she said, was that I had been very lucky to have led a relatively normal life and that the fact I had many positive aspects to my life was something to cherish, as many kids born with the same condition as me were not so lucky. They may live, but they can have many other physical and neurological conditions, such as Down Syndrome, too.

I asked what other factors could result in a better or worse outcome for patients. I had often wondered why two people with the same condition and treatment might end up having entirely different outcomes in terms of their health and length of life.

What she said astounded me at the time, but when I think about it, it makes perfect sense. She explained that how well someone goes on to, and subsequently off, bypass, which is the process that is used to keep someone alive during complex procedures such as open-heart surgery), can greatly affect their long-term prognosis.

In fact, she said, it's such a big deal that there is lots of research and studies being done on the subject. I left the lecture that day feeling blessed.

Certainly, I had been through the mill; I knew that, both from a medical perspective and psychologically, but it could be much worse. So, for me, she explained quite a fair bit about the person I am. Sure, I may have been the same had I not had a heart condition, we will never know, but I think it's fair to say that having been born with a serious congenital heart disorder, it has most definitely and definitively shaped who I am today.

In all reality, how could it not have?

THE BEST LAID PLANS

They say, don't they, that if you fall off a horse or a bike, the best thing to do, if you are physically able, is to get back on the bloody thing and give it another go.

Certainly, in the literal sense I had fallen off bikes more times than I had had hot dinners, but that goes with the territory of the sport I chose to take part in.

Another trait I know that has been shaped by my health issues is my resilience. I won't give up, ever. If you think you can beat me and I think I can beat you, then bring it on. Whether that's at Scrabble or driving a fast car.

When I was growing up, I definitely had a point to prove, I knew I didn't have the physical abilities of some others but that wouldn't stop me; if there was a race on I wanted to be first.

And so it was with relationships. I had, I think it's fair to say, a fairly shitty run with one thing and another, but I knew, I just knew Miss Right was out there somewhere.

So, I dusted myself off and got back on the dating scene but wanting this time to play the field a little more perhaps, not jump in with both feet, hoping to avoid the "buying in haste and repenting at leisure" syndrome.

I met a few women, had some dates and so on, but nothing serious. I had met one, of whom I was very fond, but she had two kids and honestly, I knew I wanted a family of my own one day. Selfish as it may sound, I wanted it to be just us, if that makes sense. So, in the end we parted ways but remained friends.

Scrolling through the profiles one night one picture really

popped out. Her long, dark ringlet hair framed her beautiful face perfectly, but it was her brilliant blue eyes. I don't think I'd ever seen eyes like them. The shape of them was a perfect oval but with an intensity that just drew you in. Well, they drew me in.

I clicked on the profile and what I read made me send her a message straight away. So much for slowing down Victor!

Her screen name was Skiwi, derived from the fact she was a Scottish girl living in NZ. Luckily, for me, she replied and within a few messages we had exchanged a bit of detail. She revealed that she was a nurse and that she had been away from the UK since 1998.

She had travelled and worked through Australia and had ended up in the far north of NZ working at a smallish hospital before deciding she needed to further her studies and career by heading to the big smoke.

Eventually, she revealed her real name, it was Sue. Bloody good to meet you, Sue, I thought.

Our online conversation developed, and we decided that it would be nice to meet. We had planned a Monday night at a local pub, which turned out to be a beautiful late summer's evening with me on the hard lime sodas.

I think she probably had a cabernet sauvignon, her go-to on such an occasion. I think it's always interesting ordering food on a first date. I mean, what do you order? Definitely not spaghetti bolognese! I can't remember what I ate, but I think we both passed the table manners test.

We got on well. She was even more good-looking in person and I found her company easy, our British senses of humour bouncing banter off one another as if we had known each other for a much longer time. It was nice. The first date wrapped up with a trip to the movies and the first date turned into a second date, and so on.

It's fair to say, probably because of my impetuous and impatient nature, that I have always been keen to move things along. If something seems right, then I usually proceed without much further thought.

As much as I liked her, I was still trying to offset that speedy Victor with a modicum of taking things easy, and to that end, I was still in touch with other women. This wasn't cool and almost cost me getting to know one of the most amazing people I have ever met. Luckily for me she saw past it, and we moved on.

While we didn't talk about our age that much, we both knew as we spent her 40th birthday in Wellington later that same year, that time was ticking for her if a family was going to happen. It needed to be sooner rather than later. Our one, and only child was conceived in Wellington and nine months later, as he entered the world, our lives were turned upside down, as they are with most new parents.

Before he arrived, though, I had taken Sue on a trip to Christchurch. It was there, on top of Port Hills, below the area I used to fly over a few years earlier in the little Piper, that I asked Sue to marry me. Now, I know what you are thinking – this was the third time. Come on, really? But, yes, it was the third time, but I had never felt more sure of something than spending the rest of my days with this intelligent, logical, caring and beautiful woman. Incredibly, she said yes!

Sue is a very loyal, very independent woman, she honestly doesn't need anyone, at least outwardly. Hailing from a family of three children, she was the youngest. Her father had sadly already passed away and her mum had retired from her physiotherapy job before we met. Her sister, the eldest, is a doctor and her brother is a lawyer. So, we used to rib her that she was "only" a nurse. She declared herself the dunce of the family, but trust me when I say this, nothing could be further from the truth.

She is very smart, has worked hard all her career and decided that her field of expertise would be in cardiac healthcare. When I met her, she was working at Auckland City Hospital both as a research nurse and on the wards to keep herself up to date with the latest nursing procedures and practices. When I first met all her family, I felt extremely inadequate. Here I was, a salesman selling cleaning stuff who was trying his best to date a girl who came from a family of high achievers. She was no slouch, herself.

It was only a few months into our relationship when the phone rang one night, my sister calling about my dad who had been severely injured in an accident while riding his bike. It was clear his injuries were life-threatening and that I needed to get home as soon as I could. My anxiety and concern around my health was still ever present and the thought of me sitting on a plane for 24 hours on my own was too much to contemplate, really. "What if I come with you?" asked Sue. "Really? You would?" "Sure, I have some leave and I can go and see my family too."

Within 36 hours we found ourselves on a plane back home via Hong Kong. It was incredible to me that this person, whom I had only known for a short time was happy to "hold my hand" both figuratively and physically as we jetted north from Auckland to London. I felt safe, I don't know why, I just did, probably because she was a nurse but not just a regular nurse, she was a cardiac nurse! This fact, in itself, would prove to be a challenge for our relationship in the years to come.

My dad survived by the skin of his teeth. If he had not been a very fit 79-year-old, there is no doubt he wouldn't have survived, but as I pointed out to the doctor, if he had not been out on his bike being fit he wouldn't have crashed! Double-edged sword I think we call that one.

D-DAY (DADDY DAY)

Sue's pregnancy had been without incident, except for Christmas 2009 when she felt disgusting and lay on the couch the entire hot day.

I was doing my best trying to cook a turkey with all the trimmings, an act that I look back on now and laugh about. What the hell was I doing? It was hot and humid, she was feeling terrible, yet I persisted.

It's funny with Christmas, it's the one time of the year I really struggle with. I have lived in the Antipodes for almost 20 years now and still I can't get used to having a barbecue, or whatever, on a day that you are supposed to be cuddled up, wearing whatever rendition of dreadful Christmas jumpers have been bought for you, eating too much and enjoying your family. Christmas Down Under is nothing like that at all. It's warm, it's shorts and T-shirts and while there is still overeating going on, neither of us had family there. It was our first Christmas together and it was a disaster. Sue still raises her eyebrows when I recount it as the worst one ever!

In March 2010, we decided to take a short break and pop over to the Gold Coast in Queensland, Australia. A friend of Sue had a time-share there and we managed to grab a week that was free. It was her last trip before she would be too far along in her pregnancy to fly safely.

It was a great week, and although she had been a little off at times, we got to spend good quality time together. I think both of us recognised it was going to be our last holiday on our own for a long time!

Back home, having sold our respective properties, we had bought a new house, which was stunning. We both fell in love with it, instantly. A double-storey with a sort of third floor which split off from the main floors to house the bedrooms. It had a huge deck out the back and a garden which dropped down to some bushland. We knew it was going to be a great place to raise a child. So, as we edged ever closer to welcoming our child into the world, we were busy getting things ready; the nursery, buying all the required equipment and so on.

Not long after meeting Sue, I had also been given the opportunity to work for the global leader in cleaning and hygiene chemistry, a company called Ecolab, which many readers may no doubt know.

The opportunity came by way of an old sparring partner when I was working back in Christchurch. He and I worked for opposing teams, but as an individual, Rod was a great guy and I liked spending time with him. He was a wise old dog, had been around the industry for a long time and was now the man in charge of the sales team in NZ. He gave me a call one day, and asked if I would be interested in working for him, running the upper North Island sales and technicians team.

Clearly my impetuous nature came to the fore yet again and I exclaimed a big fat "Yes!" before even knowing about salary and so on. Back then, negotiation wasn't my strong suit. But, as it turned out, it was probably the best career decision I had made to date.

Ecolab was, and still is, an enormous organisation with ample opportunity for those who want it. I wanted it.

My mobile beeped. It was 5am. It was a message from Sue. She had been taken into hospital the night before to be induced – because of her age the midwife didn't want her to go over her due date. But the nurse who induced her had encouraged me to go home and get a good sleep. "It will probably be your last one for a while," she reassured me, cheerfully.

I went home, via a Chinese takeaway, taking full advantage of my last night as a free man.

I called Sue. "Are you OK?" I asked. "NO!!!" came the screaming reply from the other end of the line. "Get here, now!" was the implicit instruction. I'd never been in this position before and didn't really understand how urgent it was. Even though, on reflection, "get here, now" meant exactly that!

I decided I had time for a quick shower and piece of toast. I mean, who knew how long it might be before I got something to eat. Clearly, I had a rude awakening coming. To this point in my life, I had really only needed to worry about myself. Obviously, I cared for and had loved people along the way, but what I was about to experience put everything that had gone before into oblivion.

At 6.15 that morning, weighing eight pounds or so, we were absolutely blessed to welcome our little boy into the world. Without doubt, it was the most amazing, exhilarating, emotional and quite overwhelming experience I had ever had.

At that same time my heart changed forever. I don't mean my physical heart, but rather my soul, my purpose, my entire being shifted from being self-absorbed and quite self-focused, to knowing that this little guy was now what my life was about.

He was then, he is now, and he always will be, my reason for living. I recalled my mother's voice in my head saying to me: "One day, when you have a child, you will understand, Victor." Right then, at that moment, I understood exactly what she meant.

Fergus was healthy, something I had worried about during the pregnancy. What if I had passed this genetic mutation that had afflicted me, to my child? Not that I hadn't had a good life – I had, but it would be the last thing I would have wanted, for him to have to go through surgeries, being poked and prodded, test after test, being ridiculed at school, not being able to take part in strenuous activities. All these things had worried me, but as it turned out, my worry was unnecessary as he was absolutely fine.

The first 24 hours of being a dad were a whirlwind. Sue's stay in the maternity ward at hospital was short, she was essentially kicked out a few hours after giving birth for us to be transferred to a maternity clinic where she stayed for a day or two.

Our baby was swaddled in blankets with a white hat on his tiny head. At last, he opened his eyes as I was holding him, and I saw those same incredible blue eyes that his mum had given to him. Well, son, you should be OK with the ladies when you are older, I thought.

It was, and it still is, the proudest and happiest day of my life. It was, without doubt, the best thing I had ever done. I knew there was lots of fun, love and adventures to come.

Finally, I had become a dad, something that I had been doubtful of for a number of reasons, actually living long enough was the main one. But now, my thoughts shifted to hoping I would see him take his first steps, ride a bike and be there on his first day of school. I found it hard, as previously mentioned, to see that far forward. For now, though, it was one day at a time, learning how to be parents.

I think the overwhelming feeling that I am sure most, maybe all, first-time parents have is: "My God! I am responsible for this little person." I can barely look after myself and here we are now thrust into the deep and vital responsibility that means our actions quite literally mean him living or not.

I am glad to report that 12 years on, we have managed to keep him alive, but I must confess there have been some close calls along the way! The first came a few days after he was born, and while it wasn't directly our fault, we still felt terrible when he was dropped in the bath on our kitchen worktop!

It was actually the midwife who was holding him, when he slipped out of her arms as she was showing us the correct technique and he sank under the water. It was only a fleeting moment and was quite funny, but it reinforced the fragility of the life for which we were now responsible.

I think him sleeping in our bedroom lasted two nights, Sue may say one! Either way I had no idea that babies were so damn loud when they slept. Not a snore, more of a gurgle, but it kept me awake and a Victor with no sleep is no use to anyone, sadly, a definite by-product of having a heart condition.

So, he went off to his nursery which we figured out years later was a dumb idea, he should have stayed in our room with Sue, and I should have decamped to the spare room. But we persisted with Sue being amazing as a new mum, her undying love for him shining through.

Time went by. Before we knew it, he took his first steps and was into everything. He has always been an energetic child. He would wake up, usually around 5am, sometimes 6am if we were lucky, and with the exception of an afternoon nap when he was little, it would be full-on all day, chasing him around, playing with him, keeping him safe, but above all loving him more than anything else I could have imagined.

I think it's fair to say I have always been a fairly deep person, not shy of expressing my emotion and feelings for something. Thinking about how others might feel, and so on. However, it dawned on me that I hadn't ever really understood, or appreciated, how my parents would have felt when they were told their son had this very serious condition. Or how they raised him to let him live, but also protect him too. The arrival of our son changed that and while, thank God, he was healthy, you just had that uncontrollable and eternal feeling of protection, knowing that you would do anything to protect him.

And that's when it struck me – my parents had no control over that situation, they had no say in whether I lived or died other than to grant me the lifesaving procedures I had through my younger years. The outcome of those was out of their hands, they couldn't remove me from those situations. That must have been a living hell for them.

A few weeks after Fergus was born, I was speaking to my mum and I remember saying to her that now I understood and that I was sorry for all the stress and hassle I had put her and my dad through, both in terms of my health condition and some of the silly things I had done in the past.

WHAT WAS THAT?

It was a spur of the moment arrangement to catch up with some of Sue's friends.

I had been introduced to them a couple of years earlier by Sue. An accomplished couple, we had always enjoyed their company.

The plan was to meet at a restaurant in the trendy suburb of Parnell. Not that we were trendy, well I certainly wasn't! As we were getting ready to leave, I walked up the few steps from the bedrooms of our lovely house where they met the open plan family living area. I had just reached the top step when I felt it.

What the heck was that?

I nearly fell over and, according to Sue, looked like I had seen a ghost. A huge wave of heat came over me, like a flush. I quickly became clammy and panicked. I had never felt this before.

To that point I had felt countless numbers of ectopic or missed heartbeats and sure, while I hated them, I had never felt light-headed or that I thought I might pass out. We went out for dinner, but I wasn't relaxed at all. I had been properly shaken by the episode, but little did I know there would be more, many, many more, to come.

Since meeting Sue, I had always wrongfully relied on her for advice. It's been probably the most contentious part of our relationship, so far.

It drives her mad how I will ask for constant reassurance. I am also, without doubt, a hypochondriac. Worse than this, I am well-known, to myself anyway, to catastrophise many situations. If I feel generally unwell, for example a stomach ache or a sore arm or leg, I will somehow link it to my heart. I am beyond-hyper aware of my body, which you may think is a good thing and I suppose in some ways it is, but it's also very debilitating.

Starship Children's Hospital, believe it or not, is where I used to be seen. I have always been a child, in more ways than one, plenty of people would say! But in some countries, NZ being one of them, there was no adult congenital heart clinic, at least during my time living there.

It may well have now changed. Starship couldn't have been more different to the hospital I attended in Liverpool all those years ago. A very modern building, unlike the Victorian building I knew so well, this was inviting (as inviting as a hospital can be). The inside was airy, with big spaces for internal playgrounds, cafés, shops and so on. It was decorated, as you might expect a kid's nursery to be, with pictures of animals swinging through the jungle, boats, the moon and stars, just on a much grander scale.

I described what had happened and what I had felt, to Tim, my cardiologist. He was concerned enough to order me a Holter monitor and a stress test. Oh no, I thought, not a stress test! I hated them. Ever since my 2005 episode any idea of voluntarily increasing my heart rate was not appealing! As it happened, I had just cause.

For the uninitiated, a stress test, also called an exercise tolerance test, sees the patient walking on a treadmill while wired up to various monitors and blood pressure equipment. Each two minutes the speed increases and the incline becomes steeper.

Back in the mid-1990s when I was much fitter and much younger, I managed to do the whole thing, which lasted for around 12 minutes.

By that stage you are basically running, certainly a very fast jog, up what feels like to be the side of a mountain. Similarly, a

Holter monitor is a non-invasive device that you carry around with you, usually for 24 hours, which is about the size of a large iphone. It's connected to leads that are stuck to your chest and it records every heartbeat.

This time, in my early 40s, things were very different. After a few minutes and the pace increasing I started to have the same feeling in my chest as I had done on that bloody awful day back in 2005. I was breathless, light-headed and feeling pretty average!

Ordinarily, with my state of mind there is no way I would be pushing myself, but cardiologist Tim asked me to try and push myself a bit more to see what would happen.

Well, we found out! It was a very different outcome this time, however, even though the meds I was on were a very small dose of beta blockers.

When they got me off the treadmill and sat me down on a bed, Tim gave me some reassurance that I would be OK and emphasised that they had all the equipment if things got a bit crazy. Thankfully things didn't get a bit crazy, my heart reverted to a normal rhythm and I was fine, if not a bit shaken and anxious.

Have you ever taken your car to the garage to tell the mechanic about the dreadful and terminal-sounding noise emanating from the engine or the suspension, or wherever, only for the mechanic to drive it and nothing happens? Yes, me too, and this is exactly how I felt up to that point, as all the tests and the monitoring hadn't shown anything overly untoward. There is nothing worse than saying to the doctors that you feel this and that, and whenever you wear a recording device nothing happens! But this day was a defining moment, and I don't say that lightly, it truly was. This was the day that the decision was made to give me a pacemaker. This was a good day, once I calmed down and recovered.

I realise fully from the outside looking in, that someone celebrating the arrival of a pacemaker may seem a little odd. But when you feel so terrible, and that you might keel over and die at any moment, you will do anything to help change that.

Probably one of the most incredible pieces of medical equipment ever made, pacemakers have come a very long way over their time in use. Initially developed in the 1950s, the first types of pacemakers were external and required massive batteries to power them.

They were accompanied by a trolley to allow some mobility. Hardly convenient, and primitive in their functionality. Wind the clock forward 60 or so years to when I was invited to have one installed, and things were very different.

About the size of a biscuit, they are most commonly inserted into the left pectoral muscle. Wires are channelled to either the top or the bottom of the heart, or, as in my case, both. There are many reasons to have a pacemaker, but for me what it meant was that I was able to be given higher doses of anti-arrhythmic drugs, which in turn would mean a safer and better quality of life.

And so it was that in mid-2011, I had my first pacemaker implanted. I can't begin to express the benefits I felt from having it.

Set at 60 beats per minute, no matter how many beta blockers the docs needed to give me, my heart rate would never drop below that threshold. The pacemaker also helped my heart react to exercise more efficiently.

Two parameters inside the pacemaker helped it to know when I was moving. One related to breathing, so the harder and faster I breathed the more the pacemaker would accelerate the heart, and the other which I found fascinating, was a potentiometer inside the device that sensed movement.

Like a gyroscope, it would move faster with more external force and that would tell the device to speed up the heart. Amazing stuff!

So, I was set, pacemaker on board, big boy drugs and off I went. Things were great. This was the best I had felt since 2005. I just hoped it would last.

THE WESTERN ISLE

The rivalry between Australia and New Zealand is decades old. Various sporting events have seen much anger, heartache and, of course, celebration over the years.

Some of it, no doubt, was fuelled by spurious underarm bowling back in 1981, which saw Australia deliver the final ball of a cricket match underarm to deny NZ the chance of hitting a six, which, had they done, would have drawn the game.

However, on the other side of the ledger is the unique bond the two countries have. Much of this is attributable to the two wars when thousands of young Diggers from both countries found themselves fighting on the other side of the globe.

The ANZACS, as they become known, are rightly remembered each year in April for the anniversary of the 1915 landings in Gallipoli, which saw many of them massacred as fierce fighting ensued for eight months before they were evacuated.

The result, more than 100 years on, is that Australia and NZ are indelibly tied to one another and these days that takes many platforms. Sport, business, trade, culture and defence strategies are just some of them.

My first encounter with Australia came back in 1990 when I decided to venture overseas.

On many levels I had a great time, but unfortunately, I had a frightening and, at the time, harrowing experience, too. I had been making my way up the east coast, from Sydney in New South Wales to my destination, Cairns, in the far north of Queensland.

Short on funds I had grabbed a lift with a truckie as far as

Byron Bay, where from memory he was turning hard left and heading inland towards Lismore.

It was around 4pm in the afternoon in winter, so still warm, certainly much warmer than I was used to back home, but as is the case even in those parts of the country, once the sun descends, the air temperature can drop significantly in a short period. I had been walking with my thumb out trying to hitch a lift for about 30 minutes when, at last, a car pulled up. The two front-seat occupants jumped out and asked me where I was headed. They said they were heading to Brisbane and could give me a lift that far.

I think it's fair to say that I was, by my own admission, fairly naive and by no means streetwise. I had spent most of my life living in a small community where everyone knew and trusted everyone else, where doors were never locked or at least rarely and where serious crime was someone stealing a wheelbarrow or a gnome from the garden. Even during my time living in London, while certainly eye-opening and you needed to be aware of your surroundings, it was still quite sheltered for me. I lived with my sister and her partner in West Wickham in Kent and only went to the city for work, mostly with her so she always looked after me.

In short, I was extremely trusting of people, in many ways I still am! I didn't realise that people could be so callous or nasty.

The driver asked me to put my backpack in the boot of the car, which I was hesitant about, but as I looked in the back, I could see there was another passenger, so I just assumed that he was asking me to do that for more room. With my backpack and all my worldly possessions locked away in the car I jumped in the back seat, next to the female passenger, who, it was clear, was either drugged or drunk, or maybe both, but whatever she was, she was not fully with us.

We set off and I became almost immediately worried. With a deep sense of feeling that all was not well, a few clicks down the road, I asked them to stop and let me out. At first, they told me to relax but my mind was now in overdrive, convinced I was going to be taken hostage, or worse.

Finally, we pulled over down a side road and I hopped out. Again, both guys, who were of middle eastern appearance, hopped out of the car.

One of them pretended that the boot wouldn't open and as he was fumbling around and I was watching him, the other guys punched me square in the face, smashing my nose immediately. I was on my knees as one of them kicked me in the side of the chest making me fall to the ground completely.

"Stay down," he said. I did. They jumped back in the car and made off with my backpack. Luckily there was a petrol station nearby, or "servo" as they are called in these parts, and I picked myself up off the ground, blood pouring from my face and asked if they could call an ambulance and the police.

The staff there were amazing, they took care of me until formal help arrived. What ensued was a trip to hospital, where my nose was put back in place, which was not that nice. The police came and asked me if I had somewhere to stay. "I don't have anything, let alone somewhere to stay!" was my response. No identification, no money, no clothes, in fact all my possessions including my camera, and the pictures I had taken in the months before, were gone.

I spent the night at a halfway house, and I am guessing the police got in touch with my family. As luck would have it my sister went to college with a girl who had married a doctor, and they emigrated to Australia some years earlier. My sister called them to see if they could help but being back in Sydney it was over a day of solid driving to get to me.

However, I was very close by now to the Gold Coast, famous for its miles of golden beaches, its surf, its unique culture and of course as party central in Australia. The doctor my sister's friend married, went to medical school with another guy from the UK and they connected me to them.

What took place over the next couple of months was nothing short of humanity at its best.

These people, who had never met me, or my sister, didn't know me from a bar of soap, took me in, made me feel like I was one of their family and looked after me.

Don and Liz are two of the kindest, caring and loving human beings you would ever meet. I was so, so fortunate to have found solitude with them. Their eldest kids, around my age, made me feel welcome and took me with them in their general day-to-day lives, be it shopping, to the beach or to the movies.

Suzanne, the eldest daughter, and I are still friends today. Whenever we visit the Gold Coast, we always visit them. I will never ever forget their generosity and love they showed me during what was an extremely crap experience.

It's fair to say I had been tainted by Australia, we had been back there on holiday a few times since living in NZ and I had made a few work trips over the years, but I had never really given much thought to perhaps living there.

That all changed when one day the phone rang. It was a recruitment agency wondering if I would potentially like to relocate to Melbourne to work for one of Ecolab's competitors.

I was intrigued. I knew that if I was to progress my career any further that being in Australia was probably necessary. Ecolab themselves were busy centralising their south Pacific operations into Sydney, and I could see other businesses doing the same thing. I talked to the then GM of the division I worked for at the time and told him about the call.

He urged me not to leave to work for the other company but

then said if we saw Australia as a new home that they would be very happy to move me and my family there. Before we knew it, we were on a plane for a week-long scoping of Melbourne.

My grass-is-greener trait shone through once more and all I could see was what was great about Australia and what was bad about NZ. I convinced myself and tried to convince Sue it was the right thing to do.

I had found my health once more, I felt strong, I felt ambitious, and I felt like we needed a new adventure. I got sucked into the whole vortex of excitement of moving to a new country, and even though that country had smacked me once, I seemed to have moved on from that experience. I also seemed to have forgotten just how amazing a place NZ is to live. Reluctantly, Sue agreed that we could move on the premise that if Australia wasn't what we wanted we could go back. I agreed and said absolutely, if this doesn't work, we will go back.

On reflection, that was always going to be easier said than done. It was one thing moving to the other side of the world in 2003 when I was 33 with nothing more than a backpack and my then partner in crime. This was now a whole different ball game; we had a whole life to pack up and we also had a four-year- old to think about. Even the school starting age in Australia was different, so Fergus would have to wait longer to start school in Melbourne.

At the very end of 2014, I had my first day working in Melbourne for Ecolab. I had left Sue and Fergus in Auckland, along with my dad who had come from the Isle of Man to visit. I felt it was a reprise of those years earlier when I had buggered off to PNG. My timing sucked!

I wasn't in Melbourne for long though, going back to NZ for Christmas and sharing our last time of the year there with everyone. But I had got a taste of the heat Melbourne could throw down, the thermometer had already touched 40C and it was barely summer! The heat was crazy, I had no idea that anywhere could get so warm.

They didn't tell me about this on the brochure, I thought. Early January I was back in Melbourne and work became hectic very quickly. My role was to look after some of Ecolab's biggest customers in Australia, many of whom were international clients, so not only was there much local activity there were also frequent video meetings at all sorts of crazy hours. It was good though, I enjoyed it.

I missed Sue and Fergus a lot, but I was enjoying the job and still managed to get back to NZ every two or three weeks. Fergus was growing and developing at a crazy pace, and I really felt I was missing out on that joy.

While I was on the "Western Isle" as the Kiwis like to call it, Sue was back in the "seventh state" of Australia as the Aussies like to call it. She was frantically busy, packing up the house and getting ready to rent it out. We had agreed to rent it so that if we did go back, we had somewhere to live.

In March, I drove to Melbourne airport to pick up the two most important people in my life.

It was time for them to start their new journey too. I remember watching the Air NZ Boeing 777 aircraft coming in and touching down. I was trying to guess which window Fergus would be looking out of and how excited he must be. A huge adventure for a four-year-old. Although, that said, even by that age he was a well-travelled young man, having been back to the UK twice already in his few years. I was just hoping and praying that they would both settle in. I knew eventually that Fergus would embrace it, what kid wouldn't with the Australian lifestyle, but I was worried about Sue; she loved NZ and felt very much at home there. She had upended her life for me, so that I could develop my career and chase my dreams.

The fact she was a nurse and could work almost anywhere in the world was the easy part. Leaving behind her 15 or so years in NZ, the friends she had made along the way, and the memories too, was a big ask, but I didn't give it the respect or thought that her sacrifice had been at that time.

Fergus ran towards me like a scene from the start of *Love Actually*. Hugh Grant is right as he narrates the beginning of the film– the arrivals hall at airports really are places full of love. On this day it was so bloody good to see them both.

We all settled into Aussie life. It was the end of the summer, so the weather was cooling off a bit, but there were still some lovely warm days to be had and we had fun exploring our new city and home. Like most cities these days, Melbourne is very multicultural. The variety of food is incredible.

In short if you can't get it there, you can't get it anywhere. Unlike many cities though, we quickly began to experience the four-seasons-in-one-day weather that the place is famous for. Cold, rain, sun, wind, hot and back to cold again in a day is not an exaggeration.

My work became more and more busy with me away on trips almost more often than I was at home.

I was a victim of my own success at work. I was kicking some massive goals and the more I kicked, the more the company wanted me to kick. I had "sold" Sue on the fact that I would be largely Melbourne-based with a few trips to Sydney for head office meetings, here and there, as that is what had been sold to me.

That landscape quickly changed, and three things became evident. The first was that it was relatively easy to shine here, my colleagues doing the same role as me were lazy, they were treading water, they weren't proactive. The second, because of the first, was that I could grow quickly here and pull myself up the corporate ladder if I wanted to. I wanted to, I really wanted to.

The third was that Sue and Fergus had been sold a false bill of goods. I was never at home. She was a solo parent who had no friends, knew next to no one and was feeling lonely. I felt the resentment she had towards me for dragging them both to this new country.

I was doing fine, loving life, in part due to my success at work, although I could already feel the corporate pressure. My boss in this role was a man called Paul. He was about 6 feet 4 but built like a greyhound. Born in the UK he had emigrated here at a young age but still called himself a Pom. I guess technically he is!

The first day I met him he walked into one of our meeting rooms in Sydney. It was one of the days before Christmas after I had just started the role. I had been asked to an end-of-year sales meeting. He was late, he was always late as I would find out. He arrived with his receding hairline, sunglasses covering his bald patch, dressed as he always was, impeccably, with his long tie stretching all the way down his torso, clipped on to his shirt around halfway down. Shoes shiny, he walked like he meant it and had the swagger of someone who knew their shit and was confident in his skin.

He didn't say hello to me, well, not for a while anyway. He had entered a room of eight people, all of whom did a similar role to me. The room stopped for him as he walked to the top of the long table to take the captain's seat.

At last, he acknowledged I was there. "Welcome to Wiggins from NZ." He liked to use surnames to address people, a very corporate thing to do! My initial reaction was wow, this guy is either an absolute idiot, rude and someone I will not be able to work with, or he is so good at his job that I will learn from him very quickly. I am so glad to say it was the latter.

Paul and I became friends over a period. In me he found someone who did his job as well as I could. I gave my all to the role and he saw I wanted to be the best I could be, but also that I was competitive like him and I wanted to be the best amongst my peers.

It didn't take me long to show him that he had made a good choice by hiring me. In him I saw an incredibly intelligent person, totally mad of course, quirky, peculiar. Someone that understood business and how businesses worked.

I learned from Paul like I had never learned before. I guess it's fair to say he took me under his wing because I showed effort. He used to always say to us, "meet me halfway" meaning you show him you are interested that you will work hard, and he will do whatever he could to support you. He pushed me hard, sometimes to the point of tears when he knew I could do better, that I could think of a deal-construct in a more commercially enticing way for the business. Professional to a T, never had I worked with someone of his integrity and someone that adhered to his own core values, that wouldn't allow the corporate rat-race to deter him as was easy to do. We had lots of fun together, some great trips both in Australia and across the ditch in the "seventh state".

Most importantly, though, together we won millions of dollars' worth of business for the company and that was recognised by me winning several awards, awards I would never have received without his guidance, his input, his mentorship. He was without doubt the best mentor and the best boss I have ever had.

A WHOLE NEW WORLD

Referencing the movie *Sliding Doors* again, another chance of fate came our way one morning as we rode our bikes to kindergarten with Fergus.

One of the other mums had seen him riding his bike, and, as it turned out, was pretty handy on a bike herself. "You should get that child to the BMX track," she yelled out to me.

I had no idea where the BMX track was, and while I had ridden several BMX bikes when I was young, BMX bikes these days, as it also turned out, were very different to what I had grown up with.

At that stage, Fergus had been riding a basic 16-inch wheel bike. He got it when he was just over three and it had been shipped along with the rest of our possessions from the Land of the Long White Cloud to the Great Southern Land.

I recall with a smile the day the container arrived at the home we were renting, and he jumped up asking the men to find his bike first, politely of course! They did and he had great fun riding up and down the ramp from the container to the ground, no doubt getting in their way, but they were great about it.

So, we did as was suggested, and it turned out the BMX track was not too far away from where we lived. It's fair to say that as soon as the tyres touched the track he was hooked.

Sue and I looked at each other and she agreed with me when I said: "We are in a whole load of trouble, now!" Soon afterwards, for his fifth birthday we bought him his first BMX race bike, a red, shiny Redline. The look on his face as he sat on his new steed was a joy to see, he was like a Cheshire cat, beaming from ear to ear.

What then ensued for us was a whole new world. From the race he did a month later and won everything, to the trips we have made in various parts of the world for him to race, it has been an incredible sport, not just for him, but for us too. We have met so many wonderful people (and some less wonderful) along the way.

Early in Fergus's BMX career we met a great family. Andrew Brooks, his wife Jodie and their two boys, Harvey and Ryder. Harvey was four, Ryder was barely two, I think.

Up to that point, Fergus had been the quickest kid on the track, but he had only raced a couple of times. That accolade didn't last long. Harvey was, and still is, an amazing rider. Skillful, strong and very fit. For the next few years Fergus and Harvey battled it out on most weekends at many different tracks around Australia. More important than the competition, though, was the friendship that developed between the two boys. Better yet, was the fact that Andrew and I got on very well too. A very competitive bloke but with a heart of gold. Andrew's aim in life was to be the best or the fastest at everything he did. That rubbed off on his boys tenfold.

Once he found out about my motorbike background, he asked why I didn't ride, and I explained to him about my heart condition. "Get an e-Bike," he said. "A what?", was my reply. I mean, I wasn't totally green. I knew that pedal-assist bikes were around but what I didn't know was that they were now putting the motors in properly kitted-out mountain bikes.

A couple of weeks later and a trip to a bike shop, I found myself several thousand dollars worse off but I also found myself in a whole new world, a world that had once been familiar, albeit from a motorcycle perspective.

Now I had found something I could do that wasn't too taxing for me, still allowed me to get some exercise, but more importantly it allowed me to spend time with like-minded dads and their kids. From 2016 to 2018, Andrew and I rode regularly – with the boys, but also at least once a week we would try to get out together. Andrew was fit; he was riding a normal bike with no motor, and I often still struggled to keep up with him.

Meanwhile, the boys were also getting the bug for mountain-bike riding and it was excellent cross-training for the BMX racing endeavours. At six years old, Fergus and Harvey would regularly punch out 15km-20km rides, climbing steep hills and descending terrain that many adult riders would struggle with. Their little legs were pretty tired by the end, but they loved it. Andrew would strap Harvey's younger brother on to a seat that sat just behind the handlebars, and we made it a boys' day out. Sometimes the mums would turn up too, but not often.

The new lease on life and freedom that riding gave me is hard to describe.

I become addicted quickly. I found by mid-week I was grouchy and needed to get out. Sue would pack me off for my dose of mindfulness and I returned a much happier man. But what I was doing was undoubtedly playing with fire. I realised that if something happened to me while we were riding in the middle of nowhere it could end very badly. Not even just a heart issue. An accident, or whatever, could well impact my heart too, be it from shock, blood loss etc.

But back then I decided that the pleasure, enjoyment, physical and mental benefits I got from it outweighed the potential risks.

Fergus continued to grow in his riding, becoming stronger, faster, more talented. He trained hard, he was devoted and focused on the sport of BMX racing. He joined a race team when he was six and since then has always been a member of one team or another. I, too, was passionate about his racing. I wanted for him some of the successes I didn't have. I knew he had the ability, but he needed more help with his race craft, which has to come from within. Some kids just have it naturally. Harvey is one of them, you can see on the track that nothing and no one is going to get in his way. We have known a few kids like this over the years, some still in the sport, some not.

For a few very happy years, Andrew, our kids and I had a bunch of other like-minded revellers enjoyed riding together and I particularly enjoyed visiting and experiencing new places, meeting new people and getting to know this new home.

UPGRADED BY IRENE

Someone would be forgiven for thinking that the healthcare system in New Zealand was similar to that in Australia.

In fact, it works quite differently in many ways. The NZ system is a largely publicly funded model where certain costs are met by the patient.

For example, a person pays for their visit to their GP but unlike the UK, for example, someone could almost guarantee being able to see a doctor within 24 hours.

Most residents of NZ rely on the public funded system for specific treatments such as accident and emergency and any ongoing healthcare that's needed. My pacemaker was fully funded by the government. Yes, there is private health cover for those who wish to choose it, but it's not needed and anyway, in my case, any major operation would always have to be done on the public system at a specialist heart centre, even if I was having a broken leg fixed.

In Australia there are similarities. Certainly, the core of the model is the same, most major procedures are covered by both state and federal government through a system called Medicare, funded through income tax.

However, one big difference in Australia is the almost certain need for healthcare insurance. Allied healthcare, such as dentists, chiropractic treatments and the like, are not covered by Medicare.

Without health insurance these services are very expensive, but then so too are the premiums. The premiums are arrived at by way of age and medical history, so in my case we have had to adjust what I am covered for privately because of my heart condition. If

I were to break my leg (again!) I would be covered for a stay in a private hospital, but I wouldn't be covered for anything heart related. It's not that they won't cover me, it's that we couldn't afford the premiums.

The catch is this: If someone takes out private health cover and then for whatever reason cancels it, but then at a later date chooses to reinstate it, you are treated as if you have never had it, meaning that you could have been paying for it from 18 years old and for whatever reason had to cancel it at say 30, but at 40 you could afford it again, your premiums are based on your current age with no regard for any previous cover.

I think it's fair to say, though, that I have more than had my money's worth of care over the years, and I was just about to have more spent on me.

Just as back in Auckland, when I had that nasty feeling of being about to pass out which had led to me getting a pacemaker and a grown-up dose of anti-arrhythmic drugs, now I was again starting to feel these horrible and extremely scary heart beats from time to time.

Another Holter monitor was ordered so the docs could see what was happening, if anything.

The results were in, and sure enough I was experiencing what are known as ventricular ectopic heartbeats. An ectopic beat is basically a heartbeat that is premature. It can feel like a skipped beat because the heart then must resynchronise itself which often involves a short pause.

Many people get them and for the most part they are harmless, but when there are as many as I got, and you have an underlying heart condition, it gets everyone interested.

Before this point most of the ectopic beats I was getting were originating from the top chambers of my heart, the atriums. Now, though, I was getting more and more from the bottom part of the heart, the ventricles.

As we recall from my primitive biology lesson earlier, the ventricles, or at least the right one in my body and the left in a normal heart, pump blood around the body, so it's vital it beats properly. Of course, it doesn't always beat properly, and this was the concern the docs had.

Sometimes these ventricular ectopic beats can lead to more dangerous and life-threatening rhythm problems. These are called ventricular tachycardia or the even worse ventricular fibrillation, VT and VF respectively. No one wants that and trust me when I say that even having one or more abnormal beats in this area of the heart can make you feel terrible, like the world is about to end.

So, with this news it was decided that I needed an upgrade. Unfortunately, not the type of upgrade you might find appealing, such as being moved from economy-class to business-class on a flight. No, this "upgrade" was to replace my pacemaker with an automatic implantable cardiac defibrillator, or AICD for short.

It's an interesting juxtaposition of how you feel, or at least how I felt, when faced with this kind of news, because essentially I was being told that what was working for me was not going to in the future or at the very least has the potential not to. For me, on the one hand, I felt sad that I had reached this point in my mid-40s. Of course, it didn't mean I was dead or dying, but for me it did mean I was embarking on a slippery slope. I am big enough and old enough to face the reality of my condition and that reality is that I am far more likely to die at a younger age than the general population.

On the other hand, though, I was happy. Happy that I hadn't at that point had any life-threatening rhythms and that the potential early signs had been seen and were about to be addressed.

It's important with a chronic illness that you trust the expertise, care and openness of the doctor or specialist treating you. I have always been fortunate in this regard. I have always had doctors who frankly are amazing at what they do and for those of us who are non-medical, me included, it's nothing short of wondrous how incredibly clever and skilled they are in their chosen fields.

One such woman who fits this bill perfectly is Irene Stevenson. I first met Irene soon after coming to Australia. Unlike when I arrived in NZ and basically didn't see anyone for the first two years (my fault, not theirs), this time, almost as the wheels touched down at Melbourne airport with my first flight, I was making connections with the cardiac team at the Royal Melbourne Hospital, recognised as one of the leading cardiac centres in the world. I was very fortunate for us to have chosen Melbourne as home.

Irene is one of those people who immediately puts a client at ease, who you feel safe with, and with whom you know everything will be OK. At least that's how I felt with her and still do. She is an interventional cardiologist specialising in heart rhythm disturbances and implanting pacemakers. She was my new best friend.

I had the procedure done in mid-2017. It went according to plan although apparently there was a challenge getting the new device to sit nicely into the pocket that was made in my pectoral muscle. That, and I was black and blue on my upper chest for a week or so, but otherwise it was a walk in the park.

I was upgraded. I now had a pacemaker just as previously, but now I had the added benefit of always having a mobile defibrillator with me. Surely, I could get back to life and to work quickly?

Maybe a bit too quickly. Two weeks after the procedure I found myself in the back of an ambulance, my heart having decided to go into another arrhythmia. I had been out riding my bike, just locally, nothing crazy when I felt several irregular heartbeats and then a racing heart.

Luckily, it wasn't a heart rhythm that was too dangerous, and my new device didn't need to do anything. As I sat down on the ground, things calmed down and my heart reverted to its normal rhythm on its own. But it was still a trip to the hospital to check everything was OK. It was.

THE WEAKNESS IN ME

If I had to choose one song that sums up how I have felt over the years, it would have to be Pink Floyd's *Comfortably Numb*. For a start, PF are probably in my top three bands ever, the others being Led Zeppelin and Fleetwood Mac. It's hard to choose three, and I know I am not being asked to, but I can't possibly reel off 20 or 30 bands that I am very fond of.

My taste in music is eclectic and one minute I can be listening to Hans Zimmer and his incredible pieces and then next you might hear the Sex Pistols being played on my Spotify account!

But this song, *Comfortably Numb*, resonates with me like no other. It's about a young man who was unwell as a child. While I was never humdrum about my illness as a child, now that I am older, I realise the emotional, psychological strain and pain it has caused me.

At the start of the song, they ask the child if he is cognisant and aware. This takes me straight back to my second open-heart operation, when I was coming off the ventilator, unable to talk just like the line "Your lips move, but I can't hear what you are saying". The song talks about giving "... a little pin prick" to keep him going and getting through. While I have had many pin pricks in my time, I see this more as the major procedures I have had, not so much the needles, but more so the entirety of the procedure, hoping that its intended outcome is successful and that it gets me through to the next phase in my care and in my life.

But no doubt the line that gets me every time is this: "When I was a child I had a fever, my hands felt like two balloons."

Now obviously, I didn't have that same feeling, but the fever represents my condition and my hands are the symptoms I have from it. The next line: "Now I have that feeling once again, I cannot explain, you would not understand, this is not how I am," resonates with me in my later years.

My condition became worse over the past 15 to 20 years and trying to explain to anyone how that feels both mentally and physically is an impossible task, try as I might, try as I have.

I have found myself on more than one occasion while listening to this song, in floods of tears, unable to control those feelings and I know that it's now the years and years of emotional build-up, right back from when I was young. It's not a bad thing, in fact I think it's a good thing. Whatever stirs the emotions, makes you think, reflect, ponder is worthwhile and of course for many people that's one of the magic things of music.

April 2019 saw an end for me of a relatively stable period in my health and my journey.

It saw the start of a new dawn of anxiety and a life that I was, and still am, struggling with.

If I had been out doing something strenuous, perhaps mountain biking or hiking, I would have kind of shrugged my shoulders – perhaps like a criminal would when they had finally been caught by the police and thought "OK, yeah, fair cop". (Fuck, when did I ever hike, who am kidding? To be fair, I did the Duke of Edinburgh bronze and silver awards, and there was a bit of hiking involved with that, but also some illicit hitch-hiking! Work smarter, not harder, right?)

I'm not sure, though, that driving my car to a BMX track with Fergus constitutes as excessive in the energy stakes, but it started just after I got back in the car having washed it on the way.

I could feel my pulse soaring, my heart was going so fast that

I couldn't count the beats when taking my pulse. I became hot, sweaty, my stomach was churning and my panic levels were rising quickly.

We arrived at the track, and I got out of the car still aware that something was wrong, but it felt in some ways different to previous times.

Wandering up the side of the track via a shallow incline I was like someone who smoked 90 cigarettes a day, hardly able to breathe. I sat down, hoping that it would pass; it didn't.

Now I could feel something different happening and the memories of Auckland in 2005 came flooding back; this was how it felt then, completely hopeless and me unable to do anything to correct the situation. Unlike when a car slides and is doomed to crash but the driver's reactions and skill manage to avert disaster, I was heading for a big crash and nothing I did would stop it.

I walked slowly down to the canteen, where all kinds of food and sweets were being prepared for the afternoon of BMX racing and asked the women to call an ambulance. I couldn't think straight, had I been able to, I would have called one myself, although I am not sure I would have had enough puff to speak.

By now I was dizzy, worried I was going to die, worried about Fergus seeing me in this state. He had never seen Dad sick like this before. Sure, he had seen me in hospital having procedures, but this was different, this was raw, in a non-controlled place, no doctors or nurses, no specialist equipment, this was not cool, not cool at all.

Then it happened without any warning (actually, there was warning I just didn't know then what the warnings felt like).

People have asked me what it's like when it goes off. There are lots of versions because, I suppose, everyone has a different experience. Some say it's like being kicked in the chest by a horse, but for me it felt more like an explosion inside me. It knocked me to the ground quickly.

My ICD/pacemaker which had been fitted two years earlier had detected the abnormal rhythm and thought it best to shock me back into a normal heart rhythm – for which I was grateful, in the end!

Lying on the gravel at the foot of the window to the canteen, there were people surrounding me, asking if I was OK.

Some knew I had a heart condition, some didn't, but none of them knew what had just happened. I did.

I knew that my ICD had belted me back into a normal sinus rhythm. The ambulance arrived soon after and the paramedics quickly had all manner of wires attached and needles in my arm. While my heart was now beating normally, who was to say that this might not happen again?

Fergus came over being comforted by the mum of one of his mates, tears streaming down his face, obviously scared out of his wits that something terrible had either just happened or was likely to happen to his dad.

I tried to reassure him that I felt much better now, which was true, I did, but I was still terrified. The thing that scared me more than anything else that day and what has haunted me ever since is that it was all just so random, there was no rhyme or reason as to why this happened. That and wondering when, or if, it would happen again.

I was taken to hospital. On the way the paramedics were worried that I was going to go into some disgusting rhythm again, so they stopped the ambulance on the freeway so they could get a specialist paramedic to check me over. A night's stay and I was home.

Safe, but genuinely scared out of my wits. Trying to process what had happened, being logical about it and trying to remain calm were not then and still are not now my best strengths.

I am a worrier when it comes to my health, there is no doubt.

Try as I might, try as I have, I cannot seem to stop myself from catastrophising and ultimately making something trivial into a big deal.

It's not my heart condition, it's my mental condition that is the weakness in me. Of course, having a serious heart condition is a major gig, but unfortunately, I tend to loop back to my heart condition when other things are not 100 per cent right. I might have a sore shoulder and, I think, heart attack. A sore stomach, and, I think, aortic embolism. A sore head, and I think my blood pressure is too high.

This is the danger when you know a little but don't know a lot. You join dots that aren't there, and you add two plus two, which as we all know has been and always will be the same answer, but I convince myself it's a different answer.

This part of my life, most particularly since 2005, has been my noose. It has held me back from doing that I want to do.

It isn't my heart condition in isolation, although of course there are plenty of things I can't do that are just too physically strenuous for me, but equally there's a lot I can do, should do and moreover want to do, but my head overrules and won't allow it. It's so debilitating I find it hard to find the words to describe it.

But I needed to still live, and after the incident at the BMX track, while it took me a while to get my confidence back, I did start to ride again and enjoy the things I not only had become used to but that I had assumed I would always be able to do. I didn't want to just exist, who does? We have "one lap" and I wanted to make sure that as much as possible, within the confines and boundaries of my condition that I was able to make it the best lap possible.

CHRIST, THAT HURTS!

The Mornington Peninsula in south-east Melbourne is an oasis of quirky shops, funky restaurants, vineyards and some of the best surf beaches you will find anywhere, all wrapped up by some stunning scenery. At the centre of the peninsula is Red Hill. With some elevation, pine trees and great views across the bay, it's a very popular go-to for mountain bikers most weekends, ourselves included.

A treat we look forward to each year, which was something we missed out on "back home" on the Isle of Man and in the UK, was the extra public holiday we were given each year for the King's birthday (previously the Queen's birthday).

It's always been a mystery to me that the King's birthday is celebrated in many of the Commonwealth countries, yet not in Britain. Either way, we don't mind, we are always grateful for the extra day of non-work activity, which as you might guess is almost always taken up with riding bikes at some location or other. The holiday weekend in 2021 was no exception, except to say that we were even more excited to get out and about as we had not long emerged in Melbourne from the fourth version of one of the longest pandemic lockdowns the world had seen.

There are various riding locations at Red Hill, from official tracks to, shall we say, less official, to man-made jumps, that have almost exclusively been created by boys and teenagers.

As an aside, I am always in awe of what these kids have done and continue to do. Their work ethic, their passion and their determination to build something for themselves is a testament to all of them. Some of these man-made jumps tower over me, the tops of them where the wheels leave the ramp are quite often over 6ft, very often taller. Then typically there is a landing slope, a sort of copy of the take-off side, but with some slight differences. And we aren't talking about a single jump, some of the places that have these jumps may have eight or 10 jumps in a row. That's why I have so much respect for the "kids" that build them.

Being of the age I was in June 2021, just queueing up to add a one to my fifty, I knew that some of these larger jumps were beyond my reach. Even though I have felt I can still do these things mentally, sadly my body has decided differently.

They are physically demanding and of course a crash bloody hurts. For some reason as we age the rubber in our bodies seems to deteriorate somewhat. I was about to find out just how much my rubber had deteriorated!

It looked easy, well within my capabilities and certainly I had jumped much bigger jumps in the recent past, so I was pretty comfortable that this one shouldn't cause me too many issues. This jump was the second in a series of six or seven. I wasn't intending to do them all, perhaps the first three would have been fine; much depends on how you land each one as that sets you up for the next, and so on.

The first jump wasn't really a jump. It was what is called a "roller", a mound of dirt shaped a bit like a large sleeping policeman or in Aussie lingo, a speed bump, which makes more sense. Either way, the idea is that as you crest one of these rollers you gain momentum, and the bike compresses down towards the ground. As you leave the take-off ramp of the jump, which may have anywhere from three to 10 feet of nothing between it and the landing ramp, the bike decompresses and wants to unload the energy upwards. This helps give you lift to do the jump.

All was well, the roller was fine, but then I felt something odd in my chest, an irregular heartbeat had arrived at precisely the wrong time. Not an issue in isolation but certainly distracting a moment before take-off.

My concentration wavered and I hit the take-off ramp off line, which inevitably meant I was going to land offline. I did and in fact the front wheel of my bike missed the landing zone altogether, which made it tuck under and threw me over the top of the bars in a kind of sideways motion. My body had twisted in the air and try as I might to save myself, which trust me, I did, it was in vain. I hit the ground like the proverbial sack of shit, landing hard on my left side, my chest wall, ribs and hip taking the brunt.

I knew straight away that I had done some mischief to myself, firstly because I couldn't breathe. I had no air in my lungs having had any air pushed out of me from the impact – at least it felt that way. I was just winded but maybe because of my age, maybe because of the mechanism but it felt different to being winded say from a blow to the stomach.

I sat up after a minute or so, the air slowly returning to my lungs, my surroundings becoming familiar once more. But now the pain was beginning to show its hand. Before I was aware of that though, a wave of panic came over me, "my heart," I thought. "Is my heart still beating properly?"

I took my pulse immediately; it was fast but regular. My next thought, which was irrational on reflection, but my wave of panic didn't allow for rationality, was my pacemaker; had I broken it? That was a hard fall and although I didn't land on it, I landed in such a way that it would have had a decent jolt. I then thought, well if my pulse is OK and regular then my pacemaker is probably OK too.

I was lucky that a couple of other dads were there. They had been much more sensible and opted to watch, not participate, perhaps more understanding of their age and abilities or maybe just more sensible than yours truly. One of the dads asked if I was OK. I wasn't. The pain was now in full swing, Christ it was sore, all down my left side. "Think I need an ambulance, mate," I said. They called 000, the emergency number in Australia.

I think because I was still in a state of panic and shock, I just wanted to get out of the bushland we were in. It wasn't far to roads, houses and civilisation, but I just didn't want to be in there, the terrain complicating any recovery.

A few months before, a good friend had crashed nearby when we had been out riding, in an area where it was very challenging to rescue him; 40 emergency personnel and more than three hours later they got him out.

I just kept thinking of that day, it had been horrific for us all, not least for the fact that I had heard the loudest, most guttural, raw scream I had ever heard from a man and never want to hear again. He had broken his neck and his back, so very lucky not to have had a long-lasting impact from his injuries.

I was not as broken, I was fine. Well, I thought I was fine, I just needed to get out of where I was, so I did. I stood up, got my bike and decided to ride out onto the road. Probably a stupid thing to do but you do what you do at the time right? The ambulance arrived a few minutes later, by now the adrenalin had worn off, or at least some of it had.

I hobbled into the back of the ambulance, keen to tell the paramedics about my heart condition. They seemed to be reasonably concerned so hooked me up to the various monitors they have on board. For now, all was well, at least for my heart anyway.

I had called Sue; she was on duty that day at the same hospital I was going to be taken to. "See you soon, then," she said. As we made our way to the hospital, which was about 30 minutes away, the pain started to kick in, especially down the left side of my chest. Breathing was sore, anxiety took hold, and I started to get really worried about what damage I had done.

X-rays, blood tests and CT scans later I was told the news. I had broken three ribs and chipped some bone off my hip. That all made sense in terms of the pain but certainly didn't make sense in terms of the accident. I really didn't think it would have been that bad an outcome.

A night, a very uncomfortable night, in hospital followed. The first of many uncomfortable nights over some weeks. Christ, it was sore. I had never had pain like it. No matter which way I lay, there was no getting comfortable. And because of my heart condition I was limited to the amount and type of pain relief I could have. Endone, (oxycodone) became my new best friend.

I can quite honestly say that given all the operations and procedures I have had over the years, never have I had pain like that. It was awful.

Two weeks later, I was starting to be a bit more mobile, certainly still very sore but managing now with paracetamol. We decided a takeaway was in order, so I volunteered to go and get it. It was my first outing by myself since the accident.

That same evening at 10 o'clock, just as I was trying to get to sleep, I could feel my heart rate increase, and I began to feel weird.

It was a weird feeling that I knew, I had felt it at the BMX track back in 2019. Panic set in. After a few minutes, I knew what was coming.

My pacemaker/defibrillator was trying to pace me out of the rhythm. It's a disgusting feeling, because even though my heart was already going fast the pacemaker was trying to speed it up even more to get ahead of the irregular beat. The analogy I would give is rather like how a bush fire is controlled. The firemen burn ahead of the fire to a "fire road" so that when the main fire reaches the fire road, the fire has nowhere to go.

The device is programmed to try doing this three or four times, and if it can't it determines that you need to be shocked back into a normal rhythm. I knew it was coming, it was the exact same feeling I had been through before. This time though I was sitting on the edge of the bed, Sue held my hand telling me I would be OK. I kept saying: "It will shock me! It will shock me!" And it did.

This time, though, I was kind of ready for it. Just like the previous time it was like a bomb going off inside me. It flung me on to my back, but luckily this time there was a nice comfortable bed to fall on to, as opposed to a hard gravel surface! My heart was now back in a normal rhythm and beating properly.

As is always the case when a defibrillator fires, it's recommended that you go to hospital. The ambulance was already on the way as Sue had called for one. After all the checks in the emergency ward I was transferred to the cardiac ward of the hospital, the same ward where Sue works. I spent three nights in a room that would rival some hotels. I was taken care of by her colleagues exceptionally well, all of them keen to make sure I was being looked after.

Being married to their boss had its perks, even the food was OK! Feeling better both from the injury and from the heart episode, I was allowed home.

DAMAGED GOODS

I was beginning to understand more, and trying to come to terms with it all, but my overall health seemed to be worsening.

Contrary to the reports from the doctors about the overall condition of my heart, I felt terrible. My heart remained stable in terms of a pump, but the electrics seemed to be worsening.

I wanted badly for things to get back to what they once had been, whatever that was like. I understood that would never happen, that I would never be able to do the things I used to do when I was younger, at least not without a heart transplant, but ironically, I was much too well to even be considered for a transplant.

I yearned, I still yearn to this day, to be able to ride with my mates again, to be able to at least go out for a proper ride with Fergus. Some of it is my physical ability, no doubt, but some of it, maybe most of it, is mental.

I had lived with and been married to a girl who had suffered depression. I had not understood it; I had not shown sympathy and most of all I had not been supportive when she was going through it.

To an extent, my upbringing had instilled in me that depression and anxiety were just buzz words for someone not willing to get up and get on with life. I am ashamed to say that I shunned the idea that depression and anxiety were real, that people with it should just get over themselves and get on with life.

And anyway, what did "normal" people, able-bodied people, have to be depressed or anxious about. In short, back then, I didn't understand it.

I know differently now. I know that these diseases are real, they are confronting and they are really debilitating.

In the months after the injury and the heart episode, for the first time ever I had thoughts of self-harm and suicide. We were still in the grips of Covid, and the effects that was having on us all, be it mentally or physically.

I actually didn't mind lockdown; in fact I supported it. What I was more frightened about (and initially, I was terrified) was having a wife who was being exposed to this disease daily as she and thousands like her battled to save hundreds of people at her hospital.

It wasn't being locked down that I minded, it was more that I felt vulnerable. If something happened, would there be an ambulance to get me to hospital? If so, would there be enough medical staff to treat me and if there was, would I end up getting Covid in hospital anyway? Every day my mind was racing with this stuff.

Trying, as we all were, to keep some form of normality as we balanced what was left of our usual lives, to enduring home schooling, to trying to keep safe, it was a challenge, for sure.

For me, though, the thoughts of self-harm were outside of that box, the Covid box. Perhaps they were influenced by it, I am not sure, but it was the realisation that I had, for the first time in my life, nothing to smile about, nothing to look forward to and nothing to get me up in the morning.

I could feel myself spiralling downwards and I needed to do something about it.

Additionally, I was petrified of just about everything. It was just like going back to 2005 after my first arrhythmia, except this time I felt it had compounded into something more.

First to go was my job, again. Even though I wasn't now having to travel that much, never overnight, never on a plane, I was nervous to venture too far from home or at least from a major hospital and as my job relied on me doing that, it was a problem.

Worse though was the tiredness, I was just so exhausted all the time. My brain would work overtime catastrophising, as I do, about the never-ending serious illnesses I could have and would no doubt kill me.

I knew I had plenty to live for really, my family being at the top of that list and Fergus being at the top of any sub-list.

In any case, I am far too much of a chicken to go through with anything, or is it that I am not a coward by hanging around? I am not sure.

What I do know is this though; that by leaving early, not only would I be leaving people behind that cared about me and that is truly the worst part, but I would also, I feel, be sticking a metaphorical two fingers up at the many people who have treated me medically and helped me survive over the years.

It was time to see what help I could get.

I have never been good at the psychology of anxiety. It's not that I don't understand it, I absolutely do. It's that the anxiety I experience relates to an organ in my body that no matter what I am doing, or where I am, it could suddenly decide to misbehave.

When you feel like this you (at least in my case) go into a sort of inward retreat, like a protective mode. My body is tense, my muscles hurt, my teeth grind, my lip gets bitten.

I had given many psychologists a go over the years. To be honest I probably hadn't approached them with the correct mindset (how ironic). I suppose my expectations have been out of whack with what is actually achievable.

I will offer an example of what I mean. Suppose you are unfortunate to be involved with some major trauma, perhaps a plane crash. While this would be very distressing, if you choose, you could avoid travelling on a plane again and while this could be very inconvenient and limiting, it is a choice.

With a health condition and most especially with a heart condition, there is no escape, there is no break from it, it's there 24-7, 365. And for me that has been one of the hardest things to accept and, moreover, deal with.

There have been many times when things have been relatively settled, not many irregular heartbeats, exercise tolerance quite good – lured into a false sense of being. Because just as you think, "Oh, my symptoms are abating," it will come back without warning, without reason, randomly and it throws you right back on the floor, scrabbling for hope that this is not "it".

I suppose everyone reacts differently to traumatic events.

Personally, I only ever used to think of trauma as a result of a nasty accident, bleeding all over the place, perhaps a tube down your throat, real ER stuff.

But these days, I understand that trauma takes many forms, physical, psychological or the two combined. What I have come to realise and perhaps had denied myself for many years, or perhaps I just didn't know, was the psychological damage this condition has done to me.

It's very apparent to me now that in many areas of my life I struggled to cope. Of course, it doesn't help having an over-imaginative mind. I almost constantly think the worst will happen. Why? Because many times bad stuff has happened, and it has happened so randomly. There have never been two occasions the same. For example, I can't say, if I avoid bike riding or walking up a steep hill, or doing certain types of yoga, or watching a scary film, that these heart arrhythmias won't happen.

I think for me, in many ways, that is the hardest aspect of it all, the pure uncertainty of it.

I have begun to shape my life around either avoidance or trying to control the environment if something were to happen. For example, these days as much as I love being in the countryside, it gives me anxiety, for the fact that typically the countryside means you are far away from a decent-sized hospital that could help me.

So, I stay close to metro areas if I can, tricky though when your son competes in mountain bike racing. Those events take us all over remote parts of Australia and probably what my family doesn't understand (why would they, why would anyone?) is the psychological stress this causes me. I love watching him, nothing gives me more pleasure but being somewhere that is an hour or maybe much more away from medical help is difficult for me to deal with.

From April 2019 to May 2023 when I began this book, I had eight trips to hospital either in an ambulance or had been driven there if close by (we live five minutes from our local hospital). Each time, my heart was either beating very fast or out of its normal sinus rhythm, or both.

The first two occasions after getting my defibrillator in 2017 I was pretty sick, but the defibrillator embedded in my chest fired and put me back to a normal heart rhythm. It wasn't actually set to do that, but that's another story! I am glad it did.

The third time was properly scary.

It felt different and because I was expecting to be shocked again, I had braced myself for that. Then I was frustrated that it hadn't done so. It's complicated as to why it didn't, but essentially my heart, while going fast and in an abnormal rhythm, wasn't actually going fast enough to reach the threshold of the settings that had been programmed to initiate the cycle of treatment that would have led to it shocking me.

A normal morning was us hurrying around to get Fergus off to school and me off to work. I had woken up, not feeling great.

After trying to eat some breakfast I took myself back to bed for a while, to see if the symptoms abated. One of the troubles with this stuff is that your mind, well my mind anyway, starts to play tricks. Am I really sick or am I just imagining it?

I ventured to get up and clean my teeth, then it started. As I collapsed on the bathroom floor, the first thing I thought was, gosh the floor is cold! The adrenalin kicked in almost immediately, from fright. When I am cold and I am scared it's the worst thing, my body shakes uncontrollably, like shivering, only much worse. My muscles in my legs tighten up, which in turn gives me a crap feeling. I don't want to move for fear that whatever it is that's happening will get worse.

The wailing noise could be heard as the ambulance approached our house and moments later I was greeted by two paramedics, one of whom is called a MICA. These MICA paramedics are highly trained and, in all honesty, not far off being as qualified as a doctor when it comes to emergency medicine. They can give lifesaving drugs, intubate people and do procedures that would ordinarily only be able to be carried out in the emergency department at hospital.

I am always so surprised at how relaxed they seem. I know they are there to give reassurance and comfort, (as well as saving your life when that's needed!) but you would think it was nothing more than a headache, such was their demeanour!

After I had been hooked up to their various pieces of equipment and they looked to see what was going on, it was decided they needed to get me off to hospital as fast as possible. So they packed me up and off I went.

This earned me another overnighter on Sue's ward, I was becoming a frequent flyer!

AMIODARONE BABY…

As with anything there is usually a good, better, best. You can spend money on something that will do the trick, an economy flight perhaps, but if you want a better experience, you might upgrade to business class. But if you really wanted to go all out, it would have to be first class, to have the best treatment.

This might seem an odd analogy, but my medication journey from 2009 has been similar. Initially, I was on a very low dose and "gentle" beta blocker to help my heart beat properly. With my first pacemaker back in 2011, I was given a stronger dose, a big boy's dose as I call it, but still the same medicine; we can think of this as economy.

I was upgraded to "business" a few years later and honestly, I was happy in business class. Everything I needed was there, the drug worked well for me until I ended up on the bathroom floor.

It was decided that I needed to be upgraded again. Of course, I use these terms flippantly; the reality is that as I have progressed through the past 20 years the medicine and the doses of those medications have become stronger, and as we know, there is always a flip side to everything and with medications it's usually that there are some side effects. So, we arrive now at the panacea of heart-rhythm drugs, the big daddy, the gold standard.

Amiodarone is reserved for patients who really need help controlling their heart rhythm, and sadly, I became one of those patients. Why wasn't I just given this drug years ago if it's the gold standard? It's simple.

For as much as it's a wonderful drug to control heart rate and heart rhythm problems, it also has some potentially very nasty side-effects, including but not limited to, issues with liver function, lung and breathing problems, wreaking havoc with the thyroid, not to mention that the skin can turn blue in sunlight and, as I don't wish to resemble a Smurf, it's a factor-50 day for me every day. Of course, this list of potential side-effects goes on but those are the main contenders.

It was, and is, most definitely a bittersweet pill to swallow (pun intended!). Of course, I don't want to become very unwell from the side-effects of this drug, but at the same time I also don't want to die of a horrendous abnormal heart rhythm (who does?).

It's definitely a pros and cons situation and clearly, I am guided by the very smart doctors who are there to help and support me on my continued journey, whatever that may be.

Sometimes though, even in "Business Class" things don't go to plan. There can still be some "turbulence " from time to time. (Apologies for the continued use of aviation analogies!).

The first time it happened I was definitely confused; I thought this drug was the holy grail as far as anti-arrhythmia drugs go.

We were having some work done on the house we had purchased earlier that year (2022), trying to make it better.

It's a bit of a story in itself as to why we sold the other one, but choice of schools for Fergus as he entered his high school years, the fact that Covid had caused mayhem in the building industry as well as most other areas of commerce and life generally had meant that our dream plans we had of demolishing our property to build three townhouses on the land were dashed.

It was very upsetting, especially for Sue, who had worked on this project for three years, had liaised with our financial advisor/ project manager almost continuously for that time, only for us to reach the last part of the process and be told by the council they wouldn't have anyone to sign off on the final paperwork for three months, thanks to Covid.

The knock-on effect of this was that by the time the three months would have passed, the lending, the building materials and just about everything else had shot up in price and availability. We decided to cut our losses, sell the house and buy a couple of smaller properties nearby.

I digress; the builder was there doing what builders do. I was "helping" him to move a few things out of the way, nothing heavy, nothing that should have caused me to overexert myself and all of a sudden I could feel my heart going fast and being short of breath. I was gutted. I was scared too, but mostly gutted.

I felt cheated, let down and given that I was already taking the most powerful drug to prevent these abnormal rhythms, mostly I was worried about where to from here.

The builder, a lovely bloke, offered to drive me to hospital. Our local hospital is less than 10 minutes drive from where we live, so that seemed a good option as Sue was out and who knows how long an ambulance may have taken.

One of the challenges (I suppose there are many) about having an unusual medical condition, be it heart-related or anything else, is that accident and emergency departments don't see many people like me. As a result when someone such as me turns up at the hospital they often don't necessarily understand the gravity, or at least the potential gravity, of the situation.

It's also, for me anyway, hard to articulate all the ins and outs, mostly because it's hard to talk due to lack of breath and the pure flood of adrenaline. Consequently I ended up sitting in a very busy waiting room, that was until my heart decided to help the process along by going into another and potentially more dangerous rhythm. Funnily enough this time I was taken to the resuscitation rooms immediately. After some consultation with the docs that usually see me at the main heart hospital in Melbourne, they decided to load me up with more Amiodarone. Eventually this did the trick and reverted my heart to beat normally again.

What I hadn't realised is that the drug itself takes a long time to be absorbed by the body, so the explanation I was given was that because I'd only been on the drug for a few weeks it was likely that it hadn't reached its maximum effect. After a night's stay I was sent home, panic over. All was well, until it wasn't!

Christmas of 2022 came and went, so too the summer holidays which run through the whole of January in these parts. Financially it wasn't ideal; the fact that I wasn't working at that time meant I could hang out with Fergus a bit and ferry him here and there for him to ride. It was also the downhill mountain bike race season, so we managed a couple of small trips here and there to the events, watching and supporting Fergus as he raced.

Although it was great to get out of Melbourne and see our son, in his 'oils', with his riding, for me it was at times mentally very difficult. My anxiety was awful to the point where we would take two cars to these events in case I couldn't cope with the remoteness of where we were and needed to come home. That happened once.

It really is very hard to put into words just how impactful the anxiety I experience can be.

My biggest fear is being a good distance away from a major hospital that can cope with and treat me if something goes wrong. Some at the larger hospitals scratch their heads a bit, never mind a small rural hospital that probably sees one of these things in a normal heart every Pancake Tuesday!

Of course, it goes without saying that my anxiety has had a huge impact not just on me personally but on Sue and Fergus too.

Gone, seem the days when we could just go away for the weekend or take a trip overseas. As much as I adore aviation and flying, the very last place I would want to be is 40,000 feet up in the air and having an issue with my heart. Even thinking about it fills me with dread.

These thoughts and feelings aren't new, it's just that previously I could manage it, in no small part due to Sue giving me reassurance and me knowing that if something were to happen that she was the one person who knew what they were doing. That said, as I have come to realise, there is in reality very little she could do especially in those situations of extreme remoteness.

At time of writing we have lived in Australia for over seven years. In that time I'm ashamed and sorry to say I have seen very little of this stunning country. Yes, I have been to all the capital cities with the exception of Darwin and I have seen a fair bit of Victoria. But I haven't even scratched the surface as far as exploring the country in places such as Alice Springs, or the Kimberleys or far North Queensland. I don't mind saying I'm envious, jealous even, of those that can. I don't begrudge that they can, I just hate that I can't.

And the thing is it's not that I physically couldn't do these things, it's that I mentally couldn't do it. It's a huge mountain for me to climb and get to the top. I was excited to be starting a new job the same day Fergus started his new high school. A big day for us both, him more so, obviously.

For any parent, seeing a child grow and mature into the person they will become as an adult, is extremely rewarding, emotional and of course, at times, somewhat challenging!

We are blessed with him. Sure, he's no angel. He likes to push the boundaries to see what he can get away with just like any other almost-teenager, but he has the kindest heart. He hates to see people who are struggling either with their health or their lives generally. He isn't the most outgoing kid; he can be shy, sometimes to the point where people may think he's being rude or stand-offish, but once he's comfortable with a particular person or situation look out, as it will be joke after joke and you would struggle to get him to be quiet.

One of his other attributes is that he is phenomenally active. I don't just mean like a regular 12-year-old. He struggles to sit still! It always amazes me where he gets the energy from and, yes, I know he's young and very fit, but still it's incredible that he just keeps going and going, like the Energizer Bunny!

I know it's a source of frustration for him that these days I just can't keep up. Whether it's playing basketball or backyard cricket or our mutual love of riding, he's just not getting the dad he deserves. I try to do as much as I can, but sometimes I'm just too exhausted. But what amazes me about him more than anything else is his resilience.

I had suggested a weekend away, I was feeling confident, I was feeling that this time my heart would be fine, that it would behave. We were off on a road trip to Adelaide, the capital city of South Australia. Of course, there was a mountain bike race on (typically there is always a bike involved, at least one!). We were all looking forward to it. It was going to be our first trip out of Victoria since 2019, in part due to Covid and in part due to me!

We were all set and as I loaded the last few things into the car, there it was again. The fast irregular heart rate. Honestly, I just couldn't believe it. Yes I was annoyed, disappointed and frustrated I wouldn't be going, but I was far more concerned for Fergus.

Too often already he has had to be organised at the last minute to be either taken somewhere (usually a race) or stay at someone's house for the night while Sue sits with me in hospital.

It now seemed like water of a duck's back to him, even though I knew it wasn't. He's like Sue in that respect, thinks it inside but is reluctant to express how he feels, which sometimes isn't great; 90% of his personality is Sue's, for which I'm grateful but sometimes I wish he'd have a bit more of my DNA and be a little more expressive!

So, there we were, off again for another trip to the hospital in what now seemed to be a regular occurrence. It was getting so ridiculous that we could have had a bag ready-packed! Meanwhile we needed to get Fergus to Adelaide, there was no way I would let this stop him from going, it's his passion, as he calls it, it's his mindfulness.

You definitely know who your friends are at these times. We have been lucky to have met some wonderful people since living in Australia, almost all of whom have been connected to either BMX racing or mountain bike racing, or both!

Our close friends know about my condition and have always helped us out with either having Fergus to stay or taking him to an event, but as grateful as I know Sue and I are, it's just not the same as having your parents there with you, although he may disagree!

Fergus was quickly organised to head to Adelaide with another family and off he went.

Meanwhile back at the ranch, AKA the hospital, where I was becoming a proper frequent flyer, more drugs were shoved into me.

This time there was no waiting, this time Sue was with me and talked to the triage nurse. It's probably a professional courtesy thing, I'm sure it is, and I'm also sure that it's not admitted, recognised or otherwise by anyone, anywhere, but I was taken in almost immediately.

The same rigmarole, the same questions, the same tests, the same amount of time! Eleven hours later and nine hours after being "topped up" with Amiodarone and I was on my way to the ward Sue works on. Not that it was relevant as she was on leave, but in any case, she isn't allowed to look after me and definitely not allowed to give me a bed bath! Dang it!

The weekend came and went, Fergus came home, I came home, life carried on, a bit more dented, a bit more shaken up, a bit more uncertain.

I was by now six weeks or so into my new role.

It's really not the best start to any career with any company to be taken to hospital so soon after I started. I had been upfront about my heart condition during the interview process – I would never dream of hiding that.

And I genuinely thought the worst was behind me in terms of hospital visits. My boss and the owner of the company were very supportive and understanding, but like any business they have to make commercial decisions regardless of the health and wellbeing of their staff.

It's just an unfortunate but understandable fact of life that no one person is bigger or more important than the business itself and with or without them life goes on.

Then, just as we thought, hoped and prayed (in our own way), the ugly beast reared its head again. This time, I had accompanied Fergus to the parent-teacher interviews which were concluding his first term at his new school. I was very keen to see how he was getting on.

He isn't the kind of kid that comes home each night and talks freely about what he has done for the day and how things are going for him at school. Blood from stone I think is the expression!

Extremely uncharacteristically Sue was ill and had spent the previous two days in bed. So, I was on parent duty on my own.

As we strolled from one classroom to the other, I could feel the now all too familiar fluttering in my chest. The shorten of breath wasn't far behind and adrenalin, the shaking and general state of panic were there for company too. Another ambulance, another trip to the hospital. But this time as I had been taking the golden, first class, drug for several months, my heart managed to revert itself back into rhythm without the need for more drugs.

Another first was that I was then transferred to the main congenital heart hospital in the centre of Melbourne. This is where all the specialists who look after me are based and the feeling was that such was the frequency of these arrhythmias happening that I needed some closer inspection!

That inspection came by way of the lead cardiologist coming to see me on the same day I was discharged, promising me that I had "earned the right" to an ablation. This made me chuckle to myself. Here I was being told that in essence I had to earn my right of passage to even be considered for one of these procedures, but at last it sounded like the procedure I have long been wanting may in fact get done.

That isn't to say it is the golden egg or the panacea. This is to say that there is a chance, seemingly a good chance, that I can be rid of these terrible, debilitating and very frightening abnormal heart rhythms.

I should explain this right of passage. It's all to do with risk versus reward. Up until this point, it was felt that, yes, while I have indeed had a number of major heart rhythm disturbances, they have never been life threatening (apart from the very first one back in NZ all those years ago), and they have not been so frequent. I went from 2005 until 2019 without having a sustained episode. Ongoing, I endured daily irregular heartbeats, or ectopic beats and even some short runs of irregular beats, but nothing that gave those in the know enough concern to wheel me and set about trying to find a needle in a haystack, essentially what they would be doing.

However, more recently, the occurrence of them became such that it was felt the tide may have turned, and that the risk/reward balance was now in the favour of reward.

The risk however, hadn't diminished in any way. This procedure, the ablation procedure, involves inserting a catheter into the groin of the patient, or in my case it would be the neck and carefully guiding tiny wires through the veins until they reach the heart. When the catheter arrived at its destination, the cardiologists would go on a fishing exercise to find the area of the heart that the abnormal rhythms were coming from, a veritable needle-in-a-haystack search. When located (and there is usually more than one area) they burn the area to cauterise it. The analogy is that of taking a pair of snips and cutting a wire to break an electrical circuit.

In a heart of normal anatomy the procedure is fairly straightforward with an excellent results record.

But as expected, nothing would be normal for me!

My anatomy doesn't lend itself to allowing a direct route from my groin to the search area within the heart and this is the reason the risk versus reward ratio has always been out of kilter.

I left the appointment hopeful, very hopeful, and happy that I would at least now be able to have the chance to rid myself of these abnormal heart rhythms and, fingers crossed, start to get back to a more normal life.

Back to the school visit. The first teacher we saw was really lovely, she praised Fergus no end for his attitude, his respectfulness and his desire to help others. I asked her if she had the right child! Of course she did, he's a good lad.

We moved to the next classroom to have a chat with the teacher who took his class for technology. That was fine too. As Fergus and I headed to the third classroom, it started. The same symptoms, a fast heart rate and breathlessness. He was absolutely amazing, calm, caring and while I'm sure he was worried about his dad, he didn't show it. Maybe it helped him because he was at school in a familiar environment or maybe he'd become more numb to these events, I'm not sure which, but when one of the teachers who came to my aid asked me what year he was in, she was taken aback that he was only 12.

Each time one of these episodes happened another little piece of me died, not physically, at least I hope not, but certainly mentally.

It had become a real battle and one I felt that I mostly was losing, without being too melancholy or over-dramatic. The control that the anxiety had over me and continued to envelop me into its dark, nasty grasps, was in charge of my life, in many ways.

I felt broken, but at the same time I felt determined; determined to overcome the huge burden of my anxiety.

I felt there were three steps to it. The first was having the ablation procedure and praying it would be successful. To rid myself of these arrhythmias would certainly go a long way to restoring my confidence. The second was contingent on the first, which was to stop, or at the very least, reduce, the dose of amiodarone that I was taking. The side effects this drug has, particularly long term, are too many to list, but I didn't want them, any of them! Last, I focussed on regaining some of my physical strength, but again this would only happen if I could be free (or much freer) of those rhythm disturbances.

PART THREE

A SOLUTION TO THE PROBLEM

Several days after my release from hospital in July 2023, I got a call. Not "the call," but a call nonetheless.

"Victor, it's Mandy, Professor Grigg's secretary, I have her on the line for you."

Susan was with me; she was sitting at our dining room table as we had just made our lunch. I began to shake. It's not every day that the lead of cardiology calls you – it's either really bad or maybe there is a plan? I put the phone on the loudspeaker so that Sue could listen.

"Hello Prof," I said, "How are you?"

"Victor, we believe we may have an option to help you," the Prof explained. Prof. Grigg is not one for small talk, in all reality she probably doesn't have time for it, so she cut to the chase. "We would like to look at carrying out what is quite a rare procedure, certainly not without risk, but if successful it will rid you of the symptoms of these consistent arrhythmias. Given your unique anatomy, it's very difficult for us to treat these issues in the way we normally would."

She explained the procedure she had in mind, what it would involve and some of the potential risks. She suggested I take a bit of time to think about her proposal.

"I don't need time Prof, I want it done and the sooner the better please."

What she had proposed was, essentially, to disconnect the electrical system between the top and bottom of the heart. The persistent rhythm disturbances that had been plaguing me more and more and giving me regular entry to hospital were emanating in the top chambers of my heart, but causing the bottom chambers (the chambers that push the blood around the body) to become fast and irregular too and hence that was making me feel so terrible on a, by now, almost fortnightly basis.

She was at pains to explain though that I would still get the rhythm disturbances but because the electrical pathways connecting the top and bottom parts of the heart would be "disconnected", it wouldn't cause the symptoms I had been plagued with for a long time. The procedure is called an AV Node ablation.

It's Tuesday 7th August 2023. I am on my way once more to the Royal Melbourne Hospital, although at least its voluntary and not in the back of an ambulance this time. I am in the passenger seat of our car with Sue at the helm. It's a cold dark winter morning and I needed to report to the cardiology day-stay unit at 6.30.

With the formalities done, the relevant pre-op tasks complete, such as IV lines in, ECG done and so on, I am wheeled off to the catheter ("cath") lab waiting area. Any procedure is risky, the list of "what can happen" is read out to me once again, then my signature applied to the paperwork.

Ablation procedures are very much part of an interventional cardiologist's bread and butter. In these days of incredible technology, such as 3D X-Ray mapping, which allows the cardiologist to guide and see the catheter lines from the groin or neck into the various parts of the heart, the risk is very low for something to go awry.

Most ablation procedures are done with the patient awake, although usually sedated, and if the patient feels fine post procedure, they often go home the same day. Not today though – this is no ordinary ablation procedure. Due to the complexity and anticipated length of time the procedure will take, I am going to be given a general anaesthetic.

A few deep breaths of the gas provided by the cardiac anaesthetist, and I am off for a sleep. I woke up four hours or so later. The tube that was breathing for me was removed with the help of a cough which I had been instructed to give and I could breathe for myself again. Four hours is a decent amount of time for an ablation procedure, but this was an ablation procedure with extras!

When I was a little more *compos mentis*, I asked about the success (or not) of the procedure. I was told that while it was not without its challenges, the AV node was successfully destroyed, leaving me pacemaker-dependent, but fingers crossed it would also leave me symptom-free of the arrhythmias.

IT WAS GOOD WHILE IT LASTED

I was discharged from hospital the next day and I left with a spring in my step, eager to be able to get back to living my life. Perhaps I would be able to return to my love of riding my bikes and hanging out with Fergus on the trails.

These past few years had seen a huge decline in my ability to exercise, mostly because I was terribly frightened of having an arrhythmia episode and because of that lack of exercise, I had become so deconditioned, muscles diminished, my body weak compared to just a couple of years before.

It was going to take time to regain strength and increase my exercise tolerance, but I felt confident I could restore myself to what I once was, or close to it.

For the first few days I remember being ever so tired, unusually so, even given the fact I had a general anaesthetic.

I could barely get off the couch, I just wanted to lie down and sleep. I decided I needed to get going and start to rebuild myself. Sue had taken our dog for a walk on the beach.

We are very lucky we live very near one of the best beaches in Melbourne, but the sand is mostly soft, especially when the tide is in and I have always struggled to walk on it. I opted for the walking track that runs parallel to the beach and while still sandy, it is compacted and is much easier to walk on.

I hadn't gone 100 metres and I felt I needed to stop. I took my pulse as was always my go-to, expecting it to be fast or irregular, or both, but it was fine, although I felt far from fine. I carried on trying to push this feeling to the back of my mind. Another few metres and I had stopped again. This time, I opened the oxygen app on my watch. I let the device measure the amount of O2 in my blood stream, again it was fine, again I felt weird. I decided that perhaps I was doing too much too soon, but then I reasoned I had walked less than 300 metres on the flat and I was out of breath.

This wasn't right. So, I headed back to our car for sanctuary. When she returned with the dog, Sue tried to reassure me that I was just recovering and that I should feel better soon. She didn't know, she couldn't have known, none of us could have known what was to come.

Perhaps five or so days had passed since I'd been home and it was bedtime. I always looked forward to bedtime. I could lie down, guilt free, not worried about my inner voice asking why I was lying down. This was lying down time, I didn't need to feel bad. It was early though, maybe 8.30 or so in the evening. This was my normal, I was always just so exhausted by this time of the day. That evening I felt worse than normal and soon after lying down and turning off my reading light I started to experience a strong and persistent pain in my back.

Added to that, I was just struggling to breathe properly. I sat up and put a couple of pillows behind me. It was better, not great, but better. The pain eased a little and I didn't feel so much that I was drowning.

Perhaps I drifted off to sleep, perhaps I didn't, I can't actually remember. Either way, being in bed was short-lived. I got up and the act of standing up gave me almost instant relief. Sue wanted to take me to the after-hours urgent care clinic, so she got me into the car and drove me the short distance to wait my turn to be looked over.

It has always been such a fuss explaining my medical history to doctors and nurses who are unfamiliar with me. It's complex and so rare in fact that often I am the only person with such a cardiac history that a GP (doctor) may have seen. They are however always very interested to hear it!

The British doctor listened to my chest and back and declared that my lungs sounded clear. The oximeter confirmed that same diagnosis. I was reassured that the likelihood was that indeed I was still recovering from the procedure and that things should settle down.

Things didn't settle down. The next day I went to my own GP clinic, and while my usual GP wasn't available, I saw a different doctor. I was still feeling pretty terrible, short of breath when I walked, pain in my back, the same symptoms as the previous evening. Yet the results of the tests were the same. Frustrated, I went home and tried to relax. Bedtime rolled around again, my favourite time of the day remember!

What crap existence was this that I was living when all I really looked forward to was going to bed each evening.

Yet again my time in bed was short, the symptoms had come back and they were worse than the previous evening. I asked Sue to take me to the hospital. Thirty minutes later I was sitting in the waiting room of the emergency department (known as the A&E back in the UK) with an oxygen probe on my finger. It was around 85%, way too low.

At last, I thought, some data to correlate my symptoms. I was taken inside, a place I had become far too familiar with over the past couple of years. I knew the drill. ECG stickers on, gown on, bloods taken. Eventually a stream of doctors would come by, some junior, just learning their way under the watchful guidance of their mentor or consultant, the boss, as they would commonly refer to them.

I was admitted to the cardiac ward; there was no way they could or would be sending me home with an oxygen saturation in the mid-80s. As I waited for a bed to become available on the same ward where Sue spent her professional life, I started to contemplate what was happening and what my fate may be.

I had a sneaky feeling that far from this journey being over after the success of the recent ablation procedure. In fact, I felt a whole new set of complications and challenges were about to come my way.

I was right!

LAZY BOY

I don't think I had ever slept in a recliner chair. I certainly couldn't recall doing so and I think if someone had suggested that I try it, I would have politely declined.

But when one of Sue's colleagues who was looking after me that first night in hospital suggested it would be better and more comfortable for me, I could have kissed her as it was so nice.

I was sitting upright, the fluid which had been accumulating in my lungs (confirmed by way of an X-ray) over the past few days was now at the bottom of them, allowing me some relief.

As comfortable as it was, I didn't get much sleep; my mind wouldn't settle, I was scared. Scared because I didn't know why this fluid had accumulated or indeed what the consequences of it would be.

I kept looking at the monitor over my shoulder, the telling-machine as I called it. The numbers didn't lie. The heart rate was OK, but of course that was because I was now being permanently paced by my pacemaker. Blood pressure would cycle every 30 minutes or so and I was happy if my systolic blood pressure was up over 90 – that's the top number on a BP machine! My oxygen saturation was at least now in the 90s but that was because I was being given extra oxygen, about three litres if I recall correctly.

I am sure I dozed throughout that first night, but I certainly felt devoid of sleep when the morning nursing staff came in to take my obs. I suppose a perk or two of being married to one of the Nurse Unit Managers of the ward I was on was that I was treated like royalty and I was given my own room.

The latter had become a bit of a standing joke as room 17 seemed to almost always to be mine whenever I was "in town". Although not this time. This time I was down the corridor a bit but still in my own quarters; a change was as good as a rest, right?

Once the formalities of the morning were complete, I was visited by the on-call cardiologist. This of course was not the doctor, nor indeed the hospital where my usual care was. I was well known to the doctors that looked after me under the congenital heart disease team at the Royal Melbourne Hospital, but other than the connection my wife had with the hospital, I was as new to this doctor as she was to me.

She explained that my heart had failed, and this was the cause of the fluid buildup in my lungs. "You are in heart failure Victor" she told me. Heart failure?! How could this be? I had just had a procedure to prevent that very thing. My mind started to swirl and questions were mounting, the biggest one of all being, how? How had this happened, it was only around a week since I had returned home from hospital? "You will be staying with us for a while, the first thing we need to do is try to remove the excess fluid from your lungs."

I was introduced to my new best friend, a drug called Frusemide. Just when I thought it wasn't possible to pee any more, I did! The issue the doctor had with me, however, was that Frusemide was well known for further reducing blood pressure, due to the removal of fluids. She told me that this would be a slower process than normal so she didn't completely drop my blood pressure. Next, she wanted to speak to my regular cardiac team to discuss a plan.

Sometimes when in hospital there's a feeling that nothing is happening, that anything and everything takes forever to happen. The hours roll on and progress in terms of a definitive plan or direction is sometimes missing. For five days I felt like that. I was going to be transferred to the Royal Melbourne, then I wasn't, then I was etc. I slept for the first two (possibly three) nights in the recliner until enough fluid had come out of me that I could in fact lie down comfortably again. Although I was no longer able to lie flat, I needed an extra pillow to help prop me up, something that would be in play for a long time to come.

Five days later I was allowed home. I can't really say I was terribly excited as I didn't really feel better. I mean sure I could breathe better and I no longer needed supplementary oxygen. But I suppose in terms of feeling like there was a spring in my step, that feeling was eluding me. It would become clear why all too soon.

GROUNDHOG DAY

I am a firm believer in the fact that nobody knows their body like the person inside that body!

I knew something had been wrong when I was admitted to hospital a week before. Patients tend to listen and pay attention to doctors, but just like in any other role or profession, as amazing as they are, it's possible for them to misdiagnose or even just miss the problem all together, which had in fact been the case until at last I went to the emergency department, had an X-Ray and the diagnosis confirmed.

The first couple of days back at home I recall were OK. By OK, I mean I wasn't gasping for air and while I was certainly not active, I was functioning. It was, however, short lived and soon I was back where I had started 10 days or so before my symptoms arrived.

It was a Monday, I know this, because the next day was of course going to be Tuesday, the relevance of that was that I was due to have a follow-up appointment at the Royal Melbourne Hospital after my recent AV Node ablation procedure.

At 3am on Tuesday, I was woken by the same symptoms that had plagued me a week or so ago. I decided it was bad enough to bother Sue and while she possibly protested at the time, soon she understood that my need for medical attention was high.

Because I already had a planned clinic appointment at 8am, we decided that rather than drive to the local hospital (where I had been a week earlier) we decided to go into the city and to the Royal Melbourne, where not only I was due to be in a few hours anyway, but where all of the congenital heart team were based. At 3.30am, or thereabouts, we set off for the 40-minute journey into the city. The only advantage of driving around at this time of the day is of course the lack of traffic, the journey would normally take well over an hour at peak hour.

We left our son fast asleep in bed, oblivious to the goings-on outside of his bedroom. We had become quite good at putting some essential items together for these long hours of waiting in emergency rooms and eventually sitting in a ward bed. I was sure that I would be staying, so my iPad, phone, book, headphones, charging cables, some pajamas and toiletries had all been gathered and thrown into a backpack. I gave Fergus a kiss that he would not have been aware of and off we went.

By 4.30am Sue had dropped me off at emergency and she was heading home so that she could be there when Fergus woke up and get him ready for school.

Meanwhile I was being assessed by the attending doctor, who while sure of the return of the heart failure was equally adamant that he wasn't going to do anything that the cardiologists might not want him to do!

I found this quite interesting to begin with, but I soon began to understand the reluctance to treat me given my complex and extensive cardiac history, but moreover the fact that in a couple of hours I would be seeing the cardiology team.

I was sent off to sit in the café area, which I will say I did find to be a bit strange given my situation, and I was told to make my way up to cardiology for 8am. Exhausted by now, I was ushered in straight away, seen by a cardiologist I hadn't met before, who was lovely and extremely effectual. She picked up the phone to the cardiology ward and explained to the Bed Manager that she needed a bed for me immediately and within 10 minutes I was lying in a bed, being hooked up to monitors, bloods being taken, weight being taken, multiple questions being asked and several doctors coming and going all terribly interested in me! Top tip: If you want some attention from doctors, get yourself a rare congenital heart defect and they will all gather around like bees around a honey pot!

So here I was again, in a hospital bed, not quite knowing where to go from here, but trusting as always in the incredible medical care and science that surely would see me through this latest bump in the road.

BE CAREFUL WHAT YOU WISH FOR

I have always jested with the many cardiologists I have seen, saying just give me a new heart. I suppose I have said it to provoke a reaction, to hear what their response might be.

The response has always been, "your heart is doing fine and we want you to keep yours for as long as possible." Or it might be along the lines of "oh I think you are a long way off needing a transplant".

On the one hand this has reassured me that I wasn't on the verge of death, but at some level I have kind of always secretly hoped they would say, yes, let's give you a new heart! A transplant is a huge deal and a much bigger deal than I had realised.

As a friend who was a transplant recipient once said, you close the door to one set of problems and you open the door to a whole new set, rejection of the new tissue being the most significant.

Two days into my latest hospital stay, the ward rounds were underway as they usually were each day. The cardiologist on-call for ward rounds was Dr Stacey Peters. A lovely lady that I had met once, perhaps twice before at my regular clinic appointments.

With a relaxing demeanour, she made me feel comfortable and at ease, a skill that perhaps not all doctors have regardless of how good a physician they may be. We chatted casually at first; she asked how I was feeling, which by now two days in, having started new medication, was much better, thank you!

She went on to say, "the team have discussed your case in detail and we believe the correct course of action is to assess you for a transplant!"

My God! There I had been all those years asking for one, with that tongue firmly in my cheek, and getting those "oh I don't think we are there just yet" answers. Now, she was suggesting a transplant. More than suggesting really, she was telling me we had reached that point.

It was sobering as you probably can imagine. I began to cry and she reached out her hand to touch mine and held it tight. It was scary but at the same time it was also a little exciting.

Would this now be the start of my transplant journey? How long would it be before I got a new heart? What would it be like? I remember having these and many other questions, none of which could be answered yet, but they all would be in time.

The stark reality was I knew next to nothing about heart transplants. In all my jesting and half-joking I hadn't even bothered to actually do much (or any) research about it at all. Maybe that was a good thing? Maybe I should be starting this new journey fresh, fresh of any preconceived ideas about what was involved? On the other hand, is it not better to be at least a little prepared?

Both questions were soon to become academic. Over the course of the next couple of years there would be many more questions and answers, some of which would be hard to accept, some of which would give me hope and keep me going through some pretty tough times, both mentally and physically.

Stacey finished her time with me saying that they would be contacting The Alfred Hospital in Melbourne which is where all heart and lung transplants are carried out. And with that, my journey to a promised new life began.

Typically, there are two reasons fort heart transplants. The first is end-of-life heart failure, meaning that unless the patient is given a new heart, they will die. There is of course a timeline which I understand is around a year, so the patient is likely to die within a year if they don't receive a new heart. The second reason is that the arrhythmias a patient gets are so debilitating and/or life threatening that medications and other interventions such as ablations had not worked or were less effective than they once were. Mostly I was falling into the latter category, but of course I had heart failure too. It was a double whammy!

The main thing for me was to understand why this heart failure occurred at this time? After all, my understanding was that the recent procedure I had should have made things better if anything, certainly not worse!

Sadly, as it turned out, the procedure had done just that. To say it's complicated is an understatement but here is a shot at trying to explain what went wrong. In a normal heart the flow of the electrical current which causes the heart to beat happens in an orderly fashion, starting at the top and flowing down through the middle of the heart. Its beat resembles a jellyfish in terms of the movement. In one word, it is synchronous.

Because my heart was now relying on an artificial electrical impulse (the natural pacemaker system had been wiped out deliberately to try to stop the many arrhythmias) there wasn't the same synchrony that there once had been. In short, my heart didn't like that and rather than resembling the jellyfish-type heartbeat I was now more like a pendulum with my heart swinging from side to side. This clearly wasn't conducive to a happy heart! In another single word, I was now dyssynchronous!

In isolation the procedure probably didn't specifically cause heart failure, but it was the straw that broke the camel's back, if you will.

It's likely, more than likely, that my heart was failing and I knew that. I knew with the way I had been feeling, with my reduced exercise capacity and my increased fatigue, that all was not well in the engine room! But at that time, it hadn't shown its hand fully.

It was still lying quietly in the background, waiting for the right moment to pounce and try to wipe me out!

In a sliding-doors moment during my stay in hospital, the team had tried to start the ball rolling and get some of the many tests done, to speed up the process. One of these tests (and there would be many) was to do what is called a right-side heart catheter. Basically, that's an angiogram to measure the pressures in the right side of the heart. Why do they need to measure the pressures? Well it's important that the pressures aren't too high as that can impact the pulmonary system and lead to further complications.

Dr Will Wilson explained this procedure to me. A charming, and extremely skillful physician, Dr Will had seen me in the clinic many times over the years and had in fact also done some other procedures on me. I trusted him implicitly.

As I waited in the "holding pen" outside the Cath labs for my turn to be wheeled in, another doctor happened to be nearby. A very welcome face, it was Dr Irene Stevenson, the person who I had come to know and trust the most in terms of rhythm disturbances to my heart. Irene had already done some work on me back in 2017 when she upgraded my first pacemaker.

"Victor!" she exclaimed as she wandered over to my bed in the holding pen, "What are you doing here". I explained what had happened. She picked up my hand and calmly said, "Don't worry it will be OK, wait here I am going to talk to Dr Will; there may be a way we can help you feel better."

I managed a smile through my tears. "Well, I am not exactly going anywhere!" I tried to joke, poorly, no doubt!

Before understanding what that help might be I was wheeled off for my procedure, which as it turned out revealed normal pressures, so that was one thing I could tick off!

Now, what was this help Irene was talking about?

THE GOOD DOCTOR

I know it's a cliché that is used all the time, but "Isn't it amazing what they can do these days?" was so relevant to me then.

The procedure Irene suggested to me a couple of days later when she came up to see me on the ward had never been performed on a person with my complex heart anatomy, certainly not in Australia, possibly not anywhere. So by default she had never given it a go either!

What she was suggesting was to remove the pacemaker/ defibrillator that was installed in the top left of my chest and replace it with a different type of device. The new one would do all the things the current one was doing, so it would be pacing the top chambers of my heart as well as having the protective therapy of being able to shock my heart back into a normal heart rhythm if that was necessary.

Crucially, the new device would have another lead that would be placed in the bottom part of my heart near the existing lead. The idea was essentially to balance the heart so the electrical pulses from the pacemaker would help make the heartbeat more like that desired jellyfish motion rather than the pendulum that it had been doing since early August.

I think in this day and age we have come to just expect medical science will find a way. Very often it does, thankfully.

But some things can't be fixed, it's just a fact of life sadly. And should everything be fixed? And if so at what cost both financially, physically and emotionally. I am neither qualified or intelligent enough to be answering big questions such philosophical or ethical aspects of modern medical science. On the flip side, imagine a world where we didn't try, where a status quo was accepted. How then do we advance, how are the boundaries of medical science ever stretched?

I think in this area, just as much as the research, the medical equipment, the drugs and medications, doctors willing to push those same boundaries, arguably more so, are needed. The obvious analogy is there is no point in having the most technically capable car, plane, spaceship etc. if there is no one willing or able to drive or fly it.

In the 21st century we are at a point where "almost anything" seems to be possible medically, from rebuilding people after serious trauma to replacing broken hearts, lungs and other major organs to even being able to separate conjoined twins. It really is remarkable, but none of it would have been possible without those doctors and other medical teams putting, at times, their own careers and reputations on the line in the name of progress.

This is how I saw Irene when she told me she didn't know if the procedure would work or if it did work whether it would make a difference to me. I saw her as a pioneer, as someone who was willing to push the boundaries to get a result. Without trying we will never triumph.

December 6th 2023 was the day.

Like all those other times where I had been booked in for an elective procedure, things started early, reporting for duty at silly o'clock (around 6am I seem to recall).

Ordinarily, a pacemaker device is inserted with some local anaesthetic and some sedation to keep the patient calm.

But due to the anticipated complexity and thus the time that the procedure was expected to take, I was to be given a general anaesthetic, part for my own comfort and safety and part for Irene to be able to take her time without the possibility of me becoming sore or agitated. Lying on a Cath lab bed for an extended period of time isn't the most pleasurable of experiences, trust me!

So, with the appropriate lines in veins and a suitable level of medications loaded up, off I went for a snooze – for four hours.

I don't really like to overstate, but when Irene came to see me as I was recovering back on the ward and she showed me the ECG of my new device I was so incredibly emotional. What she had managed to do was nothing short of amazing. It sounds corny I know but I could feel the difference almost immediately. Now my heart was beating in a much more organised and synchronous way. It was like someone had flipped a switch; from feeling really awful and unable to do much at all, I found myself in the following days being more like my old self with better colour and more energy and motivation to do things. However, she was at pains to tell me that this wasn't a fix. This was to give me a better chance to get me to the point of a transplant.

My heart was still very unwell and certainly wasn't going to support me for many years to come. This was a bridge to get me to that new life that by now I was yearning so much for.

Irene saved my life that day; I have told her a number of times. I know it. I know I wouldn't have been here if it wasn't for her intervention, her skill, her judgment and, above all, her willingness to give her patient the best possible chance of survival. That can be a lot to bear and get your head around. I have had many tearful moments reflecting on what she did to save my life.

WAS IT JUST A HOAX?

Feeling as if nothing could hold me back, I left hospital and Irene's care the following day and headed home for a few days' rest before my next adventure.

My date had come through from The Alfred Hospital for a week-long stay to go through all the testing I would need to have done to see if I was a suitable transplant candidate.

I had arrived at this point several weeks earlier after my first consult with the heart-failure team at The Alfred, meeting for the first time Professor James Hare, someone who could make you smile even if you were at a low point.

It soon became clear to me that The Alfred was the place to be for anyone needing a heart transplant. The infrastructure they had by comparison to what I had so far experienced was incredible. It's a huge team as can be imagined. Everyone from the consultants, through to social workers and psychologists were on hand, there to help a patient through the massive journey.

To be considered for transplant, I had some work to do!

On the 12th December, 2023, which was a Sunday, I checked into Ward 3 West for my week-long stay.

They wanted me there first thing on Monday. They wanted me the night before to do all the admin tasks, make sure I was who I said I was and so on!

I was given my own room with a sort of view of the helipad where those in need of the most urgent care often arrived, so that was pretty cool! Well, I thought it was cool until the roar of those engines of the helicopters woke me up at all hours!

Monday morning, and it was full-on. There are of course a whole barrage of tests and work-ups that need to be done before even getting close to having a transplant. Ensuring the donor heart has the best chance of success in its new body is of course extremely important.

First order of the day was a blood test and by "a" I don't mean singular!

Oh no, the phlebotomist rolled in with at least 20 test tubes to be filled, could have been more! Crikey I thought, this could be a struggle as unfortunately I have never had great veins and overly generous with my blood giving!

I am not in anyway worried or anxious about needles, I couldn't care less as I have had so many of the years, I had become so used to it but for some reason my veins have become somewhat resistant to them and they do really cool things, like roll away or collapse as soon as a needle approaches!

It's also to do with the fact that by this point my circulation was not that great and of course arms and hands are at the end of the line in terms of circulation and that doesn't help!

So, with me giving a heads-up to the poor person tasked with being the vampire, I wished her good luck and off we went. Sometime later all vials were filled, and they were off to the lab. First test done!

To say that the team was thorough would be an understatement. They were of course trying to determine a number of things, not least of which is whether a patient was even likely to survive a transplant.

I no particular order and no doubt omitting some, the tests included; Full body bone density scans, dental check up, echocardiogram, ultrasound of other major organs, cardiac CT scan, sleep study, exercise tolerance test (absolutely horrendous), psychology assessment (presumably to ensure I was crazy enough!), assessment by the social workers, visits by the surgeons to make sure they were happy with operating given my previous open heart operations, X-rays of just about everything ... I could go on.

During this time though, I had suddenly started to feel much better. Perhaps it was because I was in a safe place or, more likely, it was because the device that Irene had inserted the previous week was helping my heart so much more, or maybe it was the hospital food! Unlikely the last option I think, although I had no complaints; I was getting what I felt like the royal treatment and I was just happy to have been given this chance.

I mentioned this to one of the doctors on their morning round one day and asked if I would still need a transplant, because now I was feeling so much better.

Was this just a hoax?

"Oh no it is not a hoax and oh yes you certainly will need a transplant," the doctor confirmed. "It's fantastic you are feeling better, that's what we want because the healthier you are now the better your chances are of recovering from the transplant. The new device you have is to help get you to transplant, it's not by any means a long-term fix."

So, that was me told and I started to understand that the ethos was in fact to get patients to a transplant in a relatively healthy state, not with the wheels and doors falling off with big clouds of smoke emanating from the exhaust pipe, to use yet another analogy, but in a state of knowing that the engine isn't good but all the other parts are relatively OK and with the right mix of medications and close-care there would be a good chance of making it to the garage to get that new engine fitted.

Any thoughts I had of feeling a bit fraudulent were soon wiped away after that little chat! There were a few other little chats that week too that started to cement a few things in my mind. The biggest of them all though was beginning to understand the gravity of an operation such as a heart transplant.

It's a massive deal. Medical science doesn't really get more complicated or cutting edge than having a transplant, of any type. Perhaps the separation of conjoined twins might trump this, but a transplant is certainly "up there" with complexity and risk.

The mere fact that we are in an age where life-giving procedures are possible, I find truly remarkable.

In 1967 the first transplant was performed on a 54-year-old man who was in chronic heart failure. The donor heart was from an 18-year-old female who had sadly died in a car accident. While the operation was a success, unfortunately the recipient passed away a few weeks later from a lung infection. The heart itself was working well, however.

Winding the clock forward more than 50 years and these days, the success rate of transplants is more than 90% for recipients in the first-year post-transplant and greater than 80% after five years. It's astonishing really.

But it's not a panacea. It's a mechanism to increase and enhance someone's life and quality of that life. So, I thought that if and when my turn came to receive a gift of life, I would do it understanding the risks and the benefits and be grateful for the opportunity to be able to make the decision.

I also declared to myself there and then that I would do everything I could to look after that heart and follow the instructions of the medical teams to the letter.

LISTED

I was discharged a week after my transplant work-up tests. It was Christmas. Fergus was excited as any kid would be and I had managed to divert some of my thoughts away from my health issues to seeing him enjoy himself.

Down here in Australia it's summer and while I will never become used to seeing Father Christmas represented in flip flops and a pair of board-shorts, it's the summer holidays and for Fergus that meant no school for six weeks and riding his bike as much as he could.

By this time, I had not been working since February of that year, so for me in some ways, one day rolled into another. I had been working on building him a new bike for his Christmas present. That had been great and I had also been helping out a friend a little at his bike shop.

But life had become quite mundane and mentally I was struggling a bit. I was restricted physically in terms of what I could do. My own bike riding was pretty much non-existent by now and even those times I did throw my leg over the crossbar, I was confined to relatively flat terrain and only able to pedal for short distances.

My "fix" was to take Fergus and his mates riding as much as I could. I would drive them to their destination and they would ride to the bottom of the hill and I would take them back to the top again. We called this doing shuttles.

I felt strongly that I needed to stay connected, not only to Fergus by grasping on to any dad-and-lad time, but to my other bike friends. It was definitely very hard not to be jealous of other parents who were able to ride with their kids or at the very least be able to be the veritable mountain goats climbing up hills and down dales to watch and support their kids at race days or just when riding recreationally.

I was quite pleased once the festivities had drawn to a close and we were into 2024. Christmas, New Year and well into January in Australia sees such a slow-down in all aspects of activity and included in that would be all the relative departments that would be involved in my care being on skeleton staff and things taking longer than they often did in hospital settings.

After the first perhaps 10 days of January the phone started ringing again with me needing to attend this or that appointment to finalise some of the tests the team needed me to have. One of these tests couldn't be done during my work-up because of the surgical procedure I had the week before. Finally though I had a tick on all the tests, and all I had to do now was to wait to hear if I was going to be accepted on to the transplant list, or not.

My appointment letter telling me to attend the Heart Failure clinic arrived on February 9th, 2024.

I would at last find out if I would have a grasp on a new life. Dr Sarah Gutman, one of the senior heart-failure cardiologists, was taking the clinic. I was fidgeting as I waited for my name to be called.

I knew there had been a meeting of all the various departments who would be involved in my care. This is called a Multi-Disciplinary Meeting where my case would be discussed and everyone from the senior doctors to the physios, dieticians and psychologist would have their input and thoughts discussed so that all the team were agreed on any decision made. It is almost like a jury! Guilty or not guilty was what I was waiting to hear!

My name was called and Dr Gutman introduced herself.

She put her hand out to greet me and asked me how I was.

"Nervous."

"Fair enough," she said, "but it's good news Victor, we will be listing you today for transplant".

I could hardly believe my ears. I did it. It felt like I had been accepted into a very rare exclusive club. The first major hurdle was done. As she pulled out all the various pieces of paperwork for me to sign to give my consent to all manner of operations and procedures including a transplant itself, I could sense that from this moment on life would never be the same. I didn't know what it would be like, I just knew it would be different.

I felt so safe with this team, I knew they had my back, I felt that they had a genuine interest in my future healthcare, and I knew that they would do all they could to get me through this and help me start a new exciting life. I just didn't know when that would start. No one did!

What followed was a list of dos and don'ts.

First thing was to swap me off the blood thinner I had been taking in favour of warfarin (aka rat poison!). When I asked why, Sarah explained that when I (hopefully) received a heart the surgeons could give me some Vitamin K which reversed the effects of the warfarin, so I didn't bleed to death on the operating table. Fair enough I thought, sign me up! The only real downside to warfarin is that the levels of it in your blood must be checked regularly which involves a blood test, but heck what's a few more pin pricks among friends?

Some other interesting things I needed to change included no probiotic foods, no travel beyond two or so hours from home without approval from the hospital and definitely no travel out of the state, unless I was happy to be taken off the list for that period I would be away.

I wasn't going to risk that. Knowing my luck, it would be the very time I'd get the call!

After the news had sunk in and I had come back to earth and had a 30-minute talk with the pharmacist about how to manage the warfarin I suppose reality set in.

My reality was that I would now maybe, possibly, hopefully, have a chance to experience and enjoy a much more normal life.

It was quite overwhelming having come this far, within touch of the finish line. Yet there was such a long way to go.

GREEN BANANAS

One of the questions I asked at my very first clinic appointment with Professor Hare was how long I would have to wait, and back then, as most people would, I sort of expected a definitive reply.

Of course, it's a transplant, and to facilitate that, someone sadly has to lose their life. No one knows when that day will be or under what circumstances.

Prof. Hare talked to me in averages.

He said the average wait time in Australia was six months. Then came the caveats. The first was that my blood type was super common, O+.

Now, like me, anyone might think this is a good thing – it's not! You see, an O group person can only receive blood or tissues from another O, and because most of the population is O, those hearts (and other organs) are in high demand.

On the other hand, if you happen to be an A or a B, you can receive organs from your group, but also from O groups. So, if you had a choice, A or B would be preferable. Ironically, I had to that point journeyed through life believing I was a B+. Maybe I had confused this with most of my school grades!

The other caveat was that I was a congenital patient and that can lead to some longer waiting times, due to the complexity of our anatomy and sometimes a specific size of heart is needed.

In my case, Prof Hare thought that wouldn't be too much of an issue. One thing I did have in my favour was my size of body. I was neither large or small, basically just average! And while none of us aim to be average, now was a good to time be so!

He was clear in not giving me false hope; some people get a heart almost immediately and others can wait years, sometimes more than 3-5 years, he explained. I was "lucky" in the sense that I would (hopefully) be arriving at transplant time in a relatively healthy state. Aside from my heart, all my other organs were functioning well, especially the liver kidneys and lungs. Sadly for so many, sometimes a transplant is not an option because of the state of other organs, or as I have since found out, multiple organ transplants are required. Kidneys seem "popular". If a person's kidneys are not working well, as is often found in diabetic individuals, the kidneys potentially won't cope with the post-transplant rejection medications and often in such cases a new kidney is needed too.

I recall being called a green banana at one of my clinic appointments by the consultant. I understood what he was inferring, but in case of any doubt he explained:

"We want you to be not too sick and not too well. If you are too well, you probably aren't at the stage of needing a transplant, but on the other hand if you are too sick you may not have a good outcome".

He told me the analogy of a green banana was a good one because by the time I got a transplant the banana was probably yellow and therefore ripe. However, if they waited to list someone who was already a yellow banana, that person might be brown or even black by the time they receive a heart. That is what they were trying to avoid.

In fact, there had been a big shift in the timeline of listing someone in recent years. The Alfred had been educating other hospitals to send them patients as early as possible to be assessed so that all of those pre-tests could be done as early as possible, just as happened with me. The patient hopefully then had time on their side. So, I was now called Green Banana, and I was happy with that!

I had been told by a couple of my friends who had been through this process and out the other side, that this phase, the waiting phase, was by far the hardest. It wasn't long before I began to understand why they had felt that way.

For the first few weeks I literally had my phone strapped to me, it felt like 24/7. In the shower, on a loud setting at night and yes, I am not ashamed to admit it, the phone even came with me to the loo!

One of the issues was that any calls I would get from the hospital would always come up "No Caller ID". So, I had to answer these too.

Most of the time they were from companies trying to sell solar panels or give me better energy rates. Every call had to be answered but the "end" button was very often hit promptly after taking a non-important call.

The feeling I referred to earlier of maybe this being a hoax had long since disappeared.

I knew I needed a new heart and that was being reinforced to me by the day. My energy levels were low, I would get extraordinarily tired even after what most would consider to be a menial task or activity. I had to decide what I could do during those days. If I washed my car, for example, that would be my activity for that day. It would probably be followed by a lie down, sometimes a little nap.

When in March 2024 I was approached by a company I had once worked for to help them out a bit I thought that maybe it would be a good distraction, but I was concerned about being able to actually be effective due to fatigue.

I had cabin fever; I was frustrated that I couldn't function properly and moreover contribute to our household. Sue was propping us all up on her own and I really felt useless. Actually, the company had been seeking me out for a while but before the pacemaker upgrade I had in December 2023 there was no way I could even consider working, I was just too sick.

At least now I felt a little better and this opportunity could take my mind off things a bit. I met the GM of the business for a coffee (soft drink for me!) and we agreed that I would work on a consultancy basis starting at just one or two days per week, because that was all I felt I could truly manage. I think that arrangement lasted less than a week!

One day rolled into another and before we knew where we were I was doing 40 hours or so a week. I was tired and I found myself needing very early nights to recharge for the following day, but it gave me what I needed – a sense of purpose and a distraction from all of the health issues I had going on.

The year rolled on and the work became more and more involved and eventually in order to protect myself I said to the business that they needed to employ me full-time.

I knew, or at least I hoped, that one day my turn would come for a heart, and I also knew that after a recovery period I would need and indeed want to return to work. As a contractor, the business was within its rights to terminate my services without notice or reason; as an employee it would be much harder for them to do that. There was no hesitation on their side and by October of 2024 I became a fully-fledged employee of the business once more. I couldn't have asked for more, the business was extremely supportive of my health issues. Sometimes things just work out.

As much as returning to work was a fantastic distraction and I felt like I was contributing to our little family once more, there was an ever present "I wonder if I should be doing this? Am I doing myself more harm than good?" I was tired a great deal of the time and work basically took everything out of me that I had to give. I was just hoping that the phone would ring and I could put all the exhaustion and suffering behind me.

Many people might assume the only person feeling the effects of this whole process is the one waiting for the transplant.

This is definitely not the case, but it's also easy to forget that other people, in my case, Sue and Fergus, were directly impacted by this whole journey.

I recalled back in the transplant work-up when we met so many of the care team, the transplant nurse was emphatic about the fact that just like a child was raised by a village, so too many people were impacted and indeed needed to help a patient get through the whole process.

We didn't have the luxury of a whole village. In reality there were the three of us in this boat and we were all doing our bit to navigate the waters as best we could.

Regardless of numbers we, too, were emphatic that we would all do whatever was needed to get to the outcome we all so wanted. The commitment we had made was a real one, not just getting to the point of a transplant, but also in terms of commitment when the real work began after the transplant, More on that later!

We all felt the impacts of the waiting. For poor Fergus, what it meant for him was that he was going off to mountain bike events with other families as I was not able, or in some cases allowed, to go. The able part came from the fact that while I was functioning on a day-to-day basis with work and some normality in family life, I had become extremely anxious about travelling to remote places out of metropolitan Melbourne.

I was worried that if something happened to me I would be too far away to get medical help. But there was also the adherence to the rules that had been set by the transplant team, that travel further than maybe two hours or out of the state would mean would risk losing the chance of getting a suitable organ if one became available. There was no way I would ever risk that.

As a consequence, that also meant Sue needed to be on hand if the phone rang with that important call, to take me to hospital and be by my side, not an easy thing to do or sign up for by any means.

We did our best to mitigate the newfound intrusions and inconveniences to what should otherwise be considered a normal family life. There was nothing "normal" about life right now.

The year rolled on, I had regular clinic appointments at the hospital to ensure I wasn't declining too quickly and that my Green Banana status was still valid!

I also met the amazing Rosalyn, the cardiac team's clinical psychologist. What an amazing help she was; someone who finally understood what this whole thing felt like.

As anyone who hadn't been through a life journey such as mine, she couldn't know exactly what it felt like and nor did she pretend to, which was so refreshing. Instead, she was there to offer strategies for coping and help me when it was all becoming a bit too much, which at times it did.

She also helped me understand where all the trauma had come from because it wasn't from the immediate and current situation I was in; it had all started from when I was a kid, the procedures, the check-ups, the teasing and bullying at school, the fact I never thought of myself enough, that I thought I had let down my parents and my family by being a sick child. She uncovered all of this with me and it was so enlightening.

It was so important that in the end I realised that it wasn't my fault I had been born this way and that this life journey of mine had been navigated the best way I knew how; that I had a very uphill start to life and she showed me my perceived failures weren't in fact failures at all, they were strengths because I had to that point not only survived but thrived.

I think I drove her crazy each time I saw her though, as I would seek reassurance, asking her if she thought I would ever get a heart. Clearly it was an unfair question, how would she possibly know, she only had statistics to go on? The statistics said yes, that in all likelihood one day I would get a heart, but it was data, nothing more.

At one of the regular check-ups I met a new doctor. Her name was Su Ling Tee. I had been told about her from a new friend who had been through the same process and who had recently had a transplant.

Su was amazing! She is probably the best cardiac doctor I have ever met, not because she is necessarily any better clinically than anyone else because, let's face it, all of these cardiac consultants are incredible, but more because of how she was with me. First, she was somewhat unique in that she was a heart-failure doctor who specialised in looking after patients with congenital heart defects, such as me. I felt an extra layer of comfort and security with her.

Most importantly for me, she never ever sugar-coated anything about the situation I faced, that my heart was unwell and also in the sense of how hard the transplant, if I was to get one, could be.

It was at our first meeting that she laid out some potential treatment options that could be considered if my health deteriorated further.

One option was to treat me with inotropes, which she described as being happy juice for the heart. These would be permanently attached to my arm and injected through an intravenous drip. I didn't think much of that idea!

Another potential option would be to consider what is called an LVAD or a Left Ventricular Assist Device. It is a pump that is attached to the heart to relieve some pressure and allow the patient to stay well enough to be given a transplant.

The only issue for me was that my systemic ventricle was on my right side, not my left so it was unclear as to whether this would be a viable option. In any case I liked this idea even less than the inotropes.

I left the appointment really deflated. Was I really that sick? Was I fast approaching the end of options if a transplant wasn't going to happen?

I was sad and I was scared. A couple of days later Su Ling called me, to apologise if she had scared me. This had been prompted by me talking with one of the heart-failure nurses after my appointment and telling her how worried I was.

"I am so sorry if I worried you Victor" she said, "you are doing well and you are holding your own, but I wouldn't be doing my job properly if I didn't make you aware of all of the options and potential complications you might face."

I was instantly reassured I was still OK, I was still working, functioning and as far as I was aware I was still a green banana.

Su Ling became someone I really relied upon as I knew she would tell it to me straight but in a kind, compassionate and reassuring way.

As was now my custom, I would ask almost anyone and everyone if they thought my turn would come.

Su Ling actually gave me the biggest hint of all and if she had put some money on it she would have won; "I think you will wait around a year from when you were listed," she told me at a clinic appointment. This was the most any doctor or medical team member had given me. Maybe she did it because she knew I needed something to grasp, or maybe somehow she just knew.

Weirdly though, at a different appointment with another cardiologist a few weeks earlier, Caitlin (the doctor) had told me that they thought they had recently had a heart for me, but it wasn't viable.

It didn't matter that it wasn't viable, it just mattered to me that I was in the running, that I was being considered and that the team wanted me to be transplanted as soon as possible so that my green banana status didn't got to yellow and then brown too quickly.

RING, RING…

The year rolled out, Christmas along with all of its trimmings came and went. We actually had a very quiet Christmas, just the three of us. Sue had booked us a night at the Crown Hotel in the heart of Melbourne, one of the best-known city hotels, for Christmas Eve, which was lovely and a real treat.

Christmas Day itself was modest in terms of celebrations, with friends with whom we had planned to spend some time being otherwise engaged. So, we headed to a local restaurant and then back home to unwrap some presents.

As is common in the Antipodes, many businesses shut down for much of the summer holidays. Thus, I had a couple of weeks off which was great and while I was no longer able to do a huge amount of activity, it didn't stop me from being able to take Fergus and some of his mates riding at our local mountain-bike park. I would do anything to keep connected to him and to that whole community. I needed desperately to not lose touch with the people I knew, for I knew, or at least I hoped greatly, that one day I would be back.

For some reason, I'm not too sure why other than a state of optimism, I felt 2025 would be my year. Perhaps it was because of what Su Ling had said to me about her thinking I would wait for a year, or was it that I had been told the average wait time was six months and I was well and truly past that point, or maybe it was all the friends who had said it would happen for me this year? Either way Sue, Fergus and I had a little wager. I think I said April. That was more around me thinking it would be a convenient time with summer over and Fergus's riding season finished, Fergus I think said March and Sue said February. She won the prize. She is still waiting for the prize!

It had been an ordinary Friday. I had been at work as had Sue, and Fergus had been at school, just finishing his first week back after the summer holidays.

Sue and Fergus were getting ready to head off the following day to New South Wales for a week-long trip to a mountain bike festival at a place called Thredbo, around eight hours drive from where we lived. I should explain that we had by now come up with all manner of contingencies if the phone rang, as we had also decided it was not fair or right in many ways to be sending Fergus off with various families with the onus of responsibility for his welfare put on their shoulders, regardless of whether they were comfortable with it or not.

The final straw came when, during the preceding school holidays, he had been over in New Zealand with another family who had very generously offered to take him riding and he had an accident. Initially we thought he had hurt himself quite badly and luckily it turned out not to be the case. Regardless, the distance was just too great for us to help properly. Sue ended up having an unexpected trip to NZ on a bit of a rescue mission, something we hadn't planned on financially or otherwise!

Because I was unable to go to New South Wales as it was much too far away from the hospital, we had decided that Sue would take him and if (it was a big if) the phone was to ring for me, I would Uber my way to the hospital and hopefully Sue would have enough time to get there.

It was, I agree, a bit of a floored plan, but what we were both trying to do, perhaps not very well, was to maintain a level of normality in Fergus's life. He shouldn't have to be uprooted and disadvantaged because I might, one day get a heart transplant. His life needed to go on.

The usual Friday night rituals were in full swing, getting some dinner organised, Sue running around chasing Fergus up trying to get him to organise his "shit" ready for the trip the next morning. I had just sat down to watch a little TV after dinner.

The phone rang.

Interestingly, all those "No Caller ID" call numbers I had answered, most of which were scams, had amounted to nothing. The call I was answering this time had a number. It wasn't a saved number, it wasn't a number I recognised either, but I was going to answer it.

I will never forget the first words I heard: "Victor, it's Tricia from The Alfred. Are you at home? Is Sue with you?". I replied "yes" to both. "Can you please get Sue and put me on speaker phone?" Tricia asked.

I called out to Sue who replied with "What?!" She was already stressed trying to get Fergus and herself ready for next day.

"It's Tricia from The Alfred, she wants to speak to us both".

I knew it was THE call. I had known instinctively from the moment she had said it was Tricia. From that moment on I could neither absorb what Tricia was saying, nor could I say, from that day to this, how the conversation panned out. Except for two details. The first was that Sue and I had to do a Covid test and send a picture of the result to her; the second was that we needed to be at The Alfred by 5 o'clock next morning. Talk about timing!

They do say things happen when you least expect it. I couldn't agree more!

When the rest of the instructions were given to us (which luckily Sue managed to absorb) and we had put the phone down, reality started to sink in. Actually not sink in, rather hit me like a ton of bricks.

Oh my God, I am about to have a bloody heart transplant!

It's really very difficult to put into words just how I felt but it was now finally going to happen for me, for us, for our little family,

Hopefully that would mean that we could all have the opportunity to enjoy life together and get back to doing the things we all wanted to do but hadn't been able to do as a family. We had very little time to process the five-minute conversation and, crucially, to begin to figure out what the next 24 hours would look like.

First, what the hell are we going to do about the trip that Sue and Fergus were about to take? As the telephone call had been happening, Fergus was in the shower. He was now out and as he came through from the bathroom he looked at us both and said "what?!" "We have some news" I said and told him about the phone conversation.

He thought we were winding him up. "You're joking" was his first response, which was fair enough, as this moment was every bit as surreal for him as it was for us. He had waited just like Sue and I had, him hoping that his dad would one day be well again. We huddled together tightly and held each other, probably all thinking that this could on the one hand be our last night together, ever, but hoping that this could also be the start of an amazing new adventure, for us all.

The next task, after discussing with Fergus what he wanted to do about his trip, was to try to arrange for another family to take him. This was far from ideal, especially given what had happened four weeks earlier in New Zealand, but we decided that in fact him being away from all of the trauma of hospitals would be a good thing.

Not knowing at this stage how that might all work out; would I live or die, to put it bluntly, would be more emotional stress that he didn't need.

Going with another family and allowing his thoughts to steer more towards having fun and riding his bikes, we decided, would be a good thing.

A few phone calls later Sue had arranged for some good friends to take him, which was very kind of them.

With that organised, we then had to repack his gear and needs for the week. I went off to make a couple of calls of my own.

I needed to talk to my family back home. My dad had been in hospital himself since before Christmas with various ailments that come with being the ripe old age of 94! It was impossible to speak to him directly, which I was sad about, but I knew that my sister would be relaying all the news coming from this side of the world courtesy of Sue.

The last thing that Tricia had said to me before putting the phone down was to try to get some sleep. Yeah right! I knew I had to be up at 4am to make our way to the hospital, I also was sure that there was little to no hope of getting much, if any rest, but try I did. I lay my head on the pillow around 11pm. I was right, my mind was all over the place, all manner of thoughts from the positive to the terrified.

Most nights I'd want the time to pass slowly in order to get more rest, but that night, 4am could not have come fast enough. I was done with the what-ifs, the pontificating, the self-reassurance in the shape of telling myself I would be OK. I just wanted to be wheeled into that operating theatre and for the incredibly talented medical teams to take things from there.

NEW HEART DAY

I hadn't slept a wink when 4am arrived, so while I was really tired, I was also raring to go. I was up, showered (although I knew I would be having another one when I got to hospital), dressed and eager to get the show on the road, the nerves and reality of it all sinking in.

Before I left there was one more extremely important and incredibly hard thing to do. I had to say goodbye to Fergus. He was going to be collected in a few hours. Would this be the last time I would ever see him, talk to him, tell him I loved him? As positive as I tried to be, it was hard to not let those thoughts creep in.

I sat down on the edge of his bed and leaned over to hug him. We exchanged "I-love-you" and held each other tightly. I told him I would be fine and that we could look forward to lots of riding together when I'd recovered. He agreed I would be fine and that he would have a great time away riding. I said goodbye. What more can you do?

The drive to the hospital was quiet. Sue did the steering, I took up space in the passenger seat, each of us in our own thoughts I suppose. We met in 2009 and spoken often of this day in a hypothetical context. I am not usually one to just sit; I like conversation. Sue is the opposite. But what was there to say anyway? Here we were, both arriving at this part of our lives; the hypothetical was now real, we both knew what was at stake, we knew the risks and were aware of the various possible outcomes.

One of the most surreal things of the whole experience was arriving at the hospital and checking in at the Emergency

Department and saying to the nurse, "Hello, I am Victor Wiggins, I am here for a heart transplant!"

By their very nature, a transplant of any organ is not a planned procedure in the sense of you having a date or a time to report for the procedure.

A transplant can happen any time of day or night and the only department in a hospital that is open 24/7 is, of course, the Emergency Department. Also, I was still walking, talking and functioning, which is a little at odds with an emergency department where in the main their "customers" are acutely unwell, potentially unable to talk or walk.

Nevertheless, the nurse who checked me in seemed to have been expecting me and promptly provided me with an arm band, an A4 sheet of stickers with my name and date of birth on and instructions as to what to do next, which was to proceed to Ward 3 West, one of the cardiology wards. I waited for Sue as she had gone to park the car, then we made our way to the ward.

It's sometimes hard to understand that the doctors, nurses and indeed all the allied medical staff are used to seeing people like me, on an almost daily basis. After all, this was a large cardiology hospital, so why should my arrival be anything but a normal day, and to them of course it is. To me, however, this was anything but an ordinary day.

After being greeted by the nurse who would be looking after me, at least for the immediate future, she started with the usual pre-operation customs; blood tests, vital observations such as blood pressure, oxygen saturation, heart rate and so on. I had also by this stage put on the ever-so-flattering hospital gown, although it came off almost as quickly as it went on when I was directed to have a shower using a special antimicrobial body wash.

Then followed an electric razor whizzing over my body. I had in fact shaved the night before as experience has taught me that it's best to do a full shave because the medical staff tend to only shave what they need to shave, and the patient ends up looking like a moth-eaten piece of cloth!

It was now around 6am and I was back in bed, no chance of sleep though. Worry not; I would be getting an induced one very soon. The next couple of hours saw various activities and various people coming to see me, from the heart transplant nurse to the surgical team to the anaesthetist, all asking mostly the same questions but with a slightly different angle according to their specialties.

In between the various coming and goings, I tried as I might to take my mind off the impending procedure but in all reality how could I?

I felt sorry for Sue, she no doubt felt obliged to stay by my side and indeed I know she would have wanted to, but the wait must have been torturous for her, too. This guy, her husband, laying in a hospital bed about to have the biggest operation anyone could have. Not only that, but she also had insights from her own profession. Not specifically this ward or hospital, but this environment is where she had spent the past 25-plus years. She knew exactly the drill which I suppose had its advantages, but it must also have had its drawbacks, ignorance being bliss on occasion!

I hadn't eaten or drunk anything since around 9 o'clock the previous evening, some brie and biscuits, chosen specifically as I knew I would never be allowed to have brie ever again.

If it had been a different time of day when I had received the call, I would have chosen a platter of sushi as my "last supper" for the same reason. Alas, there were not many sushi shops open at that time.

Therefore, I was absolutely starving and thirstier than a camel by this stage. There was no relenting from the medical team; I was fully nil-by-mouth until the operation.

The process of retrieving a heart, or indeed any organ, is extremely complicated. The process begins long before the phone rings telling the recipient that there may be a suitable organ available.

The grace, professionalism and care with which this is done I have since come to learn is remarkable. In Australia, there is an opt-in mandate to organ donation; a person signs up to become a donor and upon their death if any of their organs are viable for transplant, they have previously consented for that to happen. But it isn't as straightforward as that, sadly, as the person's family is still able to override their loved one's wishes. This doesn't happen often, but it is a possibility.

When all treatment options for the potential donor have been exhausted, a specialist team of nurses approaches the person's family/next of kin and begins what can only be one of the most delicate conversations one person can have with another.

How you even approach that subject and conversation I wouldn't know. If the family would be happy for their loved one's organ(s) to be used for transplant, then a whole range of tests are started.

Most importantly, a donor must have passed away in hospital, most likely on a ventilator and brain-dead. Their heart and other organs need to be functioning.

The test results are then run through a database to cross-check with a national register of people waiting for an organ, be that a heart, lungs, liver, kidneys, etc. By far the organs most needed for transplant are kidneys.

When it's decided that a donor organ is suitable for transplant, a whole lot more wheels are put in motion, not least is determining the location of the donor heart and how long it might take for the retrieval team to get to the organ and deliver it to the hospital where the recipient is. Often, organs are flown to the hospital. Sometimes a police escort is called upon to help get the organ to where it's needed as expeditiously as possible on land.

We weren't aware of where exactly the heart I was going to receive was coming from. We had assumed that it wasn't The Alfred where it was and by what means it was being carried means we were even less sure. It was something to talk about.

By mid-morning we had been told there would be a delay. This gave me some trepidation – would I actually be having an operation at all?

Apparently, there may have been a delay with the retrieval team which gave weight to our theory that the heart was coming to The Alfred from somewhere else.

We never did find out what had caused the delay. It was after all a Saturday morning and a whole team of medical staff had to have been called in for my operation and perhaps there may have been a delay there. There could have been many reasons.

However, no sooner had we stopped hypothesising and stressing about the delay, than one of the nurses brought me a small cup of tablets and a glass of water.

Someone I had met a few months back in the clinic and who had now become a friend and, importantly, had received his new heart around six months earlier, had told me that when those tablets are given, the operation is going ahead.

Whether that was right or wrong, I still don't know but I took it as read, and I also took a pic of the tablets and texted it to him. He replied almost immediately with a heart emoji and wished me luck. I swallowed the first anti-rejection tablets that I would soon become very acquainted with, and a nurse from the theatre arrived to get me.

This was it.

In the words of the very talented David Gilmour from Pink Floyd, "there's no way out of here, when you come in you are in for good."

Not to put too fine a point on it, I was about to die or live. I was planning on the latter, clearly, but my fate was now in the hands of those incredibly talented doctors and surgeons.

Sue was allowed to come with me down to the theatre doors. From there we had to say our goodbyes. How do you even do that? We hugged, we held each other tight, and I told her the new me would see her soon.

She was stoic, she didn't want to show her inner emotions, but I could see them clearly. She was as terrified as I was.

The theatre wasn't really what I was expecting. I am not sure why, but I had assumed it would be enormous with all manner of equipment everywhere, but from my limited view all I could see was a window. One of the medical team joked about us being in the penthouse suite that day as that theatre was the only one with a window.

Of course, they were doing their best to relax and calm me, more successfully I am sure than an executioner would do, but I can't help but draw a parallel with such a situation when a life is at stake. A difference is that one person knows their fate and one still has to find out. Either way, both were going to sleep.

I had asked quite a few times after being put on the transplant list whether I could keep my native heart. Some might think this is a bit weird, possibly it is, but it had been with me for over 54 years at that point. We had been through a great deal together and strange as it may seem, I had become attached to it, even though the bloody thing had given me no end of grief, especially in recent years, but still it is (or was) a part of me.

Anyway, I had been told that the answer to that question was a definite no! When I pleaded my case based on my friend in New Zealand who proudly displays his old heart for all to see, it didn't seem to help. So as a last-ditch effort I asked just as the final preparations were being made for my long sleep if at least I could have a photo of it. A doctor said he would see what he could do. Of course, that meant no and on reflection I get it.

First there aren't many phones inside an operating theatre, and they wouldn't be sanitized anyway and second, I am quite sure the team had more important things to do just at the time, removing my old heart, than worrying about taking pictures of it!

Alas, I didn't get to keep it or indeed get a picture of it. It was a similar story with my pacemaker; I had asked if I could keep that, the reply was the obvious one.

One of the last things I remember, perhaps even the last thing, was being asked how many surgeries I had previously. Two, I replied. They of course will have known the answer anyway but attempting some humour the surgeon asked a colleague to get the big saw as they'd need it! I thought it was funny.

And with that, it was lights out ....

LEARNING TO WALK AGAIN

The surgical team had told Sue they expected the operation to take around 11 hours.

As I understand it, they thought they would encounter some obstacles along the way, mostly to do with the plumbing of my native heart and the amount of scar tissue that would need to be dissected from previous operations.

I went into the theatre around 12.30pm, so I suppose she was expecting to hear something of my progress much later that night, perhaps around 11pm or so.

When Sue's phone rang around 7pm the butterflies in her stomach were no doubt working overtime!

Almost five hours earlier than she thought she would be, she answered the phone. It was the surgeon.

Sue is a very calm person by nature, but even so I can imagine her trepidation as she was about to receive the news. Surely it was way too early to be hearing that the operation had finished?

"Good evening," announced a calm voice on the other end of the line. "It's Chris Merry speaking; we are just finishing up with Victor. The operation has gone very well, much better than we had expected in fact. The team are just closing him up and he will be through to recovery within the next hour. You can come and see him then".

There was no doubt a huge sigh of relief as Sue ended the call. The operation had in fact only taken 7.5 hours. By all accounts, my new heart fitted perfectly and there were no hiccups or issues along the way. That must have been because they used that bloody big saw to make room for it!

After I had been sewn up I was taken from the theatre to a recovery area, before being moved to the Intensive Care Unit (ICU). As would be usual after an operation of such magnitude, I was hooked up to all manner of monitors with wires and tubes akin to a bowl of spaghetti protruding from almost every part of me.

There was a plethora of medications to help support my heart in its new environment, along with medications to assist with fluid, keep me hydrated, help me pee and of course I was now being pumped full of anti-rejection medication.

There is no specified time someone is kept asleep; it ranges from just a few hours to weeks, depending how well the patient recovered and how their body was coping with its new heart.

The operation had finished at around 7pm on Saturday evening, but I was kept asleep for another 20 or so hours, with the sedation being reduced during that time so I would wake up gradually. By 3pm the following day I was conscious, my eyes opened, but the ventilator was still breathing for me.

Possibly one of the worst experiences anyone can have after a general anaesthetic is when the body wants to breathe for itself again. It's quite a hard thing to describe; on the one hand you have a machine that is breathing for you, but there comes a point as you wake up when your body wants to take over as the intrinsic need to breathe kicks in.

It feels a little like trying to breathe against the ventilator, but it doesn't last long as the ventilator support is being turned down to meet the body's ability to start breathing by itself. Nevertheless, it's not a particularly pleasant feeling!

When I was fully extubated, an oxygen mask was put on me and I was going solo.

Still very drowsy, I found it hard to focus. In fact I was really struggling to see clearly at all, everything was a blur and that started to scare me a little. I asked Sue for my glasses; they made little difference. I then asked for my reading glasses; again they didn't help much. I kept asking Sue to clean the lenses, it was as if they were smudged or something. No matter how much she cleaned them, there was no difference and in the end Sue asked the doctor about it. He said it was a common issue after being on heart bypass and that my sight should improve in the coming weeks.

It didn't really matter that much really as I wasn't going anywhere and was spending more time with my eyes closed than open at that stage. But I didn't really want to gain a heart only to lose my sight.

My recovery in those first few days progressed well, with perhaps a couple of small hiccups regarding my heart rate.

I can clearly recall my new heart having lots of ectopic beats (missed or skipped beats), something I used to get very frequently. I recall thinking, oh no, not again.

Luckily, what was happening was my new natural heart rhythm was fighting the pacing that was being delivered via an external pacemaker. This was an easy fix, they turned the external pacing off and I was fine.

There was also a concern about one of the chambers of my new heart that was "sluggish", so I was taken for a CT Scan and then I also had a special kind of scan called a transesophageal echo, where a camera is put down the throat and pictures of the heart taken to give a much more detailed view compared to a traditional echo which is done by using a device akin to a roll-on deodorant with jelly on the chest wall. Everything looked normal which was a huge relief.

On Monday, two days post-transplant, I had some of the

tubes removed, including the drain from my old pacemaker site and the pulmonary artery catheter that was there to continually monitor pressures inside my new heart. Also removed were my two intercostal chest drains. Slowly I was becoming less reliant on the various wires and tubes and beginning to look more like a human than a machine!

As is often the case when someone is in hospital, their bowels decide not to work as well as usual. I was no exception! It was now Tuesday and I hadn't been to the loo for a number two since Friday morning, so I was feeling pretty blocked up. The med team decided to give me drain-unblockers as I called them!

Well holy moly, I went from the sublime to the ridiculous. I can't recall never not making it to the loo; first time for everything I guess and so there we were, the lovely nurse, who had just started her night shift and me in what felt like knee-high in my excrement! I had shat the bed!

I was mortified, but the nurse was so lovely about it and reassured me that this was just another day at the office for her. Still, I was so terribly embarrassed. My embarrassment soon passed as it had been the start of what was to be two weeks of what can only be described as liquid poos!

A combination of the medicine they had given to me to help me go and the effect of one of the new anti-rejection drugs had induced an almost endless need to call for the commode. My inhibitions soon passed and I became adept at using a bed pan or commode, something I had never done before having this surgery.

It reminded me that it's best to leave one's dignity at the door of the hospital, and also that these amazing medical staff are just so caring and understanding. They deserve a bloody medal for what they do on a daily basis, especially in the environment of ICU where the patient is almost fully reliant on them for everything, be it passing a glass of water to cleaning your backside post commode visit!

By Wednesday there was some further concern about my new heart, due to some weird heart rhythms overnight. To make sure all was well, I was taken for an urgent biopsy. It had been planned for the next day, but the consultant brought it forward.

Obviously, rejection of the new organ is the biggest concern, especially in those early days, weeks and months; in all reality, the first year of having a transplant is extremely critical as it's during that time the recipient is more likely to have organ failure due to infection and rejection.

As a new recipient, a "freshy" as I like to call me, the education which is given long before even receiving a new organ by the transplant team is extensive.

Patients are highly encouraged to read and reread the literature they are given, as it can quite literally save a life. Everything is covered from how to wash the hands correctly, to the correct preparation of food to knowing what signs and symptoms to look out for regarding infection or rejection.

Luckily for me, my very first biopsy came back as zero rejection. There would be many more biopsies to follow, with around 15 to be completed in the first year post-transplant.

The process is quite straightforward really but it's not without some discomfort. A catheter (tube) is inserted into the neck and a wire is sent down into the heart. At the end of the wire is a sort of snipper that can take a piece of heart tissue that is then drawn back up the catheter. The sample of tissue is then sent off to the lab for analysis. This is done four times per biopsy. The whole process takes around 30 minutes or so. Not surprisingly the neck is somewhat tender for a few days afterwards! Later the same day the results are sent to the patient to indicate if there is any rejection.

Thursday of that week was a big day. It was to get out of bed and have a walk day.

I had heard it said to me a few times by people who had gone before me on this journey, that when a patient first gets out of bed standing on their own is not possible. What baloney I had thought, of course I will be able to stand on my own and I will be able to walk on my own too. How hard can it be?

I found out just how hard it was, and the answer is very! I had by now been in bed for five full days, except for being moved from my bed to sit in a chair or on the commode a few times, but those had been a transfer-aided by the nurses. I only needed to stand very briefly. Two physios came to set me up for a walk. I was very nervous but also extremely excited to be able to take my first steps with my new heart.

Well good God, it was as if I had to learn to walk again, as if my body had forgotten how to do so. With their help I managed to "walk" (more of a shuffle really) out of my bedroom and up the ward for about five metres. I had been given a walking trolley, the ones you stand behind and push along. I felt and probably looked like I was 105! I made it back to the bed and was told I had done exceptionally well. Really, I thought. I thought I was terrible, I hardly went anywhere and now I am tired!

That was possibly one of the first times the full magnitude of what I had been through and more poignantly, the amount of recovery I was facing, really hit me. This was not tea and biscuits by any means; this was as big a deal as it gets. But I was motivated to get going and that first little walk lit a fire in me that I believe helped me recover as quickly as I did.

Later that day, just as the sun was about to set, I had a treat. I had been booked into the viewing window overlooking the large woodland park opposite the hospital. Most excitingly, it also overlooked the helipad where critically ill people were unloaded after being flown to The Alfred from all over Victoria for life-saving treatment.

It was quite the service, I was pushed around in my bed and parked up. Unfortunately (or fortunately I suppose) I didn't get to see any helicopters land during my visit. We did, however, see a good rainstorm which was equally impressive.

The ICU at The Alfred is one of Australia's largest and probably the leading one in the country. With around 60 beds it hosts over 3,000 patients per year, all needing life-saving treatment and intervention. The unit is split into three sections, areas for cardiac, trauma and general. Each unit has its own dedicated teams to look after patients.

The ICU alone has more than 40 consultants and 600 or so nurses. I cannot express enough how safe I felt knowing that if there was one place I could choose in which to have this operation and the care that followed it, it was this one. To say that I was in good hands is an understatement really. I will be forever in their debt.

No sooner had I arrived back at my bed than I was being wheeled off again, this time to a new room. The room I had been in was now needed for someone sicker than me, so in one sense it was a good sign that I was being shifted across the hallway.

It wasn't far, but one interesting thing I encountered that night was that firstly I could hear the coming and goings of the helicopters and I could also smell the aviation fuel, something I hadn't experienced before. My old room was only 20 metres or so away. Odd! I didn't know it at the time, but this was to be my last night in the ICU.

On the Friday of that week, I woke up and was again met by the physiotherapists who took me for another walk. This time I managed to go much farther without the aid of the trolley. I felt like I had turned a corner, and I could start to see the finish line.

At that time, the finish line was getting to the ward, because each step meant I was that bit closer to going home and starting my new life with my new heart.

The highlight of the week was being discharged from ICU and sent on my way up to the ward for further recovery.

By now I was free of all IV lines and tubes with my epicardial pacing wires removed after I arrived at the ward.

Having things pulled out of the chest is a strange sensation. This was the second time in the week that I had this experience, the first being when my drain tubes were removed. These tubes are about the diameter of a drinking straw but much longer and they reach up inside from just above the navel to the heart. It sort of tickles when they are pulled out. I had to take a deep breath and hold it while the nurses quickly pulled them out. The inside of the tube is filled with blood which then comes out looking something like a sausage. Not for everyone, but I found it fascinating!

OVERCOME WITH EMOTION

On the 14th February, Room 2 of Ward 3 East became my new home. It was the first room on the left after entering the ward. I had my own room because not only had I just had a heart transplant, but I was now immune-compromised and there needed to be as much control as possible over the risk of getting an infection. Hospitals obviously are full of sick people with all manner of bugs, so if I could be kept away from that the better were my chances of staying well.

My focus now was on getting out of hospital, not because I hated where I was, I didn't. I may be one of only a few people who doesn't mind being in hospital. It isn't because of the amazing sleep you get or the wonderful food or even the various noises that occur at all hours with alarms and beepers going off.

It's because I know that if I am in hospital there are reasons for me to be there, it's the best place for me at that time and I resign myself to that and understand that they don't want me there one moment longer than necessary. There would be plenty of people queuing up for my room!

The daily routine was quite a usual one in most hospital stays I imagine. The doctors' daily rounds followed stabbing each day by the phlebotomist assigned to take the daily bloods.

There was usually quite an entourage of doctors, nurses and other medical staff who would form a sort of train as they travelled through the ward pushing their mobile computers and visiting each of their patients. One thing that had mirrored previous admissions to hospital was the frequent visits by junior or student doctors keen to interview me about my life and wanting to learn more about what people like me had been through and how medicine had allowed me to live as long as I had.

Almost without exception they were keen to examine me, although they were a little late now as I no longer had a wonky heart! Equally almost without exception they were blown away that I had managed to survive well into adulthood with the heart I previously had.

The doctors' visits would be followed up with any changes to my care or instructions they had made and were executed diligently by the amazing nursing staff.

One such change came in the form of anti-anxiety medication. Ironically, I was anxious about taking it. I suppose I felt I had enough medications to take and to be honest I also felt a bit of a stigma around taking meds for mental health. However, it turned out that I had been prescribed it to help me sleep, which was a common issue in hospitals but also because one of the anti-rejection medications, prednisone, was notorious for keeping patients awake. I relented and allowed myself some decent rest.

The remainder of each day would be swallowed up, taking meals, rest and having some walks around the ward to try to slowly build my strength up and get my body moving again.

But there was now also a lot of time to sit and think about the enormity of what I had just been through.

In ICU there hadn't been any down time, primarily because there was always a nurse with me who was either checking my vitals, changing settings on the machines, ensuring the right medications were being given, or else I was sleeping.

That week had been a blur and honestly, I couldn't have said what day of the week it was at any given point. There is no daylight either, so in true Las Vegas-style you have no idea if it is morning, noon or night.

My thoughts started to turn towards the donor and the family.

What must they be going through right now? How unbelievably generous a gift they had given to me. The selflessness of such an act is quite hard to understand. In their darkest hours, grief-stricken with the loss of their loved one, how they found the strength to see the possibility of someone being able to continue a life is remarkable.

I sat for many hours in a reflective state listening to music that has deep meaning to me with tears streaming down my face. These tears were shared with happiness and sadness. I was sad that someone had died to save me, but I was also immensely happy that I had made it through the operation and though it was still very early days, I was tracking well.

It was (and still is) very hard for me to be able to fully process what had happened over those 10 days.

I had been at work, an ordinary day, then the following morning being at hospital and six hours later going through the biggest surgery a person can have, then recovering in ICU for a week, with large chunks of that time missing from my memory, with only pictures or Sue filling in the details for me.

I was then sitting, walking, breathing for myself, rid of the machines that were keeping me alive. It was all somewhat overwhelming. I needed to try to process this, but it would take time, and that was OK.

As all this had been going Fergus had been enjoying himself up in New South Wales, but his trip was almost over and selfishly I couldn't have been happier about that. He'd had a good week of riding and was safe and was to return on Sunday 16th February. I was counting down the hours until I would see him again.

When he came to see me, I was overcome. I just held him so tight and never wanted to let go. With tears streaming down my face as I realised the reality that I might not have been able to see him ever again 10 days earlier when I said goodbye to him that morning as he lay in bed. It could well have been the last time.

He told me all about his trip, how cold it had been at the top of the mountain, how much it had rained on one of the days, but mostly about how much fun he'd had with his friends riding.

For me that was all that mattered. It had been great that he hadn't had to stay in Melbourne, being dragged backwards and forwards to the hospital and having to see his dad with countless numbers of tubes and other gadgetry sticking out of or on him. A 14-year-old doesn't need that trauma, at least that's how we felt about it.

We started to talk about all the things we were going to do together again, riding mostly, but also things such as camping and going on adventures together, things we had both missed out on. He was now 14 and needed me to help him navigate into the adult world, so this beautiful gift I had been given came just at the right time. When I recovered we would be packing up the car with bikes and hitting the road to explore and spend quality time together.

I had two other very special visitors that week who also brought me to tears. Roz, the amazing psychologist who had helped me through so much mental trauma and who had always been a beacon of hope and had a general air of positivity around her, popped her head in just as my bowels decided they needed to join the party. How embarrassing! Like all the medical teams though, it didn't phase her, she gave me some privacy and came back for a chat once all had been sorted out! We had a wonderful reflective talk which resulted in yet more tears!

Just as I thought I may have run out of visitors, on the

Wednesday of that week, the lovely Dr Su Ling Tee called by my room. I was already out of bed standing up as she came through the door. She gave me the biggest hug and told me how proud of me she was.

It's not too much to say that I credit three ladies with getting me through this journey – my lovely wife of course, along with Roz and Su Ling. Each of them was able to bring their knowledge, compassion and, of course, love from Sue.

This had not been easy, this was not yet over, but I knew that with people like this by my side, I would recover and go on to live that life I had long yearned for.

REHAB

At 16:38 hours on February 21st, 2025, thirteen days since entering hospital, I walked out on my own.

The staff videoed the moment for me. The whole journey had by all accounts been one of the fastest the hospital had seen. There may have been faster, but I reckon I still got a podium!

Of course, there were no prizes but when one of the nurses had told me that I was well on track with my recovery, I kind of got the bit between my teeth and thought to myself, yep, I am going to do everything I can to do this whole thing within a fortnight.

Being back at home was of course lovely, but it did take some adjustment. Foremost, I had to remember I had just undergone open heart surgery so I was a bit of a waste of time when it came to domestic duties.

Poor Sue had been and continued to be running around like the proverbial headless chicken, tending to me, Fergus and trying to keep everything going. Meanwhile I was to do plenty of resting, something I had always found difficult to do but certainly knowing that it was important that I did.

The weekend passed as we all tried to get used to my being somewhat cantankerous and emotional.

This was being fuelled by the prednisone of course, but still it was hard not to be shitty and obtuse some times and breaking down in tears at others. It's quite remarkable how certain medications can cause such a change in aspects of personality.

Monday arrived, two whole days at home and I was now heading back to hospital with Sue.

This day marked the start of my rehab at the gym. This was a 3–6 month program that all transplant recipients go through. I signed up to this as part of getting a new heart. The program runs three times per week, Mondays, Wednesdays and Fridays. I had been really looking forward to this; I saw it as my first step to being able to achieve the level of fitness I wanted. I had made a list of things I wanted to do if I ever received a new heart way back at my transplant work-up in December 2023. I had (probably) bored the social worker who was silly enough to ask me what things I would like to do, and I had reeled off a list as long as my arm. Then of course I had no idea when or even if I would receive a new heart and here I was now with it inside me and I was ready to put it to use.

My bravado was soon brought back to earth. I felt as if I could have done anything but again this was very much the prednisone talking. It soon became clear my mind was writing cheques my body couldn't cash!

The first day at the gym was just an assessment day, what could I do as a baseline? A six-minute walk test soon determined that. I managed to walk around 380 metres in that time, neither good or bad I thought, but when I reflected on how far I had managed just over a year earlier which was around 240 from memory, I realised that, OK, it was a reasonable effort and something for me to work on.

The rehab gym at The Alfred is one of the world's leading centres. It's run by the incredibly talented and extremely-driven Dr Louise Fuller, who is respected the world over in the area of cardiothoracic rehabilitation.

I had been told what I could expect during my stay in hospital. Perhaps intentionally Lou had been painted as someone who would not stand for anything less than 100% effort which was fine by me as all I was interested in was being able to become fitter and stronger in a safe environment where I was being closely managed.

As it had turned out Lou was away on leave that first week of gym, but her wonderful crew of very able physiotherapists had already drawn up a program for me to start on the Wednesday of that week. The program was broken down into two sections, cardio and strengthening exercises. The cardio consisted of walking on a treadmill and then on an exercise bike, both for 15 minutes.

The idea of this was to have my heart pumping and my body warm before moving on to strengthening exercises such as weights, squats, step-ups and so on.

This is because a transplanted heart does not react to heart-rate inputs in the same way that a normal heart does. Behind a normal heart is a whole web of micro nerves that are connected to the spinal cord and then to the brain. These nerves are responsible for controlling the sympathetic and parasympathetic system which in turn help the heart to know what to do, be it beat faster as if a person needs to run away from something (flight or flight response) or perhaps help a person calm down with a dampening response.

During the transplant operation, as the native heart is removed, so too are the micro nerves, leaving the new donor heart to be what is known as a denervated heart. This leaves the newly transplanted heart relying on the body's hormones to help control its heart rate. Therefore, a few things happen; a transplanted heart takes longer to respond to exercise and equally it takes much longer to slow down after exercise. Also, the resting heart rate is usually much higher than a normal heart – mine for example sits around 100 beats per minute at rest. This does take quite a bit of getting used to and can be quite disconcerting as you get used to it (I still am!). It wasn't long before the program became longer in terms of the number of exercises, but also harder in terms of the intensity of the exercises.

When Lou returned from leave, she told me that in a few weeks I would be running on a the treadmill. "Running?" I needed to repeat that to her. I hadn't run in over 35 years, the concept of me running on a treadmill was utterly foreign and actually quite ludicrous to me. But I knew that if she thought I could do it then I would and so my focus changed from there is "no way I can do that" to "I can't wait to do that."

A few weeks had passed at the gym and as the program kept building I began to notice a real difference in my ability and the strength I was gaining. I recalled to myself that at the start of the gym program I could barely do five squats without my legs screaming at me to please stop, I was now doing 40 of these squats and while my legs were still not terribly happy with me, I could get through them and enjoyed feeling my leg muscles burning. I was making progress and that's all I needed to see.

Run Day. 31st March 2025. This was it, the day my two legs would go faster than they had in decades, if only by a small amount! A couple of days earlier at a gym session Lou had pulled out the small trampoline for me to jog on. I didn't quite understand why I was being made to bounce up and down on it, but all became clear when Lou explained to me that yet another of the many side-effects of the medications that all transplant recipients are on is weakened bone density. Running or jumping on a very hard surface can cause issues with tendons, so it's important to train them first.

I started on the treadmill with my normal walk which then became progressively faster. The incline was dropped all the way down so the treadmill was flat and at 6.4km/h I started to jog.

I couldn't believe it. It was as if I was flying. It was by no means easy though and I felt all the sensations that Lou had warned me of: the sore legs, the strange motion in my chest, the exercise-induced breathlessness that I hadn't experienced for so many years. They were all making themselves known; so too was my heart rate, which the last time it was so high I was in the back of an ambulance being rushed to hospital. Now I was safe, it was supposed to be doing this. After a minute of jogging I was allowed to slow down back to a walking pace. I felt tired, but I felt alive, more alive than I had felt for many years.

All my co-gymgoers applauded my efforts as is the tradition when someone does their first run on the treadmill.

Lou came in with a huge high five. She saw the emotion on my face as what I had just done sank in. I had just run/jogged on a treadmill for a minute and to most people that is no achievement, but for me I could have just won the Olympics. More importantly I now knew I could do those things and that was just the start for me.

At the time of writing about this I was almost 12 weeks post-transplant and still on the gym program. It continues to grow in terms of the workout, but it also continued to push me and I was becoming stronger and fitter. At some point I was going to graduate and I would really miss it.

With my confidence and strength/conditioning all growing nicely I asked Lou if I could ride my bike again. Gently, was the reply. By now she had seen pictures of Fergus doing his thing, I had shown her them to give her an idea of what I wanted to get back to at some point, perhaps with not quite the same level of skill and ability that Fergus had, but I needed her to see the idea.

"Yes ma'am" I agreed with a small salute. "Don't be falling off," she warned, "that's not going to do anyone any good, least of all you!" I agreed to her terms and conditions and the following day I was out pedalling my bike along some easy bike paths. It was flat and it was easy, but I didn't care, I had made it.

I had managed to go from the strong likelihood that I would never be able to ride again, in the way I wanted to anyway, to being at the beginning of yet another journey, a delightful one. It truly was the best feeling; what could better it?

Well, I did manage to better it when a couple of weeks later I progressed from bike paths to a little bit of off-road cycling, more like proper mountain biking.

But the real joy came in the form of having my boy with me, the moment we shared riding along a forest track together, chatting as we went about all the places we wanted to go and ride. He was patient with me. This was not the type of terrain or level of difficulty he was used to, but we found lots of fun things for him to seek out and try and in fact the verdict was that he'd had fun.

I, on the other hand, had been having much more than fun. For me all the years of being unwell, the many trips to hospitals both planned and unplanned, the procedures, the worsening of my symptoms, the anxiety of waiting for a new heart, the operation, the pain, the recovery, feeling terrible from the side effects of the medication, all of it was more than worth it, even if this was going to be the one and only time I could ride with him.

This was 100% why I had fought so hard, why I kept pushing all the way through my life.

This was the moment it all made complete sense.

ONE DOOR CLOSES

When someone is born with a very complex congenital heart problem, as I was, and who then subsequently one day might need a transplant, again as I did, it's not a cure.

The issues, problems and challenges that the person faced as a congenital heart patient may be closed down by a new heart. But there comes a new set of issues, problems and challenges.

Just as that original diagnosis and condition needed to be closely managed, so too does the new condition that comes with a new organ doing its best to function and support the body in an environment it was never meant to be in.

From the early days of having regular biopsies to ensure no sign of rejection, to becoming used to some of the most toxic drugs known to man and to ongoing MRI, CT, annual angiograms and other procedures, the medical journey is by no means over.

However, these new challenges bring with them the opportunity of a new, different life for the patient.

The advancement in medical science around heart transplants even in the past 20 years or so is nothing short of miraculous, from enhanced organ preservation via machine perfusion, to advances in drugs such as tacrolimus which have seen huge improvements in the reduction of rejection and creating better survival rates.

Improved surgical techniques combined with better donor and organ selection have also greatly contributed to better, long-term outcomes for these patients.

As I bring my story to a close, I am looking forward to a healthy, full life. I recall one of the doctors telling me when I asked how long I would be around if I didn't get a transplant, "perhaps five or ten years" was her stark reply.

I am 55 this year (2025). I am very hopeful of many more years of bike riding, travelling, ticking off that very long list I gave the social worker almost 18 months before and, most importantly, to see Fergus follow his dreams on whatever pathway he chooses, while Sue and I can enjoy a long retirement together.

These are my hopes, but either way, I have lived a life that I was never expected to live. I have been lucky, very lucky.

I am quite sure that if someone told the doctors back in 1970 that I would have kept my native heart for 54 (and a bit) years and that I would then have been blessed with a new heart, I am not sure they would have believed them.

We are fortunate to live in an era where modern medicine can achieve things that were unimaginable just a short time ago. Be that the drug therapy, the imaging of the human body, the techniques that are available today for surgery, which were quite literally science fiction in very recent years.

And, of course, the training and dedication of all the medical staff who have worked so hard to save not only my life many times, but the lives of thousands of my peers who have had the same condition that I was born with and who are all on their own journey facing their daily challenges.